Introduction to Logic
Propositional Logic

Introduction to Logic
Propositional Logic

second edition

Howard Pospesel

University of Miami
Coral Gables, Florida

PRENTICE-HALL, INC., Englewood Cliffs, New Jersey 07632

Library of Congress Cataloging in Publication Data

POSPESEL, HOWARD, (date)
   Introduction to logic.

   Rev. ed. of: Propositional logic. 1974.
   Includes index.
   1. Proposition (Logic)   2. Logic, Symbolic and
mathematical.   3. Reasoning.   I. Pospesel, Howard,
(date).   Propositional logic.   II. Title.   III. Title:
Propositional logic.
BC181.P64 1984   160   83-19256
ISBN   0-13-486167-1

Editorial production, supervision,
   and interior design by Lisa A. Domínguez
Manufacturing buyer: Harry Baisley

For Carmen

Printed in the United States of America

10   9   8

ISBN 0-13-486167-1

Prentice-Hall International, Inc., *London*
Prentice-Hall of Australia Pty. Limited, *Sydney*
Editora Prentice-Hall do Brasil, Ltda., *Rio de Janeiro*
Prentice-Hall Canada Inc., *Toronto*
Prentice-Hall of India Private Limited, *New Delhi*
Prentice-Hall of Japan, Inc., *Tokyo*
Prentice-Hall of Southeast Asia Pte. Ltd., *Singapore*
Whitehall Books Limited, *Wellington, New Zealand*

Contents

Student's preface   ix

Teacher's preface   xi

Acknowledgments   xiii

1   LOGIC   1

   1.1   Introduction, 1
   1.2   Key Terms, 3
       Exercises, 7

2   IF   9

   2.1   Compound Statements, 9
   2.2   Symbolizing Conditionals, 10
   2.3   Arrow Out, 14
       Exercises, 20

3   AND   **24**

    3.1   Symbolizing Conjunctions, 24
    3.2   Ampersand In, 28
    3.3   Ampersand Out, 30
        Exercises, 33

4   IF (AGAIN)   **41**

    4.1   Symbolizing Difficult Conditionals, 41
    4.2   Arrow In, 45
        Exercises, 53

5   NOT   **62**

    5.1   Symbolizing Negations, 62
    5.2   Tilde In, 66
    5.3   Tilde Out, 70
        Exercises, 74

6   IFF   **84**

    6.1   Symbolizing Biconditionals, 84
    6.2   Double Arrow In and Out, 85
        Exercises, 88

7   OR   **95**

    7.1   Symbolizing Disjunctions, 95
    7.2   Wedge In, 97
    7.3   Wedge Out, 100
        Exercises, 104

8   RÉSUMÉ   **114**

    8.1   Summary of Inference Rules, 114
    8.2   Proof Strategy, 117
    8.3   Definitions, 120
        Exercises, 123

9   DERIVED RULES   132

9.1 Eight Additional Rules, 132
9.2 Proof Strategy, 137
9.3 Substitution Instance, 141
     Exercises, 144

10   TRUTH TABLES   153

10.1 Constructing Truth Tables, 153
10.2 Testing Arguments, 158
      Exercises, 161

11   BRIEF TRUTH TABLES   168

11.1 Proving Invalidity, 168
11.2 Proving Validity, 171
      Exercises, 174

12   STATEMENTS   179

12.1 Logical Truths, 179
12.2 Contradictions, 182
12.3 Contingent Statements, 184
      Exercises, 186

13   LOGICAL RELATIONS   188

13.1 Entailment, 188
13.2 Logical Equivalence, 190
      Exercises, 194

14   NATURAL ARGUMENTS   199

14.1 Identification, 199
14.2 Formalization, 202
14.3 Evaluation, 205
      Exercises, 206

appendix 1   IS PROPOSITIONAL LOGIC   214
                RELIABLE?

appendix 2   ALTERNATIVE SYMBOLS   218

appendix 3   SOLUTIONS TO STARRED   219
                EXERCISES

Index   230

Student's Preface

I intend this book to accomplish three ends. The *first goal* is to introduce you to an exciting branch of knowledge: contemporary symbolic logic. I shall do this by explaining in detail the elements of propositional logic, the fundamental part of symbolic logic. The *second goal* I have set for the book is to increase your awareness of the arguments you read and hear every day. Being aware of arguments is a precondition for assessing them. The means I have chosen to increase your awareness of arguments is to fill the following pages with actual examples of arguments that are very like the arguments you encounter. These examples have been drawn from newspapers, magazines, books, term papers, posters, television programs, films, records, and conversations. The *third goal* of the book is to sharpen your native ability to evaluate arguments. This is a goal of utmost consequence; one of the marks of a well-educated person is the ability to assess correctly the worth of arguments. I hope to achieve this goal by providing you with two important logical instruments: the method of *formal proofs* (in chapters two through nine) and the method of *truth tables* (in chapters ten and eleven).

I enjoyed writing this book; I hope you will enjoy reading it.

Teacher's Preface

Any logic text written in English today should give some account of why it deserves to be added to the mountain of available material. The most important feature of this book is its *application*—from first example to final exercise—of the techniques of symbolic logic to arguments of the sort students encounter in their reading, conversing, and televiewing. In this respect the present volume differs from all other logic texts with which I am acquainted. The book was written in the belief that a study of propositional logic can improve one's rational skills, and it has been designed to help college students achieve such improvement.

The book is organized around natural-deduction formal-proof procedures. I am convinced that these procedures, because of their similarity to native patterns of inference and their emphasis upon plotting strategy, are well suited as instruments for accomplishing the end described above. In this regard formal-proof procedures are far superior to truth-table and truth-tree techniques. Two truth-table tests are developed in the volume, but only after an extensive treatment of formal proofs. I have adopted Suppes' proof format, which employs a column to keep tabs on assumption dependence. I have found this format pedagogically preferable to Fitch's indented-columns format.

Statement connectives are introduced gradually, one per chapter. Students are afforded an opportunity to master both symbolization and proof moves involving a given connective, before adding more connectives to their logical vocabulary. This approach has proved successful in my own logic classes.

For several years I used E. J. Lemmon's outstanding text, *Beginning Logic*, in my introductory logic course. Those familiar with Lemmon's book will recognize the extent to which I have been influenced by it.

A word about the symbols employed in the book. As a step toward the (still distant) goal of notational uniformity in logic, I have selected commonly used symbols: ~, &, v, →, ↔. With the exception of the tilde, this is the set employed by Hacking, Lemmon, Mates, and Suppes. I prefer the tilde to their dash because the latter symbol invites students to confuse the logical operation of negation with the arithmetical operation of subtraction.

The second edition differs from the first chiefly in these ways:

1. More than one third of the exercises and examples have been replaced by better ones, and most exercise sets have been expanded.
2. The Wedge Out Rule has been simplified.
3. I have extended the brief-truth-table technique presented in chapter eleven to valid arguments.
4. There is increased emphasis on proof-construction strategies.
5. The sexist language that crept into the first edition has been eliminated.

James Shelley, Director of Academic Computing at the University of Miami, and I have developed a computer program keyed to the second edition of *Propositional Logic*. This program helps students learn to symbolize, construct formal proofs, and devise truth tables. For more information regarding this program contact the Philosophy Editor, Prentice-Hall, Inc., Englewood Cliffs, New Jersey 07632.

Acknowledgments

David Marans has read and criticized each of the several drafts of this volume; many pages have been improved by his suggestions. David created the crossword puzzles in exercises 57, 113, and 247, and supplied twenty-five additional exercises.

The book has benefited from critical reading by Samuel Gorovitz, Gene James, Tom O'Kelley, Mark Woodhouse, and Greg Young. The following friends contributed exercises: Raymond Beck, Arnold Burr, Don Carignan, Debby Conrad, David Cooper, Laurie Dimun, Barbara Hecht, Barbara Irwin, Joan Kilpatrick, William King, Ernest Kloock, Hon-Fai Lee, Jeffrey Marcus, Robert McCleskey, Jorge Mederos, Jorge Morales, Denise Oehmig, Jon Ruse, Yolanda Sánchez, Alan Simpson, Linda Sumarlidason, Maria Valdez, Maria Vidaña, Edith Watson-Schipper, Fred Westphal, and Harold Zellner.

The second edition has been improved by suggestions from Ila Eisenberg and Professors William Hanson, David Harrah, Owen Herring, David Randall Luce, Wayne MacVey, David Marans, and David Sanford. Howard Goldberg supplied elegant proofs for the "superchallenge" (exercise 231) and the "maxichallenge" (exercise 235). Each of the following friends contributed several examples new to this edition: Juan Aldea, Carol Casey, David Marans, Denise Oehmig, Carmen and Michael Pospesel, and James Rachels. Other new exercises were supplied by Kaoru Abbey, Fabio Arber, Rondus Bennett, Nancy Cain, Marika Christ, Nancy Day, Bill Finlay, Noel Gianelli, Owen Herring, James Humble, Sharon Klein, Steve Klimacek, Scott Morrison, John Murray, Leo de la Peña, Jon Reynard, Jesús Rodríguez, Charles Rogers, Catherine Schmitt, Richard Talda, Bill Webber, Todd Williams, Michael Young, and Harold Zellner.

Introduction to Logic
Propositional Logic

1

Logic

1.1
Introduction

A close friend of mine who suffered from dizzy spells underwent tests by a neurosurgeon. When they met to discuss the test results, this conversation took place:

> DOCTOR: David, you have a benign tumor in your inner ear. It's called an *acoustic neuroma*.
> DAVID: How can you be sure it's benign?
> DOCTOR: Acoustic neuromas are always benign.[1]

The neurosurgeon was advancing an argument that can be stated formally as:

> All acoustic neuromas are benign.
> David's tumor is an acoustic neuroma.
> Therefore, it is benign.

[1]My friend, ever the logician, recorded this dialogue and mailed it to me (while awaiting brain surgery) because he knew of my interest in sample inferences. His tumor was removed successfully.

Every day, each of us advances arguments and encounters arguments put forward by others. Of course, few are as dramatic as the example above. A more pedestrian example comes from my own experience. There is one rest room on each floor in the stacks of the University of Miami library. Those on the even-numbered floors are for women; the remainder are men's rooms. One day recently as I absentmindedly passed through the doorway of one of these rooms, I was gripped by the neurotic fear that I was walking into the wrong kind of rest room. The anxiety dissolved when I spotted a urinal. In an instant I made an inference which can be given this formal statement:

> All rest rooms with urinals are men's rooms.
> This rest room has a urinal.
> Therefore, it is a men's rest room.

Arguments can be assessed in two quite different ways. On the one hand, we may determine the truth or falsity of the premises occurring in an argument. This may be called assessing the argument's *content*. On the other hand, we may determine whether the conclusion follows from the premises. When we evaluate an argument on this score we are assessing its *form*.[2] In general, *logic* is concerned with evaluating the form rather than the content of arguments. For example, it is not the business of logic to determine the truth (or falsity) of the premises in the above argument about tumors; this job falls within the province of neurology. The logician is interested in identifying and assessing the form of the argument. When we remove the content from the "tumor" argument, this form remains:

> All $\mathcal{D}$ are $\mathcal{E}$
> $\mathcal{I}$ is $\mathcal{D}$
> Therefore $\mathcal{I}$ is $\mathcal{E}$

'$\mathcal{D}$', '$\mathcal{E}$', and '$\mathcal{I}$' mark the gaps that remain after content expressions like 'acoustic neuromas' are removed. The "rest room" argument also has this form. The form is a good one; if an argument exhibits it, its conclusion follows from its premises.

This distinction between form and content may be further illustrated with the help of these examples:

ARGUMENT ONE	ARGUMENT TWO
If Atlanta is the capital of Florida, then Atlanta is in Florida.	If Atlanta is in Florida, then Atlanta is south of Detroit.
Atlanta is the capital of Florida.	Atlanta is south of Detroit.
Therefore, Atlanta is in Florida.	Therefore, Atlanta is in Florida.

[2]The notion of an argument's "form," explained here only informally, is clarified in section 9.3.

Since these two arguments have false conclusions, each must incorporate some error. The mistake in Argument One is obvious: its second premise is false (a mistake of content). The premises of Argument Two are true. However, it has a different type of defect: its conclusion does not follow from its premises. The argument exhibits the following defective form:

If $\mathcal{P}$ then $\mathcal{Q}$
$\mathcal{Q}$
Therefore $\mathcal{P}$

What is the form of Argument One?

An argument does not establish the truth of its conclusion unless it has *both* correct content *and* a good form. One purpose of a college education is to prepare people for the job of evaluating the content of the arguments they encounter. One purpose of a logic course (and perhaps the main purpose) is to enhance people's native ability to evaluate the form of the arguments they meet. Another purpose of a logic course is to impress upon the student the importance of identifying arguments and assessing them in both of these ways (in terms of content and form).

But why should we assess the arguments that come our way? Because we want (as far as possible) to believe only what is true. The best way to establish the truth or falsity of many of our beliefs is to assess the arguments that can be advanced for or against those beliefs. And why do we want to believe only truths? Because actions based upon false beliefs are often unsuccessful; and because—practical considerations aside—people find distasteful the idea of believing to be true what is actually false.

1.2
Key Terms

Before proceeding further, it will be helpful to clarify some of the terms that have occurred above and to introduce additional ones. Each term in this list requires comment:

argument
conclusion
premise
statement
deductive logic
valid
invalid
true
false
inductive logic

Argument is a fundamental logical concept. An **argument** is a set of statements, one of which (the **conclusion**) supposedly follows from the others (the **premises**). (Including the word 'supposedly' broadens the definition so that it covers bad arguments as well as good ones.) Arguments are the expressions in language of pieces of reasoning. The constituents of arguments are statements. The question of the nature of statements is an unresolved philosophical issue.[3] Fortunately, this working definition suffices for our purposes: a **statement** is a sentence that is true or false. The class of statements is roughly the class of declarative sentences. Some examples:

STATEMENTS	NONSTATEMENTS
Ted Kennedy is a Democrat.	Do you have the time?
All acoustic neuromas are benign.	Don't cross the street.
Some Egyptians are blonds.	Please help me find my brother.
	Look out!
	Bless this food.

The two main branches of logic are deductive and inductive logic. In **deductive logic** we are concerned with dividing arguments into two classes: (1) those whose conclusions follow with necessity from their premises; and (2) all other arguments. Arguments in the first class are called **valid**; those in the second class are called **invalid**. Here are two equivalent definitions of 'validity':

A valid argument is one ~~having a form~~ such that *if* all its premises are true, *then* its conclusion must also be true.

A valid argument is one ~~having a form~~ such that it is impossible that its premises are all true and its conclusion false.

Because "validity" is such an important concept in deductive logic there are several equivalent ways of saying that an argument is valid, for example:

The premises of the argument *entail* its conclusion.

The conclusion of the argument *follows with necessity* from its premises.

The conclusion of the argument *follows logically* from its premises.

Note that *validity* as we have defined it is a matter of form, not content. A valid argument may contain false statements, and an invalid one may be composed exclusively of truths. These examples illustrate:

[3]If you wish to pursue this issue, you might read (as a start) Richard M. Gale, "Propositions, Judgments, Sentences, and Statements," in *The Encyclopedia of Philosophy*, ed. Paul Edwards (New York: Free Press, 1967), VI: 494–505. This article introduces the problem and will direct you to further readings.

VALID	INVALID
Norman Mailer is a Greek and he is also a dentist. Therefore, he is a Greek.	Joseph Heller is an American. Therefore, he is an American and he is also a novelist.

Both statements in the "Mailer" argument are false. In spite of this defect, it exhibits impeccable form. If the premise of the "Mailer" argument *were* true, then the conclusion *would also be* true. Both statements in the "Heller" argument are true. But in spite of this virtue, its form is poor. The conclusion of the "Heller" inference simply does not follow from its premises. The "Mailer" and "Heller" arguments have these forms:

"Mailer"	P and Q Therefore P	valid form
"Heller"	P Therefore P and Q	invalid form

Within the class of invalid arguments one can find all the possible combinations of the truth and falsity of constituent statements. Here are several examples:

false premise and false conclusion	Sandra O'Connor is a Cuban. Therefore, she is a Cuban and she is also a brickmason.
false premise and true conclusion	All Protestants are Lutherans. Therefore, all Lutherans are Protestants.
true premise and false conclusion	Ted Kennedy is either a Protestant or he is a Catholic. Therefore, he is a Protestant.

In the class of valid arguments one can find all combinations except one. Here are some examples:

true premise and true conclusion	Some Lutherans are Democrats. Therefore, some Democrats are Lutherans.
false premise and true conclusion	Ted Kennedy is a Protestant. Therefore, he is either a Protestant or he is a Catholic.

Among deductive arguments one combination—namely, "(all) true premises and a false conclusion"—is excluded by the definition of 'validity'. The virtue of validity lies in this feature—that it is *truth preserving*. A valid argument can never take you from truth to falsity.

The term 'valid' as we have defined it does not exactly correspond to the term 'valid' of ordinary discourse. (Since the technical term has a precise meaning and the ordinary term does not, their meanings could not correspond completely.) The principal difference is that the ordinary term encompasses both form and content while the technical term is restricted to form alone. When we assess a piece of reasoning as "valid" in nontechnical discourse, we mean to praise both its structure and its substance. The 'valid' of everyday language would not be applied to arguments that are defective in either respect.

To avoid confusion, let's agree (while we are engaged in logic) to apply the adjectives 'valid' and 'invalid' only to arguments and to assess statements, but not arguments, as 'true' or 'false'. According to this proposal, nothing will be called both *valid* and *true*, as the following argument proves.

> Only arguments are valid.
> No arguments are true.
> Therefore, nothing is both valid and true.

And, of course, nothing will be called both *invalid* and *false*. A statement is *true* when it accords with the actual state of affairs, and one that does not accord is *false*.

In *inductive logic* we are concerned with locating arguments on a continuum that has at one pole arguments whose premises provide no support whatever for their conclusions, and that has at the other pole arguments whose premises provide the maximum support for their conclusions. (The deductive logician would label arguments at the latter pole *valid*.) The inductive logician is not primarily concerned with the arguments falling at either extreme but with those falling between the poles; that is, arguments whose premises provide some—but not absolutely conclusive—support for their conclusions. The seventh scene of Tennessee Williams's *The Glass Menagerie* provides a nice example:

> AMANDA: ... What is the young man's name?
> TOM: His name is O'Connor.
> AMANDA: That, of course, means fish—tomorrow is Friday! I'll have that salmon loaf—with Durkee's dressing![4]

Under one possible analysis Amanda's reasoning may be expressed as two linked arguments:

[4] *The Glass Menagerie* (New York: New Directions, 1949), p. 61.

The Gentleman Caller is named "O'Connor."
All people named "O'Connor" are Irish.
Therefore, the Gentleman Caller is Irish.

The Gentleman Caller is Irish.
Most Irish people are Catholic.
Most Catholics do not eat meat on Fridays.[5]
Therefore, the Gentleman Caller does not eat meat on
    Fridays.

The conclusion of the first argument follows from its premises with necessity. The premises of the second argument provide some support for their conclusion, but that conclusion does not follow with necessity.

A major difference between the two branches of logic lies in the standards used in assessing argument forms. The deductive logician employs all-or-nothing standards; each argument is valid or invalid. The inductive logician employs standards that permit graded assessments. Since the form of the second "Gentleman Caller" argument has some merit, but not maximum merit, that argument is more usefully evaluated in inductive logic.

Both branches of logic are important. Unfortunately, inductive logic is not as well developed as its older sibling. The remainder of this volume is devoted exclusively to deductive logic.[6] Actually, its scope is further restricted to a branch of deductive logic called *propositional logic*. Many of the preceding examples fall within the scope of propositional logic; others belong to another branch of deductive logic called *predicate logic*.[7] What distinguishes propositional logic from the rest of deductive logic is explained in the next chapter.

EXERCISES

1. Consider this valid argument form:

    P and Q
    Therefore P

    ('P' and 'Q' mark gaps to be filled by statements.) Invent an English argument with a true premise and a true conclusion that exhibits this form. Here is an example:

---

[5]This dietary prohibition was dropped in 1966 following the Second Vatican Council.

[6]If you want to learn some inductive logic, begin with Brian Skyrms, *Choice and Chance: An Introduction to Inductive Logic* (Belmont, Calif.: Dickenson, 1966).

[7]See my *Introduction to Logic: Predicate Logic* (Englewood Cliffs, N.J.: Prentice-Hall, 1976). This book presupposes familiarity with propositional logic.

> Ted Kennedy is a Democrat and he is a Catholic.
> Therefore, Ted Kennedy is a Democrat.

Devise two more English arguments exhibiting this form such that one has a false premise and a true conclusion, and the other has both a false premise and a false conclusion. Can you invent an argument having the above form that has a true premise and a false conclusion?

2. Consider this invalid argument form:

> P and Q
> Therefore P and R

('P', 'Q', and 'R' mark gaps to be filled by statements.) Invent four English arguments exhibiting this form such that the first has a true premise and a true conclusion, the second has a false premise and a true conclusion, the third has a false premise and a false conclusion, and the fourth has a true premise and a false conclusion.

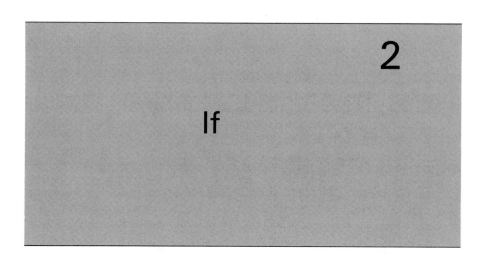

2

If

2.1
Compound Statements

We will call a statement that has no parts which are themselves statements *simple*. Some examples:

> Some Lutherans are Democrats.
> David's tumor is an acoustic neuroma.

Any statement that is not simple we will call *compound*.[1] Some sample compound statements:

> *If* the fan belt breaks *then* the generator stops turning.
> Joseph Heller is an American *and* he is a novelist.
> *Either* one of the children is up *or* there is an intruder in the house.
> Belief in other minds is rational *if and only if* belief in God is rational.

---

[1]Grammarians use the term 'compound' (also 'simple') in a different sense. A number of expressions employed in this book have other meanings in grammar.

Each of these four statements consists of two simple statements and an expression that connects the simple statements. These connecting expressions (which are italicized in the above examples) are called, naturally enough, *statement connectives*. The following statement is also compound:

It is not the case that Norman Mailer is a dentist.

It consists of the locution 'it is not the case that' and a simple statement. The locution is called a *statement connective* in spite of the fact that it attaches to one statement instead of connecting two.

There are many statement connectives in English (or in any natural language), but these five are of special importance in logic:

if ... then
and
it is not the case that
if and only if
either ... or

The remainder of this book is a study of these five connectives, the compound statements that can be constructed with their help, and especially the arguments that involve these compound statements. The study of the forms of arguments whose validity or invalidity rests on the pattern of compound statements composing them is called *the logic of statements* or, more commonly, *propositional logic*. (I shall use the terms 'statement' and 'proposition' interchangeably.) Now you can see why some of the arguments considered in chapter one belong to propositional logic, while others do not.

In this chapter (and chapter four) we devote our attention to the statement connective 'if ... then'. In chapters three, five, six, and seven we shall concentrate on the other four connectives listed above.

2.2
Symbolizing Conditionals

October 18, 1977. ©1977 United Feature Syndicate, Inc.

A statement composed of two constituent statements and the connective 'if ... then' is called a *conditional*. The component statement that precedes 'then' is called the *antecedent* (meaning "that which precedes"), and the component following 'then' is termed the *consequent* ("that which follows"). The antecedent and the consequent may be either simple or compound. A sample conditional:

> (S1)   If the fan belt BREAKS, then the generator STOPS turning.

We facilitate our work by employing symbols. Three kinds of symbols will suffice for the present. (1) *Capital letters* are used to abbreviate simple statements. Where possible, the letter chosen to abbreviate a statement will be the first letter of a prominent word in the statement. In this text the words I have selected to supply statement abbreviations are printed entirely in capital letters — this will help us keep track of the symbols chosen. An example: The antecedent of S1 will be symbolized by the letter B. Although the convention I have chosen for indicating letters involves printing *words* in capital letters, do not think that an abbreviating letter represents a word or any linguistic expression shorter than a statement. For example, in S1 B abbreviates 'The fan belt breaks' — not 'breaks'. Simple statements (occurring in one problem) that convey the same information[2] or have the same content shall be abbreviated by the same letter. For example, these three statements would be symbolized with the same letter:

> Marvin struck Norton.
> Marvin hit Norton.
> Norton was struck by Marvin.

Simple statements (occurring in one problem) with different content shall be abbreviated by different letters.

(2) The statement connective 'if ... then' is abbreviated by the *arrow* symbol ('→'). The arrow is preceded by a capital letter (or letters) representing the antecedent statement and followed by a letter (or letters) representing the consequent. S1 is symbolized by the formula F1.

> (F1)   B → S

This formula is read "If B then S" or "B arrow S."

(3) A formula containing three or more letters requires *grouping symbols* in order to avoid ambiguity. For example, it isn't clear whether F2 (below) symbolizes a conditional with a simple antecedent and a com-

---

[2]The concept "conveying the same information" is difficult to analyze. However, this is more a theoretical than a practical problem; in most cases we can tell whether two statements convey the same information.

pound (conditional) consequent or one with a compound antecedent and a simple consequent.

(F2) $A \rightarrow B \rightarrow C$

Our primary grouping symbols are the *parentheses*: '(' and ')'. These can be used in an entirely natural fashion to eliminate the ambiguity present in F2.

(F3) $A \rightarrow (B \rightarrow C)$
(F4) $(A \rightarrow B) \rightarrow C$

F3 represents a conditional with a simple antecedent; the conditional represented by F4 has a compound antecedent. Speaking metaphorically, the parentheses in F3 are fences that limit the range of the second arrow. This indicates that the first arrow, which is not similarly limited, is the primary connective in F3. We say that the first arrow has greater *scope* than the second. Its scope is the entire formula, while the scope of the second arrow is the string of symbols lying between the parentheses. This emphasis on the use of grouping symbols is not (as it might seem) academic nitpicking, for, as we shall prove later (in section 13.2), F3 and F4 are not equivalent. Our policy will be to avoid ambiguous formulas such as F2.

In the punctuation of some formulas we shall need *brackets* ('[' and ']') in addition to parentheses; in a few instances we shall even require *braces* ('{' and '}'). F5 illustrates the use of all six grouping symbols.

(F5) $D \rightarrow \{ [E \rightarrow (F \rightarrow G)] \rightarrow H \}$
$\phantom{(F5)   D \rightarrow \{} 1 3 4 2$

The grouping symbols in F5 assign varying scopes to the four arrows. The numbers beneath the arrows show their rank in terms of scope. If we employed all the grouping symbols in punctuating a formula and needed still more, we could start over again with parentheses.

English provides many ways of expressing S6.

(S6)   *If* MARVIN stays, *then* NANCY leaves.

The sentences in the following list are equivalent to S6:

If Marvin stays Nancy leaves.
Nancy leaves *if* Marvin stays.
Provided that Marvin stays Nancy leaves.
Nancy leaves *provided that* Marvin stays.
Should Marvin stay, Nancy will leave.

Marvin's staying will *result in* (*bring about, lead to,* etc.) Nancy's leaving.

Each of these statements is correctly symbolized by F6.

(F6)   M → N

It is particularly important to realize that not one of these statements is correctly rendered by F6'.

(F6')   N → M

The order given to the components of a conditional is critical. We may employ this symbolization guide:

The statement following the word 'if' (or its synonym 'provided that') is the antecedent; accordingly, its abbreviation is placed before the arrow.

If you apply this guide to the above statements which contain 'if' or 'provided that', you will arrive at F6 (not F6') in each case. (Unfortunately, the guide breaks down when applied to the locution 'only if'; however, we will not encounter any "only if" statements until chapter four.)

Let's consider a somewhat more complicated symbolization problem. This sentence is quoted from a logic textbook:

If the RULES are valid, then if the AXIOMS are true, all the THEOREMS must be true.

Replacing English statements by abbreviations, we reach:

If R, then if A, T.

This is a conditional whose antecedent is 'R' and whose consequent is 'if A, T'. We move next to a hybrid formula:

R → (if A, T)

Finally, we expunge the last bit of English to arrive at:

R → (A → T)

Until you acquire facility in translating English sentences into formulas, it is a sound idea to symbolize complex sentences in stages (as I have done in this case).

As a final example I will symbolize the dialogue from this "Sesame Street" comic strip:

December 27, 1971. © 1971 Children's Television Workshop.

The girl's assertion is expressed in the *subjunctive* mood. As the logic we are developing is basically a logic of indicative discourse, my first step in symbolizing the statement is to rephrase it in the *indicative* mood.

(S7)   If I have more LIGHT, I can read a BOOK, if I HAVE a book, if I can READ.

Admittedly, there is a difference in meaning between the statement in the comic strip and S7.[3] My justification for paraphrasing a subjunctive statement into the indicative mood is that such a paraphrase is very unlikely to affect the validity of an argument in which the statement figures.

Abbreviating the simple statements in S7, we reach:

If L, B, if H, if R.

This is a *triple* conditional. Occurrences of 'if' identify L, H, and R as antecedents. By elimination we realize that B functions as a consequent. We thus arrive at F7, which is *a* (not *the only*) correct symbolization of S7.

(F7) $L \rightarrow [H \rightarrow (R \rightarrow B)]$

The L, H, and R can occur in other orders.[4]

2.3
Arrow Out

The most basic and most frequently employed pattern of valid inference is this:

---

[3]There are interesting logical and philosophical problems concerning the analysis of conditional statements expressed in the subjunctive mood. See R. M. Chisholm, "The Contrary-to-Fact Conditional," *Mind*, LV (1946), 289–307. For further references, see R. S. Walters's bibliography in *The Encyclopedia of Philosophy*, II: 215–16.

[4]Exercise 204 at the end of chapter four treats this matter.

If $\mathscr{P}$ then $\mathscr{Q}$
$\mathscr{P}$
Therefore $\mathscr{Q}$

('$\mathscr{P}$' and '$\mathscr{Q}$' mark gaps that may be filled by statements. I use script letters to represent the generality of this inference form. *Any* statements or statement abbreviations may fill the gaps marked by '$\mathscr{P}$' and '$\mathscr{Q}$'.) Observe that the second premise of an argument exhibiting this form is identical to the *antecedent* of the first premise, and that the conclusion is identical to the *consequent* of the first premise. This pattern of inference is employed by every human who reasons and has been recognized since antiquity. It bears the Latin label *modus ponens*, meaning "in the mood of affirming" (the second premise affirms the antecedent of the first premise). *Modus ponens* is so basic that its validity does not require justification. In fact, it is so fundamental that any argument that might be advanced in its behalf would be at least as questionable as (and very probably, more questionable than) *modus ponens* itself. Nevertheless, we shall suggest a justification in section 10.2.

Pope Paul VI employed a *modus ponens* argument in a Christmas message to world leaders some years ago:

> *Violence becomes fashionable again, and even clothes itself in the breastplate of justice. It becomes a way of life. Peace is possible, if it is truly willed; and if peace is possible, it is a duty.* [5]

I extract the argument, supplying the unstated conclusion:

> If peace is POSSIBLE, achieving peace is a DUTY.
> Peace is possible.
> Therefore, achieving peace is a duty.

(I have also changed the order of the premises in order to match exactly the *modus ponens* form.) The Pope's argument can be symbolized as follows:

$$P \rightarrow D, P \vdash D$$

(The premises are separated by a comma. We adopt the *turnstile* symbol, '$\vdash$', as shorthand for the word 'therefore'; the turnstile is placed between the last premise and the conclusion.)

It is important to distinguish *modus ponens* from the following invalid inference pattern:

If $\mathscr{P}$ then $\mathscr{Q}$
$\mathscr{Q}$
Therefore $\mathscr{P}$

[5] *Cleveland Plain Dealer* (December 21, 1972).

The second premise of an argument having this form is identical to the *consequent* of the first premise. This pattern is appropriately labelled *the fallacy of affirming the consequent*. The contrast between the two argument patterns is shown clearly in the following:

$$\textit{modus ponens}: \quad \mathcal{P} \to \mathcal{Q}, \mathcal{P} \vdash \mathcal{Q} \ (\textit{valid})$$
$$\text{affirming the consequent}: \quad \mathcal{P} \to \mathcal{Q}, \mathcal{Q} \vdash \mathcal{P} \ (\textit{invalid})$$

Consider an example of an argument that commits the fallacy of affirming the consequent:

> If Ralph Nader is PRESIDENT, then he is FAMOUS. He is famous. So, he is president.

Symbolized:

$$P \to F, F \vdash P$$

The first premise of the argument asserts that Nader's attaining the presidency would imply his being famous; it does *not* assert that his achieving fame implies his being president. Thus, when the first premise is coupled with the second, it does not follow that Nader is president.

    The deficiency of the "Nader" argument is especially noticeable because its premises are obviously true and its conclusion is plainly false. Some arguments which commit the same fallacy have conclusions that are true or at least not clearly false. Such arguments can seduce the unwary. The following passage from a book by Hillyer Straton provides an example:

> *Never has a book been subjected to such pitiless search for error as the Holy Bible. Both reverent and agnostic critics have ploughed and harrowed its passages; but through it all God's word has stood supreme, and appears even more vital because of the violent attacks made upon it. This is proof to Baptists that here we have a revelation from God; for we believe that if God reveals himself to man for purposes of blessing, he will preserve a record of that revelation in order that men who follow may know his way and will.*[6]

Straton appears to be advancing this argument:

> If the Bible is God's REVELATION, then it will WITHSTAND critical attack. It does withstand such attack. Hence, it is revelation.

In symbols:

$$R \to W, W \vdash R$$

---

[6] *Baptists: Their Message and Missions* (Philadelphia: Judson Press, 1941), p. 49.

Some may fail to see the formal defect in the "revelation" argument (in spite of the fact that it has the same form as the "Nader" argument). The first premise of the "revelation" argument does *not* assert that the Bible's withstanding attack implies its being revelation. This fact constitutes the basis of the argument's invalidity. A formal demonstration of its invalidity is given in section 10.2.

   Modus ponens can be used to establish the validity of certain other arguments. An argument advanced by Mr. Spock provides an example. In one *Star Trek* segment he addresses the following to Assistant Commander Matt Decker (paraphrased):

> *Continuing to attack the enemy ship would be suicide. Anybody who attempts suicide is psychologically unfit to command the* Enterprise. *Therefore, I will have to relieve you of your duty.*

Spock's argument may be restated:

> Decker is ATTACKING the enemy ship. If so, then he is attempting SUICIDE. Decker is psychologically UNFIT to command the *Enterprise* if he is trying to commit suicide. Therefore, Decker is psychologically unfit to command the *Enterprise.*

This argument is symbolized:

$$A, A \rightarrow S, S \rightarrow U \vdash U$$

One way of showing this to be a valid argument is to note that one can infer S from the first two premises and then, by combining S with the third premise, infer the conclusion. Both inferences are instances of *modus ponens*.

   We have in the above reasoning implicitly assumed a principle that should be brought to the surface — namely, that if one can proceed from the premises of an argument to its conclusion by a series of valid inferences, then the argument is valid. This principle underlies a logical technique called the method of *formal proof*, which we shall introduce now and develop in the next seven chapters. A formal proof of the validity of an argument is a list of statements that satisfies two conditions: (1) each item in the list is either a premise of the argument or a statement derived by means of a valid inference rule from statements above it in the list; and (2) the last item in the list is the conclusion of the argument. (This explanation of "formal proof" will be tightened in section 8.3.)

   The first rule of inference we adopt sanctions *modus ponens* inferences. We call it the *Arrow Out Rule* because it licenses the passage from a formula containing an arrow (and a second formula) to one lacking the arrow.

The Arrow Out Rule: From a conditional and a statement identical to its antecedent derive a statement identical to its consequent.

We can state this rule more simply if we let ' $\mathcal{A} \rightarrow \mathcal{B}$ ' represent any conditional (no matter how complex), ' $\mathcal{A}$ ', a statement identical to the antecedent of that conditional, and ' $\mathcal{B}$ ', a statement identical to the consequent of the conditional. The rule restated:

From $\mathcal{A} \rightarrow \mathcal{B}$ and $\mathcal{A}$ derive $\mathcal{B}$.

(In succeeding chapters script letters will be used in a similar way in the statement of additional inference rules.)

We are now in a position to construct a formal proof (or simply "proof") for the *Star Trek* argument:

$$
\begin{array}{l}
A \\
A \rightarrow S \\
S \rightarrow U \\
S \\
U
\end{array}
$$

To facilitate the checking of proofs and to render one person's proofs more intelligible to another, we shall include two additional columns. (Later, we shall add a fourth column.) In the column on the left we number the items; in the one on the right (called the *justification* column) we give for each item a reason or justification for including it in the list. With these conventions adopted, the proof of the *Star Trek* argument becomes:

$$
\begin{array}{lll}
(1) & A & A \\
(2) & A \rightarrow S & A \\
(3) & S \rightarrow U & A \\
(4) & S & 2,1 \rightarrow O \\
(5) & U & 3,4 \rightarrow O
\end{array}
$$

We adopt *A* as an abbreviation for 'Introduced as an assumption'. (For the time being, all assumptions in a proof will be premises of the argument being validated.) We adopt, for example, '2,1 $\rightarrow$ O' as shorthand for 'Derived from lines 2 and 1 by the Arrow Out Rule'. In justifying a step made in accordance with the Arrow Out Rule, I cite the conditional premise first. However, this subtlety is not essential, and you may prefer not to adopt it.

I shall construct a proof for another argument. Recently, Jewish students at the University of Miami petitioned the school to institute a program of Jewish studies. In support of their request they cited a statement that the academic dean had made on the occasion of the university's establishing an Afro-American studies program:

It is the duty of a university as an institution to disseminate knowledge of the cultures of the people who inhabit the section. The Afro-American Studies Program is the response of the university to this duty. [7]

It is clear that the students were advancing this sort of argument:

A university has the DUTY to disseminate knowledge of the cultures of the people who inhabit the section. If this is true, then provided that many Jews LIVE in South Florida, the University of Miami should INSTITUTE a Jewish studies program. Many Jews do live in South Florida. It follows that the university should institute this program.

In symbols:

D, D → (L → I), L ⊢ I

A proof of validity:

$$
\begin{array}{lll}
(1) & D & A \\
(2) & D \to (L \to I) & A \\
(3) & L & A \\
(4) & L \to I & 2,1 \to O \\
(5) & I & 4,3 \to O
\end{array}
$$

Line 2 in this proof is a conditional whose consequent is also a conditional. The inference of line 4 from lines 2 and 1 illustrates the point noted above that the Arrow Out Rule applies to conditionals having compound parts.

As a final example I construct a proof for this symbolized argument:

(I → J) → K, K → I, I → J ⊢ J

$$
\begin{array}{lll}
(1) & (I \to J) \to K & A \\
(2) & K \to I & A \\
(3) & I \to J & A \\
(4) & K & 1,3 \to O \\
(5) & I & 2,4 \to O \\
(6) & J & 3,5 \to O
\end{array}
$$

Note that the conditional on line 1 of this proof has a compound antecedent ('I → J') that is matched by the conditional on line 3. Also note that line 3 serves as a premise in the deduction of *two* lines (4 and 6). This is

[7] Jill H. Movshin, "SBG Supports Jewish Studies," *The Miami Hurricane* (September 28, 1971), p. 2.

permissible; any line in a proof can be used as a premise as often as needed.

   This logical technique is called the method of *formal* proof for at least two reasons. First, every step in a proof must be sanctioned *explicitly* by some rule. There is no room for informal sanctions such as "Well, I see that this follows." Second, each rule employed refers only to the *forms* of statements.

EXERCISES

3.   Symbolize each statement using the suggested abbreviations.

$P \to S$

(a)   (*Nursing text*) "If the medullary centers are DEPRESSED, then chemoreceptors in the carotid bodies STIMULATE respiration."

$T \to B$

(b)   (*Billboard ad*) "If you have the TIME, we have the BEER."

$L \to C$

(c)   (*Florida Turnpike toll card*) "If ticket is LOST regular toll from farthest point will be COLLECTED."

$S \to A$

(d)   (*Newspaper*) "Some 7,000 employees of Southern Bell in Dade County would be AFFECTED if a nationwide STRIKE of Bell System workers goes into effect."

$C \to F$

(e)   ("Mickey Finn" comic strip*) "I'll FORGET about Portiko's offer—providing you get Mother to CHANGE her mind."

$Q \to P$

(f)   (*Newspaper*) "Should the Dolphins QUALIFY as a runnerup team, they will PLAY at Cleveland Christmas weekend."

$B \to C$

(g)   (*Newspaper*) "San Diego can CLINCH the AFC West crown by BEATING Denver in their final game."

$R \to B$

(h)   (*Science fiction*) "Had the stowaway REFUSED to obey, the pilot would have used the BLASTER."

$A \to (A \to T)$

(i)   (*Logician James Carney*) "If the AXIOMS could be so selected that they were necessarily true, then, if the DEDUCTIONS were valid, the truth of the THEOREMS would be guaranteed."

$Q \to (C \to R)$

*(j)   (*Newspaper*) "If you have a specific QUESTION, we will RELAY it to him, if he CALLS in."

4.   Translate each formula into an English sentence using this "dictionary":

   A =   Salt is added to the solution
   D =   The solution's boiling point drops
   M =   The manual is correct
   S =   The solution boils sooner

*Solutions (or partial solutions) to starred problems are provided in appendix three.

(a)   A → D

(b)   M → (A → S)

*(c)   (A → D) → (A → S)

5. Complete the following proofs. Every assumption has been identified in the justification column.

(a)   (1) A → B   A

           (2) B → (C → D)   A

           (3) A   A

           (4) B   1,3 → O

           (5) C → D   2,4 → O

(b)   (1) E → F   A

           (2) (E → F) → E   A

           (3) E   2,1 → O

           (4) F   1,3 → O

(c)   (1) (G → H) → (I → J)   A

           (2) G → H   A

           (3) I   A

           (4) I → J   1,2 → O

           (5) J   4,3 → O

*(d)   (1) K → L   A

           (2) M   A

           (3) L → N   A

           (4) M → K   A

           (5) K   4,2 → O

           (6) L   1,5 → O

           (7) N   3,6 → O

Instructions for exercises 6 through 13: We call arguments stated in English concrete and those expressed only in symbols abstract. For each abstract argument construct a proof of its validity. For each concrete argument, (1) symbolize it (on one horizontal line), and (2) construct a proof of its validity. (These exercises are arranged so that the simplest problems occur first. This practice is followed throughout the book.)

April 20, 1971, McNaught Syndicate, Inc.

6.   Identify the argument in the "Mickey Finn" comic strip. Supply the unstated conclusion. Use these abbreviations:

H = The Justice Department charges Hawks with income tax evasion
R = Ron becomes the crime syndicate's number one target

*7.   The Germans have DEVALUED the U.S. dollar. If this is true, American consumers will PAY more for new Volkswagens. Provided that Americans will pay more for new Volkswagens, the value of my nearly new VW camper has RISEN. It follows that the value of my camper has increased.

8.   Argument 8 on page 43 is concerned with the problem of symbolizing sentences that contain the expression 'only if'. We use these abbreviations:

A = S1 is equivalent to S4
B = S4 is equivalent to S2
C = S1 is equivalent to S2

The argument is symbolized:

$A, B, A \rightarrow (B \rightarrow C) \vdash C$

9. $A \rightarrow (A \rightarrow B), A \vdash B$

10.   Stuffed animals can reason:

"Aha!" said Pooh. (Rum-tum-tiddle-um-tum.) "If I know anything about anything, that hole means Rabbit," he said, "and Rabbit means Company," he said, "and Company means Food...." [8]

Pooh's argument:

There is a rabbit HOLE here. A rabbit hole means that there is a RABBIT nearby. If there is a rabbit nearby, then there is COMPANY around. If there is company around, then there is FOOD available. Thus, there is food available.

The second premise is a conditional.

[8]A. A. Milne, *Winnie the Pooh* (New York: Dutton, 1926), p. 22.

11.   If we buy a PIANO, then we'll go BROKE if we also install AIR conditioning. If we buy a piano, we'll have to have an air-conditioning system installed [because of the humidity problem].[9] We are buying a piano. So, we will be broke.

12.   (C → D) → E, E → C, C → D ⊢ D

*13.   (F → G) → (G → H), F → G, F ⊢ H

3

And

3.1
Symbolizing Conjunctions

A statement consisting of two constituent statements joined by the connective 'and' is called a *conjunction*. The component statements are termed *conjuncts*; they may be simple or compound statements. A sample conjunction:

> Eric Heiden is a speed SKATER and he is also a BICYCLIST.

We introduce the *ampersand* ('&') as an abbreviation for the connective 'and'. The conjunction above is symbolized:

> S & B

This formula is read "S and B" or "S ampersand B."

In chapter two we adopted a principle of avoiding ambiguity in the formulas we write. Hence, these formulas are objectionable:

> A & B → C
> D → E & F

It is impossible to determine whether they symbolize conjunctions or conditionals. We outlaw such formulas, replacing them with unambiguous formulas such as these:

$$(A \& B) \rightarrow C \qquad A \& (B \rightarrow C)$$
$$D \rightarrow (E \& F) \qquad (D \rightarrow E) \& F$$

The formulas on the left are conditionals; those on the right are conjunctions.

Several English connective expressions are equivalent (from the standpoint of logic) to the connective 'and'. Some appear (in italics) in the following list of statements:

> MARVIN stays *but* NANCY leaves.
>
> Marvin stays, *however* Nancy leaves.
>
> Marvin stays, *moreover* Nancy leaves.
>
> Marvin stays *although* Nancy leaves.
>
> Marvin stays *yet* Nancy leaves.
>
> Marvin stays *even though* Nancy leaves.

Each of these statements is symbolized 'M & N'. The italicized expressions are not completely synonymous; nevertheless, there is a common factor in their meanings that justifies our treating them in a group. (Did you notice that the preceding sentence is a conjunction?) The meaning of each term is such that a person who assents to a compound statement built around that term is automatically committed to accepting both of the constituent statements.

I'll symbolize some more complex sentences, starting with this one from a newspaper sports story:

> *A Houston loss to Denver and a Miami victory over New England puts the playoff game in the Orange Bowl.*

This is a conditional with a conjunctive antecedent:

> If HOUSTON loses to Denver and MIAMI beats New England, then the playoff game will be in the ORANGE Bowl.

We symbolize it:

$$(H \& M) \rightarrow O$$

Two more sentences and their symbolizations:

> (S1) *(Allstate ad)* "If all cars had AIR bags, we'd eliminate 24,000 DEATHS a year, plus hundreds of thousands of crippling INJURIES."

(F1)   A → (D & I)

(S2)   *(Miami politician)* "If the bond issue PASSES, all the citizens will WIN, and if it FAILS, this GENERATION and future ONES will lose."

(F2)   (P → W) & [F → (G & O)]

Would it be wrong to symbolize S2 with the pair of formulas F3 and F4?

(F3)   P → W
(F4)   F → (G & O)

Since F2 has the same content as F3 and F4 taken together, it would not be an error to symbolize S2 with the latter two formulas. However, for the sake of uniform treatment, let's adopt the following convention:

One English sentence will be represented by *one* formula.[1]

In some contexts the word 'and' does not function as a statement connective, for example, in S5.

(S5)   Marvin and Nancy are cousins.

S5 is not equivalent to the conjunction S6. (Why not?)[2]

(S6)   Marvin is a cousin and Nancy is a cousin.

S5 is a simple statement; accordingly, it will be symbolized with a single capital letter (and no ampersand).

At the beginning of the chapter I claimed that statements built of two constituent statements joined by the connective 'and' are conjunctions. But, occasionally, one finds such a statement that is equivalent to a conditional and should be symbolized with an arrow instead of an ampersand. S7 (addressed to Roosevelt by Churchill in 1941) is a case in point.

(S7)   "GIVE us the tools [of war], and we shall FINISH the job."

S7 is properly symbolized by F7:

(F7)   G → F

---

[1]An exception to this convention must be made when both a premise and the conclusion of an argument occur in the same English sentence. In such a case, of course, two formulas are required.

[2]If both Marvin and Nancy have cousins but are not related to each other, then S5 is false and S6 is true.

(*G* abbreviates 'You do give us the tools of war'.) The moral that should be drawn from these observations is that one should *think* while symbolizing, rather than proceeding by rote. If after producing a symbolization there is any question about adequacy, you should inspect the formula and determine whether it contains the substance of the original statement. In this way one can discover that F7' is an incorrect symbolization of S7.

(F7')   G & F

It follows from F7' that the United States gives Britain tools of war. Because this does not follow from S7, F7' is not acceptable.

Before concluding this discussion of symbolization, I want to touch on one more topic: determining the gross structure of arguments. How does one tell which statements in an argument function as premises and which as the conclusion? Of course, there is no substitute for understanding the passage that contains the argument. However, certain key terms are fairly reliable indicators. These expressions follow premises and introduce conclusions:

> therefore
> so
> hence
> thus
> consequently
> it follows that
> ... proves that
> ... shows that

And these expressions regularly follow conclusions and introduce premises:

> since
> because
> for

Neither of these lists is exhaustive.

It often helps to first identify the conclusion of an argument. As there is only *one* conclusion per argument, the remaining statements (assuming they all belong to the argument) will be premises. The conclusion may appear at the beginning, in the middle, or at the end of an English argument. When we symbolize the argument, we place the (symbolized) conclusion last. The order given to the symbolized premises is not critical, but I follow the practice of symbolizing premises in the order in which they occur in the English formulation of the argument.

I shall illustrate some of the points just noted with an argument purporting to establish the identity of the world's first cheerleader. A newspaper obituary for Robert Matthews includes this paragraph:

> *A 1956 edition of "Ripley's Believe It or Not" called Matthews "the world's first cheerleader" because he organized the activity in 1898 while a student at the University of Illinois. That school says it is the first to have cheerleaders.* [3]

The argument may be set out more explicitly as follows:

> Robert Matthews was the first cheerleader at the University of ILLINOIS. *It follows that* he was the WORLD'S first cheerleader *since* Illinois was the first SCHOOL to have cheerleaders. Obviously, he must have been the world's first cheerleader if Illinois was the first school with cheerleaders and Matthews was the first cheerleader there.

The important terms for revealing the structure of the argument are italicized. The argument is symbolized:

$$I, S, (S \& I) \rightarrow W \vdash W$$

3.2
Ampersand In

The "cheerleader" example is an obviously valid argument that involves both the ampersand and the arrow. We would like to be able to construct a formal proof for it, but in order to complete this proof, we must deduce a conjunction. As yet, we have no rule of inference that sanctions such a move; so, we introduce one.

> *The Ampersand In Rule:* From two statements derive a conjunction formed from them.

The rule restated:

> From $\mathcal{A}$ and $\mathcal{B}$ derive $\mathcal{A} \& \mathcal{B}$.

The inference pattern sanctioned by this rule is so simple that we rarely employ it consciously in ordinary contexts. Still, it is clearly sound and will frequently be needed in proof construction. A proof of the "cheerleader" argument:

[3]"Robert Matthews Dead at 99; 'World's First Cheerleader,'" *Miami News* (May 15, 1978), p. 4-A.

(1)	I	A
(2)	S	A
(3)	(S & I) → W	A
(4)	S & I	2,1 &I
(5)	W	3,4 → O

The justification for line 4 ('2, 1 &I') is short for 'Derived from lines 2 and 1 by the Ampersand In Rule'. (I cite first the premise identical to the left conjunct of the statement being derived, but it's not essential that you adopt this practice.)

Next, we construct a proof for this abstract argument:

A, B, C ⊢ (B & A) & C

The proof involves a double application of the Ampersand In Rule.

(1)	A	A
(2)	B	A
(3)	C	A
(4)	B & A	2,1 &I
(5)	(B & A) & C	4,3 &I

A move sanctioned by the Ampersand In Rule involves *two* premises. Thus, the following "proof " is incorrect.

(1)	A	A
(2)	B	A
(3)	C	A
(4)	(B & A) & C	2,1,3 &I (ERROR!)

From a given pair of lines in a proof either one of two statements may be deduced by means of the Ampersand In Rule. For example, on line 3 of the following partial proof one may deduce either 'D & E' or 'E & D'.

(1)	D
(2)	E

Since the Ampersand In Rule offers the proof constructor this option we dub it a "choice" rule. Is Arrow Out a choice rule?[4]

---

[4]No. From a pair of statements one statement at most may be derived by Arrow Out.

3.3

Ampersand Out

This argument is valid:

> Jane Fonda is an ACTRESS and a POLITICAL activist.
> So, she is a political activist and an actress.

In symbols:

A & P ⊢ P & A

The order of the conjuncts in a conjunction is unimportant (from the standpoint of logic). In logicians' jargon, the ampersand is *commutative*. (Is the arrow commutative?) In order to construct a proof for the above argument, we require another rule of inference.

> *The Ampersand Out Rule:* From a conjunction derive either con-junct.

The rule restated:

> From $\mathcal{A}$ & $\mathcal{B}$ derive either $\mathcal{A}$ or $\mathcal{B}$.

It is obvious from its statement that Ampersand Out is a "choice" rule. Now we can construct a proof for the "Fonda" argument.

(1)	A & P	A
(2)	A	1 &O
(3)	P	1 &O
(4)	P & A	3,2 &I

Notice that a slightly different proof could have been constructed for the "Fonda" argument:

(1)	A & P	A
(2)	P	1 &O
(3)	A	1 &O
(4)	P & A	2,3 &I

For most valid arguments (particularly the more complex ones) there will be several alternative correct proofs. A practical corollary of this fact: If a proof you construct for a starred exercise differs from the proof given in the third appendix, it does not follow that your proof is mistaken. It would be a good policy in such a situation, though, to recheck your proof.

Where there are two or more alternative correct proofs for an argument, are there grounds for preferring one proof to another? A logician will prefer an organized proof to a disorganized one and a shorter, more "elegant" proof to a longer one. For our purposes, however, any error-free proof is wholly acceptable.

How shall we symbolize Heine's assertion that "LIFE is a disease, the whole WORLD a hospital, and DEATH is our physician"? Three possibilities:

(F1)   L & W & D

(F2)   L & (W & D)

(F3)   (L & W) & D

It will facilitate the development of our proof procedure if we agree to renounce formulas patterned like F1. Which of the remaining two shall we adopt as the proper symbolization?

Preliminary to answering this question, I note that F2 *entails* F3. (One statement entails a second when the argument that has the first statement as sole premise and the second statement as conclusion is valid. When one statement entails a second, the second *follows logically from* the first.) This proof demonstrates that F2 entails F3.

(1)	L & (W & D)	A
(2)	L	1 &O
(3)	W & D	1 &O
(4)	W	3 &O
(5)	D	3 &O
(6)	L & W	2,4 &I
(7)	(L & W) & D	6,5 &I

Not only does F2 entail F3, F3 entails F2. (Exercise 22 at the end of the chapter is concerned with this entailment.) Mutually entailing statements are said to be *logically equivalent.* Logically equivalent statements have the same content. We can now answer the question about which formula is the symbolization of Heine's statement. Because the two formulas have the same content, each is an adequate symbolization. Generalizing on this point: If any two formulas are logically equivalent and one of them is a correct symbolization of some statement, then the other formula is also an acceptable symbolization of that statement. Just as in checking proofs: if your symbolization of a statement in a starred exercise differs from the solution in the third appendix, it does not follow that your formula is incorrect. Your symbolization is right if (and only if) it is logically equivalent to the solution provided.

The logician describes the logical equivalence of F2 and F3 by saying that the ampersand is *associative.* (Is the arrow associative?)

Consider this argument:

> If four is LESS than six and EVERY number less than six is prime, then four is PRIME. Therefore, if four is less than six it is a prime number.

In symbols:

$$(L \,\&\, E) \rightarrow P \vdash L \rightarrow P$$

It should be clear that the premise of this argument is true. (The premise does not maintain that four *is* prime.) The conclusion, on the other hand, is false; four is less than six but (being divisible by two) is not a prime. Since its premise is true and its conclusion false, the "prime" argument must be invalid. If we can construct a "proof" for this invalid argument with the set of rules we are developing, then our proof procedure is useless as a method of establishing validity. It may seem that such a "proof" is possible:

(1) $(L \,\&\, E) \rightarrow P$ A
(2) $L \rightarrow P$ 1 &O (ERROR!)

Fortunately for the system we are developing, this is not an acceptable proof. Line 2 is incorrectly derived by applying the Ampersand Out Rule to a *part* of line 1 (namely, the antecedent of line 1). The Ampersand Out Rule *and all the other rules* introduced in chapters two through nine apply to *whole* lines only. This restriction can be emphasized by providing a second instance of a violation.

(1) $L \,\&\, (W \,\&\, D)$ A
(2) W 1 &O (ERROR!)

The argument that this "proof" treats is valid. A three-line proof will establish its validity.

We now have three inference rules at our disposal; some suggestions for developing strategies for constructing proofs may be useful at this point. When you are in the process of constructing a proof there will usually be two types of lines on your worksheet: (1) those set down at the top (which will be either premises of the argument or lines derived from them), and (2) those set down at the bottom as goals. Let's call lines of the first type "premise lines" and those of the second "goal lines." The last goal line, of course, will be the conclusion of the argument; but there may also be intermediate goal lines—lines that will help you reach the final goal. Here is a strategic suggestion for each of the rules we have covered so far:

ARROW OUT: If one of the premise lines is a conditional, search the other premise lines for the antecedent. If you find it, apply Arrow Out. If you do not find the antecedent among the premise lines, add it as a goal line.

AMPERSAND IN: If one of the goal lines is a conjunction, search the premise lines for the two conjuncts. If you find both conjuncts, apply Ampersand In. If you find only one conjunct, add the other as a goal line. If you find neither conjunct among the premise lines, add both as goal lines.

AMPERSAND OUT: If one of the premise lines is a conjunction, apply Ampersand Out (once or twice).

Each intermediate goal line is placed above the goal lines already on the worksheet. Note that setting down a goal line must be distinguished from deriving a line in a proof. A line added as a goal must at some later stage be derived from higher lines or the proof will remain incomplete.

EXERCISES

14. Symbolize each statement using the suggested notation.

(a)   *(To "Dear Abby")* "I am a CHRISTIAN and I also PLAY the clarinet."   C & P

(b)   *(Shakespeare,* Macbeth*)* "Drink PROVOKES the desire, but it TAKES away the performance."   P & T

(c)   *(Children's book)* "And although he was a very SMALL ghost, Georgie had a really BIG idea."   S & B

(d)   "Show us someone who likes this HASH and we'll show you someone who likes GARBAGE." (Let *H* abbreviate 'You show us someone who likes this hash'.)   H → G

January 5, 1970, King Features Syndicate, Inc.

*(e)   *(Albert Camus)* "Sunlight not only stimulates the MIND and morals but is also a sovereign cure for DIARRHEA." (Let *A* abbreviate 'Sunlight stimulates morals'.)   (M & A) & D

(f)   *(Sports story)* "If Oakland BEATS Seattle and Denver LOSES to San Diego, the Raiders would GAIN the wild-card berth."   (B & L) → G

(g)   *(Newspaper)* "If she SPEAKS, she BREAKS the spell and has to WAIT for another Midsummer."   S → (B & W)

(S → B) & (B → W)?

(h) "YOU release hamburger, I release hand." (Let *I* abbreviate 'I release hand'.)

$Y \rightarrow I$

May 5, 1983. © 1983 United Feature Syndicate, Inc.

$(O \rightarrow L) \& (H \rightarrow W)$

*(i) *(Oldtime ballplayer Goose Goslin)* "If I make an OUT I LOSE the batting championship, and if I get a HIT I WIN it."

$(I \& R) \rightarrow (T \rightarrow O)$

(j) *(Logician James Carney)* "If one can show that the axioms of system one can be INTERPRETED so as to be theorems of system two, [and] that system two has the same inference RULES as system one, then system ONE must be consistent if system TWO is consistent."

15. Translate each formula into an English sentence using this "dictionary":

A = Miami wins its last regular-season game
B = Miami loses its last regular-season game
C = New York loses its last regular-season game
D = Miami wins the division championship
E = Miami is the "wild-card" team

   (a) A & D
   (b) (A & C) → D
   (c) A & (C → D)
*(d) A → (C & D)
   (e) (A → D) & (B → E)

16. Complete the following proofs. Every assumption has been identified.

(a) (1) (A & B) & C   A
    (2) A & B   1, &O
    (3) A   2, &O
    (4) C   1, &O
    (5) A & C   3,4

(b) (1) A & C   A
    (2) B   A
    (3) A   1 & O
    (4) C   1 & O
    (5) A & B   3,2 & I
    (6) (A & B) & C   4,5 & I

*(c)
(1) D & E	A
(2) (D → F) & (E → G)	A
(3) D → F	2 $\mathcal{I}$0
(4) D	1 $\mathcal{8}$0
(5) F	3,4 → O
(6) E → G	280
(7) E	1 $\mathcal{8}$0
(8) G	6,7 →0
(9) F & G	5,8 &I

(d)
(1) (H & I) → (J & K)	A
(2) I & H	A
(3) I	280
(4) H	280
(5) H & I	3,4 &I
(6) J & K	1,5 →0
(7) J	6,4 0

Instructions for exercises 17 through 26: Symbolize the concrete arguments; construct proofs for all arguments.

17. Mother-son conversation:

> MARK: Did I feed my fish?
> CARMEN: You fed your big ones.
> MARK: If I fed the big ones, I fed the little ones.

Mark reasoned:

> I fed the BIG fish. If I fed the big ones, I also fed the LIT-TLE fish. Thus, I fed both my big fish and my little ones.

18. I fed the BIG fish, and if I fed them I fed all my fish. Hence, I fed ALL my fish.

19. W. T. Jones explains one of Aristotle's contentions about the "un-moved mover":

> *And what is the object of his thought? Clearly it can only be himself. This follows because the unmoved mover knows only the best, and the best is the un-moved mover.*[5]

Jones's argument:

> The unmoved mover KNOWS only the best. The un-moved mover IS the best. If the unmoved mover knows only the best and is the best, then he knows only himself. So, the unmoved mover knows only HIMSELF.

*20. News story:

> *Fourteen Dade County jail prisoners were held in isolation today because one of them has hepatitis, a disease he apparently contracted in the jail.*

---

[5]W. T. Jones, *The Classical Mind: A History of Western Philosophy* (New York: Harcourt Brace, 1969), p. 231.

> *Jail officials did not say the ill prisoner got the disease in jail but the incubation period for it is from 10 to 50 days, and the prisoner has been in jail more than four months.*[6]

The reporter advances an argument in this passage. The conclusion is put forward (cautiously) at the end of the first paragraph; premises are supplied in the second paragraph. A formalization of his argument:

(1) ⅃ & F
(2) ⅃ → (F → C)
(3) I
(4) F → C
(5) F
(6) C

The prisoner CONTRACTED hepatitis in jail. This is a consequence of the following facts: The INCUBATION period for the disease is from 10 to 50 days, yet the prisoner has been in jail more than FOUR months. Now if the incubation period is from 10 to 50 days, then providing the man has been jailed over four months, he must have contracted the illness in jail.

(marginal notes: A   A   1, bo   2, 1→0   1 2 0   4 5 → 0)

21. A letter to Ann Landers and her reply:

> *Dear Ann Landers: I have an average-size problem. Last week I had my ear pierced. Not both of them — just one. You'd have thought I had committed an axe murder or something. My folks raised a terrific howl.*
> *I should have told you at the beginning of this letter — I'm a guy.*
> *Why all the excitement? I'm old enough to drive a car, old enough to buy beer and old enough to fight in a war. But my folks don't seem to think I'm old enough to make this decision. What do you think? — Long Island Joe*
>
> *Dear Joe: It's your ear and if you want to hang an earring on it, it's OK with me — but I'm not excited about the idea either.*[7]

Long Island Joe's argument:

I'm old enough to DRIVE. I'm old enough to buy BEER. And I'm old enough to FIGHT in a war. Now, if I'm old enough to do all these things, then I'm also old enough to have my ear pierced. Therefore, I'm old enough to have my ear PIERCED.

22. (L & W) & D ⊢ L & (W & D)

23. Feminist Ti-Grace Atkinson, speaking at Washington's Catholic University, claimed that the Catholic Church had "used" the Virgin Mary in its doctrine of the Immaculate Conception. At this point Patricia Buckley Bozell (editor of the Catholic magazine *Triumph* and sister of William Buckley) ran to the podium and slapped (or attempted to slap) Ms. Atkinson. Afterward Mrs. Bozell said:

[6]Bill Gjebre, "Jail Inmate Has Hepatitis; Authorities Isolate Cell," *Miami News* (April 9, 1971), p. 1-A.
[7]*The Parkersburg News* (February 28, 1979). Reprinted by permission of Ann Landers and Field Newspaper Syndicate.

I think I did what God would have wanted me to do. ... Any son would want his mother protected. [8]

This somewhat weird justification can be advanced as an argument.

Any son wants his mother PROTECTED. If so then Jesus wants MARY protected. By SLAPPING Ti-Grace I protected Mary. If Jesus wants Mary protected and I protected her by slapping Ti-Grace, then JESUS wanted me to slap Ti-Grace. It follows that Jesus wanted me to slap Ti-Grace.

24. The instruction manual for my lawnmower advised me to begin cutting my lawn with three clockwise swaths and then to finish with a counterclockwise spiral; however, the booklet gives no rationale for these directions. I conjectured the following explanation (which is cast as an argument):

Mowing clockwise blows clippings toward the CENTER of the lawn; and if this is so, beginning with three clockwise circuits will keep clippings off the SIDE-WALK. Mowing counterclockwise blows clippings toward the PERIMETER; and if this is true, doing the rest of the lawn counterclockwise MINIMIZES mowing clippings. So, starting with three clockwise laps will keep the clippings off the sidewalk; moreover, doing the rest of the lawn in the other direction will minimize mowing clippings.

*25. Newspaper story:

Dr. Howard Knuttgen, a Boston University biologist, is conducting a study on the harm professional football players can do to each other.

In 1942, Knuttgen says, pro football players averaged 200 pounds a man, but last year that average was 222.

"As momentum equals mass times velocity," Knuttgen says, "there can be no doubt that these men are hitting harder and injuring each other more seriously." [9]

Knuttgen's reasoning can be given this formal dress:

Momentum EQUALS mass times velocity. Today's players have more MASS than the players of 1942, but move with equal (or greater) VELOCITY. If momentum equals mass times velocity, then if players today have

[8] Billie O'Day, "Bozell vs. Atkinson: Was the Slap Justified?" *Miami News* (March 15, 1971), p. 2-B.
[9] Charlie Nobles, "Football Injuries Could Alter Rules," *Miami News* (July 14, 1971), p. 3-C.

at least the same velocity as, and more mass than, players in '42, today's players are HITTING harder than those in '42. If football players today hit harder than players in '42, then they are INJURING each other more seriously than did the men playing in '42. All of this proves that the men playing now are injuring each other more seriously than did the players of '42.

26. When an ice cube floats in a glass of water, some of it extends above the surface. One might expect, therefore, that as the cube melts the water level will rise slightly, but this does not happen. A scientific explanation of why the water level remains constant can be formulated as a deductive argument:[10]

[According to Archimedes' principle,] a solid body floating in a liquid DISPLACES a volume of liquid that has the same weight as the body itself. If this is true, the chunk of ice has the SAME weight as the water displaced by its submerged portion. The weight of a substance remains CONSTANT through melting. If (i) the ice has the same weight as the water displaced by its submerged portion and (ii) the weight of a substance is unaffected by melting, then the ice cube turns into a mass of water having the same WEIGHT as the water initially displaced by its submerged portion. Provided that the cube turns into a mass of water having the same weight as the water initially displaced by its submerged portion, it turns into a mass of water having the same VOLUME as the water initially displaced. The LEVEL of water in the glass will remain constant if the cube becomes a mass of water having the same volume as the water initially displaced. Hence, the water level remains constant.

Note: The next three exercises are more difficult than any of the preceding ones. These problems (203 in particular) require the employment of ingenuity. If you are developing a liking for logic or if you enjoy a challenge (or both), you will want to attack these exercises. But you should not feel obligated to try them; nor should you become discouraged if your attempts fail. If you can't crack them now, return later in the term; chances are you will succeed then. There are challenging problems in most of the exercise sets in the volume. To distinguish them from the other exercises, I have (1) marked them with the word 'CHALLENGE' and (2) employed a separate numbering system (beginning with '201').

201. (CHALLENGE) Symbolize each statement using the suggested notation.

[10]This explanation is based on an example provided in Carl Hempel, *Aspects of Scientific Explanation* (New York: Free Press, 1965), p. 346.

C → {[(E⊃J)⊃I] → [(N⊃L)⊃H]} .

(a) *(Author James Boswell writing to the philosopher David Hume)* "If you will agree to CORRESPOND with me, you shall have London NEWS, LIVELY fancies, HUMOROUS sallies, provided that you give me ELEGANT sentiments, JUST criticism, and INGENIOUS observations on human nature."

(b) *(Sports story)* "The winner of Saturday's Buffalo-Miami game wins the division title, with the loser getting a wild-card spot."

> B = Buffalo wins Saturday's game
> M = Miami wins Saturday's game
> C = Buffalo wins the division title
> D = Miami wins the division title
> E = Buffalo gets the wild-card spot
> F = Miami gets the wild-card spot

[B→(C & E)] & [M →(D & E)]

202. (CHALLENGE) A Bible reference work remarks:

The first three gospels are not the earliest Christian documents, for all the genuine epistles of St. Paul were almost certainly written before the Gospel of St. Mark, which in turn provided the foundation for St. Matthew and St. Luke. [11]

The reasoning contained in this passage can be formulated as a propositional-logic argument:

The Pauline epistles predate the Gospels of Matthew, Mark, and Luke. Proof: The Pauline epistles predate the Gospel of St. Mark. That gospel provides the foundation for those of St. Matthew and St. Luke. If Mark provides the foundation for Matthew it must precede Matthew, and similarly if Mark provides the foundation for Luke it must precede Luke as well. Now if St. Paul's letters antedate Mark, which in turn antedates both Matthew and Luke, then Paul's letters obviously antedate both Matthew and Luke. Q.E.D.

B
D & E
(D→F) &
(E→G)
[B & (F & G)] →
(A & C)

Symbolize the argument and prove it valid. Use these symbols: (A & B) & C

> A = Paul's letters predate Matthew
> B = Paul's letters predate Mark
> C = Paul's letters predate Luke
> D = Mark provides the foundation for Matthew
> E = Mark provides the foundation for Luke
> F = Mark predates Matthew
> G = Mark predates Luke

[11]James Hastings, *Dictionary of the Bible*, rev. by Frederick C. Grant and H. H. Rowley (New York: Scribner's, 1963), p. 139.

203. (CHALLENGE)

(A & A) → B, A ⊢ B

A proof for this abstract argument:

(1) (A &A) → B   A
(2) A   A
(3) A & A   2,2 &I
(4) B   1,3 →O

In this proof line 2 supplies both the left and the right conjuncts of line 3. I am willing to accept the "liberal" interpretation of the Ampersand In Rule that is presupposed in this proof. However, there are proofs for argument 203 that do not employ the Ampersand In Rule in this unusual way. Can you construct such a proof?

4

If (Again)

4.1
Symbolizing Difficult Conditionals

Before 1972 the Miami Police Benevolent (?) Association categorically excluded nonwhites,[1] and for this reason some white officers refused to join the group. In view of these facts, it is clear that statement S1 (describing the situation before integration) expresses a truth.

> (S1) Roger Lane is a MEMBER of the PBA only if he is WHITE.

S1 seems to be a conditional, but which component is the antecedent? Should we transform S1 into S2 (and so symbolize it with F2) or transform it into S3 (and symbolize it with F3)?

> (S2) If Roger Lane is a member of the PBA, then he is white.
>
> (F2) M → W

---

[1] In November, 1972, the Miami PBA integrated, but only after losing a legal battle pursued to the United States Supreme Court.

(S3) If Roger Lane is white, then he is a member of the PBA.

(F3)   W → M

As S2 and S3 are not equivalent statements, only one of these restatements of S1 can be correct.

We can establish conclusively that S1 and S3 are not logically equivalent statements. If they were equivalent, they would have to agree as regards truth (or falsity). But though S1 is true, S3 is false. Lane happens to be a white policeman who refused to join the association. Hence, S3 is not an acceptable restatement of S1.

S2, in contrast with S3, is true. Both S1 and S2 express the thought that Lane's being a member of the PBA implies his being white. S3 expresses the quite distinct thought that Lane's being white implies his being a member of the association. As S1 and S2 have the same content, F2 is a correct symbolization of S1.

We can adopt the following guide in symbolizing "only if" sentences:

The expression 'only if' introduces consequents.

A sentence having the form

$$\mathcal{P} \text{ only if } \mathcal{Q}$$

is properly symbolized

$$\mathcal{P} → \mathcal{Q}.$$

The arrow replaces the words 'only if' without any change in the order of the constituent statements.

There is a good deal of confusion among students concerning the symbolization of "only if" sentences. Many are strongly inclined to symbolize S1 (for example) with F3. One source of this inclination is obvious. Generally, the term 'if' introduces antecedents. Some students apparently suppose that 'if' *always* introduces antecedents; were this true, F3 would be the proper symbolization of S1. It is important that you understand the proper treatment of "only if" sentences, for such sentences occur repeatedly in the examples and exercises of subsequent chapters. Therefore, at the risk of being tedious, I shall present three arguments designed to show that S1 is properly symbolized by F2 and not F3.

The three arguments pertain to statements S1 through S6.

(S1)   Lane is a member of the PBA only if he is white.

(S2)   If Lane is a member of the PBA, then he is white.

(S3)   If Lane is white, then he is a member of the PBA.

(S4)   If Lane is not white, then he is not a member of the PBA.

(S5) Lane is a member of the PBA if he is white.
(S6) Lane is a member of the PBA even though he is not white.

The arguments do double duty as exercises in other chapters and are numbered accordingly.

8. S1 is (logically) equivalent to S4. S4 is equivalent to S2.[2] If S1 is equivalent to S4, then provided that S4 is equivalent to S2, S1 must be equivalent to S2. It follows that S1 is equivalent to S2.

52. S3 is equivalent to S5. If S1 is equivalent to S3 and S3 to S5, then S1 is equivalent to S5. If S1 is equivalent to S5, then the word 'only' in S1 does not affect the meaning of S1. But since the word *does* affect S1's meaning, S1 is not equivalent to S3.

65. If S1 is equivalent to S3, then S1 is compatible with S6 if and only if S3 is compatible with S6. S1 is not compatible with S6. S3 is compatible with S6 [for S3 says nothing at all about the case in which Lane is *not* white]. Hence, S1 is not equivalent to S3.

These are valid arguments with true premises; thus, they establish the truth of their conclusions. (You have already demonstrated the validity of argument 8; by the end of chapter six, you will have done so for the other two arguments.)

Following the translation guide explained above, we symbolize S7 with F7.

(S7) DAVID will go to the party only if AMY goes.
(F7) D → A

Formula F7 claims that David's presence at the party is proof of Amy's presence; that is, that David will not attend in Amy's absence. It is clear that F7 expresses at least part of the content of S7, but isn't F8 also implied by S7?

(F8) A → D

Formula F8 claims that Amy's presence is proof of David's presence. Is this claim part of the content of S7? Note that F8 may well be a true statement and also that a person asserting S7 may mean to claim F8 (in addition to F7). However, neither of these observations shows that S7 entails F8. We should distinguish between what a *person* means to claim in uttering a sentence and what the uttered *sentence* actually means. Sentence S7, strictly construed, does not entail F8. Contrast S7 with the stronger statement S9:

[2]This is established in chapter five.

(S9) David will go to the party *if and only if* Amy goes.

Sentence S9 is a stronger statement precisely because it entails F8 while S7 does not. Both statements, of course, entail F7. In chapter six we will study sentences like S9.

The word 'only' should be regarded as a caution sign in logic. It causes trouble for the unwary in propositional logic and in other branches of logic as well. As an example of how tricky it is, note that 'if only' has a very different sense from that of 'only if'. S10 (quoted from a philosophy article) is symbolized by F10, and S11 is symbolized by F11.

(S10) "We could ELIMINATE certain descriptions as irrelevant if only we could DETERMINE what was essential...."

(F10) D → E

(S11) We could ELIMINATE certain descriptions as irrelevant only if we could DETERMINE what was essential.

(F11) E → D

It's useful to employ translation rules (such as " 'only if' introduces consequents"), but don't substitute them for thought.

Two other puzzling locutions are 'sufficient condition' and 'necessary condition'. If event (or state of affairs) A is a sufficient condition for event (or state) B, then A's occurrence ensures B's occurrence. If event (or state) C is a necessary condition for event (or state) D, then D cannot occur in C's absence. Sufficient conditions need not be necessary conditions and necessary conditions need not be sufficient. Consider these sentences:

(S12) Marvin's being BUSTED for "pot" possession is a sufficient condition for his being DROPPED from the team.

(S13) Nancy's SCORING above 1,000 on the GRE is a necessary condition for her ADMISSION to graduate school.

S12 means approximately the same as S14 and is, therefore, symbolized by F14. S13 means roughly the same as S15 and, so, is symbolized by F15.[3]

(S14) If Marvin is busted for possessing "pot," he will be dropped from the team.

(F14) B → D

---

[3]F14 (F15) is not a wholly satisfactory symbolization of S12 (S13), but it represents the best that can be done within propositional logic. For a discussion of the inadequacies of this rendering, see Roger Wertheimer, "Conditions," *Journal of Philosophy*, LXV (1968), 355-64.

(S15)   Nancy will be admitted to graduate school only if she scores above 1,000 on the GRE.

(F15)   A → S

We can formulate these translation principles:

Sufficient conditions become antecedents.
Necessary conditions become consequents.

For example, Marvin's being busted is the sufficient condition in S12, and so *B* is the antecedent of F14. Nancy's scoring above 1,000 is the necessary condition in S13, and so *S* is the consequent of F15. Note that the translation principle 'Sufficient conditions *become* antecedents' does not mean "The *expression* 'is a sufficient condition for' *introduces* antecedents." A similar comment applies to the translation principle concerning statements of necessary condition.

Sentences S13 and S15 are incorrectly symbolized by F16.

(F16)   S → A

S13 and S15 deal with possible or actual events: Nancy's taking the GRE and her being admitted to graduate school. In the normal case taking the GRE *precedes* admission to graduate school. This fact might persuade someone to choose F16 (instead of F15) as the symbolization of S13 or S15 on the grounds that in a conditional sentence dealing with events, the earlier event should be mentioned by the antecedent statement. In fact the arrow symbol has no temporal significance. F15 does not mean "If A then *later* S." In many conditionals the later of two events is described in the antecedent; S17 is an example.

(S17)   If the vase smashed on the floor, then Harry dropped it.

In sum, the antecedent statement need not describe the antecedent (earlier) event.

4.2
Arrow In

My brother-in-law gave me this explanation of why Volkswagen "Beetles" do not have instrument-panel lights to warn of engine overheating:

> *Virtually the only case in which a "Beetle" engine overheats is when its fan belt breaks. And whenever this happens, the "Gen" light comes on.*

His explanation is easily formulated as an argument:

The engine OVERHEATS only if the fan belt BREAKS. If the fan belt breaks, the generator STOPS turning. If the generator stops turning, the "Gen" LIGHT comes on. So, the engine's overheating is a sufficient condition for the "Gen" light's coming on.

In symbols:

$$O \rightarrow B, B \rightarrow S, S \rightarrow L \vdash O \rightarrow L$$

This is an instance of a pattern known as *chain argument*. A chain argument has at least two premises and possesses these features:

1. Every statement is a conditional.
2. The antecedent of the first premise is identical with the antecedent of the conclusion.
3. The consequent of each premise (except the last) is identical with the antecedent of the following premise. (In this way the premises are forged into a chain.)
4. The consequent of the last premise is identical with the consequent of the conclusion.

The "VW" argument seems intuitively valid, but how can we *establish* its validity? Our formal-proof procedure as developed so far is inadequate to the task. However, we might give an informal demonstration along these lines:

Look, *suppose* the engine does overheat. It would follow from this supposition and premise one that the fan belt has broken. Then it would follow with help from premise two that the generator stops turning. And with premise three it will follow that the "Gen" light comes on. To summarize: From the assumption of overheating we can conclude the burning of the "Gen" lamp. So, we are warranted in asserting that *if* the engine overheats, *then* the "Gen" lamp burns.

This is a legitimate way to reason, and we shall strengthen our proof procedure by adding a rule of inference that sanctions inferences of just this sort.

The Arrow In Rule: If from an assumption statement (and perhaps other assumptions) a second statement can be derived, then derive the conditional that has as antecedent the assumption statement and as consequent the second statement.

The rule restated:

From the derivation of $\mathcal{B}$ from assumption $\mathcal{A}$ (and perhaps other assumptions) derive $\mathcal{A} \to \mathcal{B}$.

What is meant by "deriving $\mathcal{B}$ from assumption $\mathcal{A}$"? Is it required that the deductive passage from $\mathcal{A}$ to $\mathcal{B}$ be one step long? No; we may proceed by any number of steps from assumption $\mathcal{A}$ to $\mathcal{B}$, and we shall describe this as "a derivation of $\mathcal{B}$ from $\mathcal{A}$." A more exact account of this notion will be given later in the chapter.

Since chapter two, we have been justifying the introduction of premises into proofs by calling them "assumptions." It is necessary now to state formally a rule that covers the introduction of premises, as well as certain other statements.

The Assumption Rule: Any statement may be introduced as an assumption at any point in a proof.

This rule may seem inordinately liberal; I shall explain below why it is not.

With the aid of the two rules immediately above — plus the Arrow Out Rule — we construct a formal proof of the "VW" argument.

(1)	O → B	A
(2)	B → S	A
(3)	S → L	A
(4)	O	PA
(5)	B	1,4 → O
(6)	S	2,5 → O
(7)	L	3,6 → O
(8)	O → L	4-7 → I

The first four lines are justified by the Assumption Rule. The first three statements are premises of the argument; let's call them *original* assumptions. The fourth line is a *provisional* assumption made in order that the Arrow In step can be taken at line 8. We identify provisional assumptions with the abbreviation 'PA'. The entry on line 8 of the justification column ('4-7 → I') is short for 'Derived by the Arrow In Rule from the derivation of line 7 from the assumption on line 4'. (The assumption line is always cited first.)

Notice that the Arrow In Rule differs in an important respect from the inference rules introduced previously. Each of the earlier rules sanctions a passage from a *statement* (or statements) to a statement. The Arrow In Rule sanctions the passage from a *derivation* (or inference) to a statement. That is, it is because we were able to *derive* line 7 from the assumption on line 4 that we are warranted in adding line 8. This difference is reflected in the justification entry for an Arrow In step by the use of a hyphen (rather than a comma) to separate line numbers.

When proofs were first explained in chapter two, a three-column format was provided — with a warning that one more column would be added later; we need that fourth column now. Many of the proofs that we shall construct will have assumptions of two kinds: original assumptions (premises of the argument being evaluated) and provisional assumptions (the proof just completed is of this sort). If these proofs are to be successful, their last lines must depend only on original assumptions. As a means of keeping track of this matter we add an *assumption-dependence* column to our proof format. The purpose of this column is to indicate for each statement in the proof which assumption(s) it depends upon. We locate this column to the left of the line-number column. For each rule, we will adopt a principle that determines the assumption dependence of any line introduced by that rule. The principle governing the Assumption Rule:

An assumption depends upon itself.

This principle applies to original and provisional assumptions alike. The assumption-dependence principles for the other four rules presented so far:

→O⎫
&I ⎬ :   The statement derived depends on all of the assumptions on which the premise(s) of the step depend(s).
&O⎭   (We refer to this as the "standard assumption-dependence principle.")

→I: The conditional derived depends on all of the assumptions on which the statement corresponding to its consequent depends—less the assumption that corresponds to its antecedent.

To illustrate these principles and the modified proof format, I rewrite the proof for the "VW" argument as follows:

1	(1)	O → B	A
2	(2)	B → S	A
3	(3)	S → L	A
4	(4)	O	PA
1,4	(5)	B	1,4 →O
1,2,4	(6)	S	2,5 →O
1,2,3,4	(7)	L	3,6 →O
1,2,3	(8)	O → L	4-7 →I

Each of the first four lines, being an assumption, depends only on itself. Line 5 depends on the assumptions its premises depend on—namely, 1 and 4. Line 6 is derived from line 2 (depending on assumption 2) and line 5 (depending on assumptions 1 and 4) and, thus, depends on assumptions 1, 2, and 4. A similar explanation applies to line 7. Line 8 depends on whatever assumptions line 7 depends on (1 through 4) less assumption 4; hence, it depends on 1 through 3. Only numbers of assumption lines can appear in the new column. In the above proof, lines 5 through 8 are *derived* lines, not assumption lines. Thus, none of the numbers 5 through 8 could appear in the assumption-dependence column of that proof.

The assumption-dependence column can be included in any proof; however, it is needed only in proofs that involve provisional assumptions. I will not include this column in other proofs.

You will notice that an Arrow In step reduces assumption dependence (line 8 of the above proof depends on fewer assumptions than does 7). It is by the use of the Arrow In Rule (and other rules to be introduced later) that provisional assumptions are eliminated before the proof is concluded. If we had not been able to eliminate assumption 4 from the set of assumptions on which line 8 depends, we would not have succeeded in proving the validity of the "VW" argument, inasmuch as 4 was *not* a premise of that argument. We can formulate this general rule:

> A proof of an argument is not complete if the last line depends on a provisional assumption.

It is because of this requirement that the Assumption Rule is not so lax as it might appear, for any provisional assumption introduced by this rule must be eliminated from the set of assumptions on which the final line depends.

Why does the Arrow In Rule bring about a reduction of assumption dependence? Specifically, how does line 8 in the above proof avoid depending on line 4? The key to understanding this matter is the realization that when you advance a conditional, you are not thereby committed to the antecedent. Suppose that you assert this conditional:

> If the government drafts men, then they will also draft women.

In asserting this conditional, you have not claimed that the government *will* draft men. Similarly, the statement on line 8 of the proof for the "VW" argument — namely, 'O → L' — does not assume that its antecedent is true; that is, it is free of the assumption made on line 4. What the statement 'O → L' does assert is that there is a connection between its antecedent (true or false) and its consequent. This connection has been established by passing from line 4 to line 7. The existence of this connection is quite independent of whether the statement on line 4 is true or false.

Let's turn to an interesting question about symbolization. We know how to symbolize S1 (with F1) and S2 (with F2), but how are we to symbolize S3?

(S1)   If Chip is ADMITTED to college, then if he STAYS four years, it will COST us $50,000.

(S2)   If Chip is admitted to college and stays there four years, it will cost us $50,000.

(S3)   If Chip is admitted to college, and if he stays four years, it will cost us $50,000.

$$(F1) \quad A \to (S \to C)$$
$$(F2) \quad (A \,\&\, S) \to C$$

The content of S3 appears to be caught by at least one of the two for-mulas—but which one? If we can prove that F1 and F2 are logically equivalent, this will show that both formulas are acceptable symboliza-tions of S3. And we *can* show that F1 and F2 are logically equivalent. (This is a *modus ponens* argument with an unstated conclusion. Did you notice it?) We prove the equivalence of these formulas by showing that each entails the other.

A proof that F1 entails F2:

1	(1)	$A \to (S \to C)$	A
2	(2)	A & S	PA
2	(3)	A	2 & O
1,2	(4)	$S \to C$	1,3 $\to$ O
2	(5)	S	2 & O
1,2	(6)	C	4,5 $\to$ O
1	(7)	$(A \,\&\, S) \to C$	2-6 $\to$ I

In constructing this proof, I employed the *Arrow In strategy*. When we wish to derive a conditional, we make a provisional assumption of the antece-dent of that conditional and attempt to derive the consequent. I restate the strategy using the terminology introduced at the end of chapter three:

If one of the goal lines is a conditional, add the antecedent as a premise line and the consequent as a goal line.

The Arrow In strategy is employed twice in this proof that F2 en-tails F1:

1	(1)	$(A \,\&\, S) \to C$	A	[1]
2	(2)	A	PA	[3]
3	(3)	S	PA	[5]
2,3	(4)	A & S	2,3 & I	[7]
1,2,3	(5)	C	1,4 $\to$ O	[6]
1,2	(6)	$S \to C$	3-5 $\to$ I	[4]
1	(7)	$A \to (S \to C)$	2-6 $\to$ I	[2]

I will make some suggestions designed to simplify the task of constructing proofs and illustrate them by referring to this proof. When devising a proof, concentrate first on the principal column, which is the list of statements; the other columns can always be added later. Very often, it is helpful to construct this main column by working from both the top and the bottom toward the middle. (When you write statements at the bottom while there is a gap in the middle, you are of course *setting goals* rather than *making deductions*.) The order in which I set down the statements in the proof above (the order of "proof discovery") is indicated by the bracketed numbers on the extreme right. (This column is an instructional device and not a part of the proof format.) At the start I knew what would be the first and last lines in the proof. Noting that the last line is a conditional, I adopted the Arrow In strategy — that is, I made a provisional assumption of 'A' on the second line and set down 'S → C' (as a secondary goal) on the next-to-last line. Realizing that the next-to-last line is itself a conditional, I employed the Arrow In strategy again, this time making a provisional assumption of 'S' on the third line from the top and putting 'C' (as a tertiary goal) on the third line from the bottom. At this point only a small gap remained in the middle. With a little thought I found that 'A & S' would plug that gap. Having connected the top set of statements with the bottom group, I added the remaining three columns in this order: line number, justification, and assumption dependence. These three columns were by necessity built from top to bottom.

It may be helpful to view an Arrow In proof as involving a *sub-proof*, or proof-within-a-proof. The subproof begins with the provisional assumption and concludes with the statement that matches the consequent of the conditional that will be derived by the Arrow In Rule. I illustrate by repeating the proof of the "VW" argument.

1	(1)	O → B	A
2	(2)	B → S	A
3	(3)	S → L	A
4	(4)	O	PA
1,4	(5)	B	1,4 → O
1,2,4	(6)	S	2,5 → O
1,2,3,4	(7)	L	3,6 → O
1,2,3	(8)	O → L	4-7 → I

subproof (for lines 4-7)

Note that the first and last lines of the subproof are identified by the numbers in the justification entry on line 8. The subproof shows that (with the help of assumptions 1 through 3) one can derive line 7 from the assumption on line 4. Viewed in terms of this notion of "subproof," what justifies the Arrow In deduction on line 8 is the completion of the subproof on line 7.

Viewing Arrow In proofs in this way may help to make sense of proofs involving more than one Arrow In step. Consider again the proof that F2 entails F1.

```
1          (1)  (A & S) → C      A

2          (2)  A                PA        ← larger
                                              subproof
3          (3)  S                PA
2,3        (4)  A & S            2,3 & I   ← smaller
1,2,3      (5)  C                1,4 → O     subproof

1,2        (6)  S → C            3-5 → I

1          (7)  A → (S → C)      2-6 → I
```

The smaller subproof occurs as part of the larger one; accordingly, it could be called a *subsubproof* of the main proof. The completion of the subsubproof on line 5 justifies the step taken on line 6. Line 6 completes the larger subproof, and that justifies the deduction of line 7.

I conclude the chapter by mentioning several matters pertaining to the Arrow In Rule. First, can this rule be applied to just any pair of lines in a proof? No; careful inspection of the rule reveals that these two conditions must be met:[4]

1. The first line (which is identical to the antecedent of the conditional being derived) must be an *assumption*.
2. The other line (which is identical to the consequent of the conditional) must be *derived from* the first line (and perhaps other assumptions).

The following "proof" of the invalid "prime" argument (see section 3.3) has a concluding step that violates both conditions. The argument symbolized:

$$(L \& E) → P \vdash L → P$$

The "proof":

```
1      (1)  (L & E) → P    A
2      (2)  L & E          PA
2      (3)  L              2 & O
1,2    (4)  P              1,2 → O
1      (5)  L → P          3-4 → I (ERROR!)
```

The second of the two conditions stated in the preceding paragraph is that the consequent line must be *derived from* the antecedent line. I

---

[4]These conditions are implied by the particular formulation of the Arrow In Rule presented in this book. There are other logically sound formulations of the rule that do not imply these conditions.

promised earlier in the chapter to give a more exact account of this notion.

> A statement $\mathcal{B}$ is derived from an assumption $\mathcal{A}$ (and perhaps other assumptions) if and only if (1) $\mathcal{B}$ is a derived line (not an assumption) and (2) $\mathcal{B}$ depends on $\mathcal{A}$.

Of course, $\mathcal{B}$ depends on assumption $\mathcal{A}$ if and only if the line number of $\mathcal{A}$ occurs in the assumption-dependence column opposite $\mathcal{B}$.

It was stressed above that the last line in a proof cannot depend on any *provisional* assumptions. Must the last line depend on *all* of the *original* assumptions? In nearly every case it will; occasionally, however, you will encounter arguments with one or more superfluous premises (premises that could be deleted without destroying the validity of the argument). An example:

$$A \rightarrow B, C, A \vdash B$$

The second premise of this abstract argument is superfluous. The last line of a proof for this argument will probably not depend on this premise (the assumption-dependence entry will be '1,3'). This is perfectly acceptable. If you prove that the conclusion of an argument follows from *some* of its premises, you have at the same time shown that it follows from the entire set of premises.

From this point on, proofs will be more challenging and, hence, more fun to tackle.

EXERCISES

27. Symbolize each statement using the suggested notation.

   (a)   Black will be BEAUTIFUL only if this baby finds a FAMILY. $\mathcal{B} \rightarrow F$

$Q \rightarrow E$

(b) Your having a QUIZ average over 90 is a sufficient condition for being EXCUSED from the final.

$P \rightarrow A$

(c) (*Junk mail*) "Only if we can ATTRACT readers of your caliber in these early days of *Saturday Review/Education*, can we PUBLISH the magazine we have in mind."

$S \rightarrow A$

(d) (*Philosopher Carl Hempel*) "A precise ANALYSIS of the concept of confirmation is a necessary condition for an adequate SOLUTION of various fundamental problems concerning the logical structure of scientific procedure."

$S \rightarrow R$

(e) (*Winston Churchill*) "The SETTLEMENT of the West could only take place if the Indian barrier were REMOVED."

$S \rightarrow P$

(f) (*Newspaper*) "Hannah could have PLAYED in the Orange Bowl if only the University of Miami had SHOWN more eagerness for black athletes when Hannah was a senior at Mays."

$D \rightarrow R$

*(g) (*Snoopy*) "The commanding officer only offers me a ROOT beer when there's a DANGEROUS mission to be flown."

$(A \& W) \rightarrow S$

(h) (*Editorialist Clayton Fritchey*) "If he [Ted Kennedy] really is unalterably AGAINST running, and if he really WANTS to see the nomination go to someone who shares his viewpoint, the SOONER he makes a Shermanesque statement the better."

$(W \& D) \rightarrow (m \rightarrow R)$

(i) (*Newspaper*) "Should the Dolphins WIN their division and DEFEAT the Western champion, the American Conference title game will be held in MIAMI Jan. 2 only if the RUNNERUP team beats Cleveland."

*(j) (*Ecology poster*) "Without you it won't get done."

$J \rightarrow H$

H = You help
J = The job gets done

$S \rightarrow H$

(k) (*General Lüttwitz to General McAuliffe in Bastogne, 1944*) "There is only one possibility to SAVE the encircled U.S.A. troops from total annihilation: that is the HONORABLE surrender of the encircled town."

*(l) (*Newspaper*) "If the Chiefs beat the 49ers and Buffalo (their final opponent) and should the Raiders beat their last opponent, Denver, and play to a tie against Kansas City, then the Dolphins would be eliminated by losses to the Colts and Packers."

$[(F \& B) \& (D \& K)] \rightarrow [(C \& P) \rightarrow E]$

F = The Chiefs beat the 49ers
B = The Chiefs beat Buffalo
D = The Raiders beat Denver
K = The Raiders tie Kansas City
E = The Dolphins are eliminated
C = The Dolphins lose to the Colts
P = The Dolphins lose to the Packers

28. Which of the following sentences could be *naturally* symbolized as conditionals? (The qualifier 'naturally' is added because *every* statement is logically equivalent to some—perhaps quite involved—conditional formula.) You need not symbolize the sentences.

    (a) (*Aesop*) "He [the fox] crouched down, then took a run and a jump."

    (b) (*Tennis shoe advertisement*) "Tretorn on your heel means more comfort on the court."

    (c) (*Mark Twain*) "Often a hen who has merely laid an egg cackles as if she had laid an asteroid."

    (d) (*Dickens character*) "Stand on your head again, and I'll cut one of your feet off."

    (e) (*Newspaper*) "American journalists have traditionally refused to reveal sources even if it means jail for contempt of court."

    (f) (*Advertisement for brochure on South Carolina*) "With a copy of our new book, you can do a little sightseeing before you go on vacation."

    (g) The janitor wondered if it was raining.

29. Complete the following proofs (including assumption-dependence columns). Every assumption has been identified.

(a)	1	(1)	$A \to B$	A
	2	(2)	A	PA
	1,2	(3)		
	1,2	(4)	A & B	
	1	(5)	$A \to (A \& B)$	$2\text{-}4 \to I$
*(b)		(1)	$C \to D$	A
		(2)	$C \to E$	A
		(3)	C	PA
		(4)		
		(5)	E	
		(6)		
	1,2	(7)	$C \to (D \& E)$	$3\text{-}6 \to I$
(c)	1	(1)	$F \to (G \to H)$	A
	2	(2)	G & F	PA
	2	(3)	F	
	1,2	(4)	$G \to H$	
	2	(5)	G	
	1,2	(6)	H	
	1	(7)	$(G \& F) \to H$	
(d)		(1)	$(G \& F) \to H$	A
		(2)	F	PA
		(3)	G	PA
		(4)		
		(5)		
		(6)		$3\text{-}5 \to I$
	1	(7)	$F \to (G \to H)$	$2\text{-}6 \to I$

Instructions for exercises 30 through 41 (and 204-207): Symbolize the concrete arguments; construct proofs for all arguments.

    30. In the first two panels Charlie Brown reasons:

> If we GET this last guy out, we WIN the game. We will get the guy out if Snoopy CATCHES the fly ball. Thus, if Snoopy catches it, we win!!

August 8, 1972. © 1972 United Feature Syndicate, Inc.

  *31. In section 3.3, it was pointed out that S1 does *not* entail S2.

> (S1) If four is LESS than six and EVERY number less than six is prime, then four is PRIME.
> (S2) If four is less than six it is a prime number.

Prove that S2 *does* entail S1; that is, prove the validity of the argument whose premise is S2 and whose conclusion is S1.

    32. Dialogue between Injun Joe and his accomplice outside the Widow Douglas's house:

> *"Kill? Who said anything about killing? I would kill him if he was here; but not her. When you want to get revenge on a woman you don't kill her—bosh! You go for her looks. You slit her nostrils—you notch her ears like a sow!"*
> *"By God, that's—"*
> *"Keep your opinion to yourself! It will be safest for you. I'll tie her to the bed. If she bleeds to death, is that my fault? I'll not cry, if she does. My friend, you'll help in this thing—for my sake—that's why you're here—I mightn't be able alone. If you flinch, I'll kill you. Do you understand that? And if I have to kill you, I'll kill her—and then I reckon nobody'll ever know much about who done this business."* [5]

An argument lurks in the latter part of Injun Joe's speech:

> If you FLINCH, I'll kill YOU. And if I have to kill you, I'll kill HER. Therefore, I'll kill both of you, if you flinch.

[5]Mark Twain, *The Adventures of Tom Sawyer* (New York: Grosset & Dunlap, 1946), p. 259.

33. News story:

> *PHILADELPHIA — Police attempts to stamp out heroin by attacking the suppliers of the drug may be counterproductive and lead to an increase in crime by addicts, two scientists believe.*
>
> *The two said that . . . . by aiming at the supply of the drug, police succeed in forcing the price of heroin up. Addicts have no choice but to pay the increase and if necessary turn more and more to crime in order to get enough money for the heroin.* [6]

A formalization of their argument:

> Reduction by police of the heroin SUPPLY is a sufficient condition for rising heroin PRICES. Addicts will NEED more money for heroin purchases if the price rises, and if they need more money they will commit more CRIMES. Thus, if the police reduce the supply of heroin, crimes committed by addicts will increase.

34. Abraham Lincoln had the following to say on the importance of keeping Kentucky in the Union:

> *I think to lose Kentucky is nearly the same as to lose the whole game. Kentucky gone, we can not hold Missouri nor, as I think, Maryland. These all against us, and the job on our hands is too large for us.* [7]

President Lincoln's reasoning restated:

> Should KENTUCKY join the Confederacy the Union will lose the Civil WAR, for the following reasons: If we lose Kentucky, then we will also lose Missouri and Maryland to the Confederacy. And we will lose the war if all of these states join the Confederacy.

Let A abbreviate 'Missouri joins the Confederacy' and B 'Maryland joins the Confederacy'.

*35. Exercise 3(j) in chapter two concerns this sentence:

> If you have a specific QUESTION, we will RELAY it to him, if he CALLS in.

It is not clear which of the two occurrences of 'if' is to predominate. The two possibilities may be expressed by inserting parentheses and italicizing the main 'if'.

[6]"Another Look at Heroin," *Miami News* (January 5, 1972), p. 10-A.

[7]Frank B. Latham, *Lincoln and the Emancipation Proclamation* (New York: Franklin Watts, 1969), p. 31.

(S1) *If* you have a specific question (we will relay it to him if he calls in).

(S2) (If you have a specific question we will relay it to him) *if* he calls in.

Prove that S1 entails S2. A formally identical proof would show that S2 also entails S1; hence, the two statements are logically equivalent. This establishes that in a conditional whose consequent is a conditional [such as 'Q → (C → R)'], the two antecedents ('Q' and 'C') may trade places without affecting the logical content of the statement.

36. Recently, classroom windows were bolted shut at the University of Miami because of the students' expensive habit of running the air conditioners with the windows wide open. When the windows were openable, I was accustomed to advancing the following argument in favor of either closing the windows or turning off the air conditioners:

> If the windows are OPEN we get HOT air. If the air CONDI-TIONER is on we get NOISE [noisy units]. It follows that if the windows are open and the air conditioner is on, we get both hot air and noise.

37. The philosopher Ernest Nagel writes:

> *The current claim that the principle of causality is inapplicable to the subject matter of quantum mechanics is TENABLE only if it is construed to LEGISLATE the use of special types of state-descriptions, and only if the use of statistical state variables by a theory is taken to MARK the theory as lacking a deterministic structure.* [8]

F1 and F2 are two possible symbolizations of this sentence.

(F1) $(T \rightarrow L)$ & $(T \rightarrow M)$
(F2) $T \rightarrow (L$ & $M)$

Prove that F1 entails F2.

*38. Prove that F2 entails F1 (see preceding exercise). This establishes that both are correct symbolizations of Nagel's sentence, if either is.

39. In *Brave New World*, Mustapha Mond makes this reply to the Savage's defense of chastity:

> *But chastity means passion, chastity means neurasthenia. And passion and neurasthenia mean instability. And instability means the end of civilization.* [9]

---

[8] *The Structure of Science* (New York: Harcourt Brace Jovanovich, 1961), p. 323.
[9] Aldous Huxley, *Brave New World* (New York: Bantam, 1953), p. 161.

Supply the unstated conclusion. Use these abbreviations:

C = People are chaste
P = People are passionate
N = People are neurasthenic
U = People are unstable
E = Civilization ends

Let's interpret the second sentence in Mond's speech as expressing this claim: If people are passionate and neurasthenic, then they are unstable.

40. When the circus owner threatens to fire Dr. Dolittle, the strong man stands up for him:

"If the Doctor goes, I go too. And if I go, my nephews, the trapeze acrobats, will come with me. And I've a notion that Hop the clown will join us. Now how about it?"
  Mr. Alexander Blossom, proprietor of "The Greatest Show on Earth," hesitated, chewing his moustache in dismay and perplexity. . . . Deserted by the strong man, the trapeze brothers, [and] his best clown . . ., his circus would be sadly reduced.[10]

The strong man's argument:

If the DOCTOR goes, I go too. And if I go, the TRAPEZE acrobats will leave. The exodus of the trapeze acrobats and me will cause Hop the CLOWN to leave. Our leaving (the strong man, the trapeze brothers, and Hop the clown) would result in a sadly REDUCED circus. So, if Dr. Dolittle leaves, the circus will be greatly reduced.

Let S abbreviate 'The strong man leaves'.

41. Prove that the conditional statement S1 is a logical consequence of the dialogue between Sarge and Lt. Fuzz in panels four through eight of the "Beetle Bailey" comic strip.

(S1) If Sarge squeaks his CHAIR, he will also HIT his desk and RUSTLE his papers and Lt. Fuzz will slam his DRAWER, stomp his FOOT, and SHOUT cadence.

[10]Hugh Lofting, *Doctor Dolittle's Circus* (Philadelphia: Lippincott, 1952), p. 244.

January 17, 1971, King Features Syndicate, Inc.

The argument in question has five premises.

204. (CHALLENGE)   F1 and F2 are symbolizations of the dialogue in the "Sesame Street" comic strip that was reproduced in section 2.2. Demonstrate that F1 entails F2. (As F2 also entails F1, the two formulas are logically equivalent.)

   (F1)   L → [H → (R → B)]
   (F2)   R → [H → (L → B)]

205. (CHALLENGE)

   [(A → B) → (A → C)] → D, B → C ⊢ D

206. (CHALLENGE)

   E ⊢ F → E

A five-line proof is possible. But remember the second restriction on the use of the Arrow In Rule.

   Argument 206 is demonstrably valid, but it is not clear that all English arguments that seem to have this form are valid. Consider, for example, the following:

Jane Fonda is monogamous. Hence, if she has two husbands she is monogamous.

This problem is discussed in appendix one.

207. (CHALLENGE)

   G ⊢ G

Every statement entails itself. (Why is this so?) Therefore, argument 207 is valid. There is a *one-line* formal proof for 207:

   (1)   G   A

You might check the account of "proof" given in section 2.3 (or stated more precisely in 8.3) to satisfy yourself that this does constitute a proof of argument 207. One can also devise a more ordinary proof that involves deriving the conclusion from the premise. To make this suitably challenging, don't employ the Ampersand In Rule in the liberal way discussed in exercise 203 (end of chapter three). My proof has six lines; can you improve on that?

1	1. G	A /∴ G
2	2. A	PA
1,2	3. G&A	1,2 &I
1	4. A→(G&A)	2-3 →I
1	5. G&[A→(G&A)]	1,4 &I
1	6. G	5&O

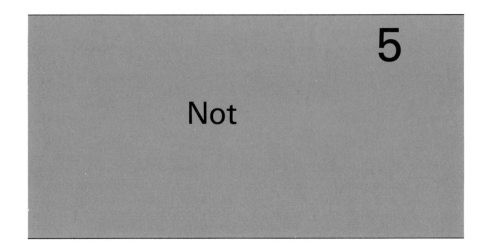

5

Not

5.1
Symbolizing Negations

A statement composed of the expression 'It is not the case that' and a constituent statement is called a *negation* (or *negative statement*). The constituent statement may be either simple or compound. A sample negation:

>   (S1)   It is not the case that Norman Mailer is a DENTIST.

We introduce the *tilde* ('~') as an abbreviation for the connective 'It is not the case that'. (We call this expression a "connective" even though it attaches to one statement rather than joining two statements. It is a *monadic* connective. Each of the other connectives we shall study joins two statements; they are *dyadic* connectives.) S1 is symbolized:

>   (F1)   ~ D

This formula is read "Not *D*" or "Tilde *D*."
The following statements have the same content as S1:

>   (S2)   *It is not true that* Norman Mailer is a dentist.
>   (S3)   *It is false that* Norman Mailer is a dentist.

62

(S4)   Norman Mailer is *not* a dentist.
(S5)   Norman Mailer *isn't* a dentist.

Accordingly, they may be represented by F1. S2 and S3 are clearly compound statements. Each contains as a part the affirmative statement 'Norman Mailer is a dentist'. Are S4 and S5 also compound? Since all four statements are symbolized by one formula, it is convenient to regard S4 and S5 as compound statements. However, this decision is somewhat arbitrary.

To avoid ambiguity when symbolizing negations, we adopt this principle concerning the use of parentheses:

> Whenever the constituent of a negation is a conditional, conjunction, (looking ahead) biconditional, or disjunction, the constituent is enclosed in parentheses (or brackets, etc.). When the constituent of a negation is either a simple statement or a negation, it is not enclosed in parentheses.

The following symbolizations illustrate this grouping principle:

(S6)   It is false that Billy Graham is both a QUAKER and a LUTHERAN.
(F6)   ~(Q & L)
(S7)   It is false that Billy Graham is a Quaker and false that he is a Lutheran.
(F7)   ~Q & ~L

Note that S6 and S7 (F6 and F7) are *not* logically equivalent. S7 entails, but is not entailed by, S6. A third example is quoted from *The New Yorker*:

(S8)   "Henry Kissinger is no FOOL, but he is not infallible, and the blockade may lead to a dreadful CONFRONTATION."

If we abbreviate 'Kissinger is fallible' with A, we can symbolize this statement with F8.

(F8)   (~F & ~ ~A) & C

Consider these eight formulas:

(F9)   ~A & B
(F10)   A & ~B
(F11)   ~A & ~B
(F12)   ~(A & B)
(F13)   ~(~A & B)
(F14)   ~(A & ~B)

(F15)   ~(~A & ~B)
(F16)   ~~(A & B)

F9 through F11 are conjunctions. Each has at least one negative conjunct. F12 through F15 are negations of conjunctions. F16 is a negation of a negation (of a conjunction). It is important to know that there are no logically equivalent formulas in the set F9 through F16. This fact emphasizes the importance of correctly punctuating negations. It also establishes that the tilde of logic does not "behave" like the minus sign of arithmetic.

Capital letters abbreviate affirmative statements, not negative ones. This is a consequence of a convention adopted previously, as the following argument shows.

> Letters abbreviate only simple statements. Negative statements are not simple. So, letters do not abbreviate them.

(Can this argument be properly assessed by propositional logic?) Examine statements S17 through S19.

(S17)   Some pilots are alcoholics.
(S18)   Some pilots are not alcoholics.
(S19)   It is not the case that some pilots are alcoholics.

The negation of S17 is not S18 but S19. S18 and S19 are not equivalent. One indication that S18 is not the negation of S17 is that both of these statements are true. A statement and its negation will never agree in truth (or falsity). If S17 is symbolized with F17, F19 will represent S19 but not S18.

(F17)   P
(F19)   ~P

This illustrates once again the necessity of symbolizing *thoughtfully*.

Organic farmer J. I. Rodale (who crusaded against eating sugar) once claimed, "I'm going to LIVE to be 100 unless I'm RUN over by a sugar-crazed taxi driver."[1] This is a compound statement consisting of two simple statements joined by the connective 'unless'. This connective occurs frequently in our discourse. We can symbolize "unless" sentences by employing two of the connective symbols already introduced, the tilde and the arrow. Rodale's statement is symbolized:

---

[1] He died at 72 while extolling his nutritional views during a taping of the Dick Cavett television show.

$$\sim R \rightarrow L$$

We employ this principle in translating "unless" statements:

Negate the constituent that follows 'unless' and make the resulting negation the antecedent of a conditional; the other constituent of the original statement becomes the consequent of the conditional.

This principle applies both to statements where 'unless' occurs in the middle (like the Rodale claim) and to statements which begin with 'unless'. My summer-school contract provides an example of the latter case:

Unless signed copies are RETURNED by the specified date, this offer of employment automatically EXPIRES.

In accordance with the principle stated, we arrive at:

$$\sim R \rightarrow E$$

Let's consider one more example. A newspaper space filler begins:

If the wedding is CANCELLED, wedding gifts must be RETURNED unless the bridegroom has DIED.

It may help to symbolize this in two stages:

(1) C → (R unless D)
(2) C → (~ D → R)

It might be suggested that a sentence containing 'unless' is equivalent to a *pair* of conditionals — not just one. Consider this newspaper headline: "DRIEST April ever for South Florida unless it RAINS." The translation principle given in the previous paragraph yields F20 as symbolization, while the suggestion in this paragraph is that F21 is the proper symbolization.

(F20)   ~ R → D
(F21)   (~ R → D) & (R → ~ D)

Suppose that there is a small rain and still April retains the record for dryness. The headline would not be falsified, but F21 would (because its right conjunct would be falsified). So, F21 is not a satisfactory symbolization of the headline. Occasionally 'unless' may be used in a strong sense so that two conditionals are required for its symbolization. In this volume, however, it is not used in that strong sense.

5.2
Tilde In

One morning at the breakfast table my daughter Amy (then aged three) announced that she was now "big." My son Mike (five), who used a table-knife, rebuked her with these words:

If you were BIG you would have a KNIFE. But you don't have a knife. That tells me you aren't big.

In symbols:

$$B \rightarrow K, \sim K \vdash \sim B$$

No one taught Mike to reason in this way. It is a basic pattern that each of us employs regularly. The pattern traditionally bears the label *modus tollens*,[2] meaning "in the mood of denying." An argument exhibiting this pattern has two premises. The first premise is a conditional, and the second is the negation of the consequent of that conditional. The conclusion is the negation of the antecedent of the first premise.

   The "knife" argument is clearly valid, but we are not yet able to establish this fact with our proof procedure. We can, however, provide an informal justification for the argument:

> *Assume* for a moment that Amy is big. From this assumption and the first premise it follows that she has a knife. But the second premise contradicts this. Therefore, the assumption that Amy is big was mistaken, and we conclude its negation.

We add to our stock of rules one that sanctions reasoning of this sort:

> *The Tilde In Rule*: If from an assumption statement (and perhaps other assumptions) a standard contradiction can be derived, then derive the negation of the assumption.

The rule restated:

> From the derivation of $\mathcal{B}$ & $\sim\mathcal{B}$ from assumption $\mathcal{A}$ (and perhaps other assumptions) derive $\sim\mathcal{A}$.

We define a *standard contradiction* as a conjunction whose right conjunct is the negation of the left conjunct; that is, the right conjunct consists of a tilde followed by the left conjunct. Examples:

---

[2]The second word is pronounced "TAH'-LENZ."

STANDARD CONTRADICTIONS	NOT STANDARD CONTRADICTIONS
A & ~A	~A & A
~B & ~ ~B	(B & C) & (~B & ~C)
(D → E) & ~(D → E)	(D → E) & (D → ~E)

Some of the formulas in the right column are contradictions and some are not—but none of them are *standard contradictions*. Note that a formula is a standard contradiction by virtue of its form—not its content. The Tilde In Rule makes no reference to the content of the standard contradiction involved; any one will serve as well as any other. As we shall prove in chapter thirteen, all contradictions (and therefore all standard contradictions) are logically equivalent.

A proof for the "knife" argument:

1	(1)	B → K	A
2	(2)	~K	A
3	(3)	B	PA
1,3	(4)	K	1,3 → O
1,2,3	(5)	K & ~K	4,2 & I
1,2	(6)	~ B	3-5 ~ I

Lines 1 and 2 are original assumptions. Line 3 is a provisional assumption made with the idea of the subsequent application of the Tilde In Rule, a move that is made on line 6. '3-5 ~ I' is short for 'Derived by the Tilde In Rule from the derivation of the standard contradiction on line 5 from the assumption on line 3'. (The assumption line is always cited first.) Line 6 of the assumption-dependence column was computed with the aid of this principle:

> The statement derived by the Tilde In Rule depends on all of the
> assumptions on which the standard contradiction depends—
> less the assumption whose negation is derived.

Thus, line 6 depends on the assumptions of line 5 (1 through 3) less assumption 3; hence, it depends on 1 and 2. The Tilde In step "wipes out" the provisional assumption.

Why is it legitimate to deduce '~ B' on line 6 of the above proof? The contradiction on line 5 follows from the assumptions on lines 1 through 3. Only a contradictory set of assumptions will yield a contradiction and, thus, lines 1 through 3 constitute a contradictory set. To avoid inconsistency, one of the assumptions must be given up. The assumption-dependence entry on line 6 shows that we are retaining assumptions 1 and 2. We can retain 1 and 2 only by rejecting the third assumption, *B*, which we do on line 6.

In the movie, *Oh God!*, when Jerry Landers (played by John Denver) tells his wife Bobbie (Teri Garr), that he has had an encounter with God, she tries to persuade him that the experience was illusory.

> BOBBIE: Did you see God or just hear him?
> JERRY: I only heard him.
> BOBBIE: Well, seeing is believing.

Bobbie seems to be reasoning in this way:

> If you SAW God, then you should BELIEVE that he was there. You did not see God. So, you should not believe that he was there.

In symbols:

$$S \rightarrow B, \sim S \vdash \sim B$$

Does this argument have a valid form? Can you construct a Tilde In proof of its validity?

The "God" argument superficially resembles a *modus tollens* inference but is in fact invalid. The first premise claims that S is a *sufficient* condition for B. That premise is quite compatible with there being other sufficient conditions for B (hearing God, for example). So, from S's denial nothing follows about B. The "God" argument has the same form as the "Redford" argument (below), but the invalidity of the latter is more obvious (because we know the premises to be true and the conclusion to be false):

> If Robert Redford plays professional football, then he is more than five feet tall. He does not play professional football. Therefore, he is not taller than five feet.

Both arguments display a pattern called the *fallacy of denying the antecedent.* Compare this pattern with that of *modus tollens.*

$$\text{modus tollens:} \quad P \rightarrow Q, \sim Q \vdash \sim P \text{ (valid)}$$
$$\text{denying the antecedent:} \quad P \rightarrow Q, \sim P \vdash \sim Q \text{ (invalid)}$$

Because the "God" argument is invalid, if you constructed a "proof" for it you committed at least one error.

The Tilde In Rule is employed in the proofs of many arguments that do not exhibit the *modus tollens* pattern. I shall further illustrate the application of the rule by constructing proofs for two such arguments. The first is advanced by philosopher Bernard Bolzano:

That no proposition has truth disproves itself because it is itself a proposition and we should have to call it false in order to call it true.[3]

The argument restated:

> The proposition that no proposition has truth is not true because if it is true then it is false.

Letting T abbreviate 'The proposition that no proposition has truth is true', the argument is symbolized:

$$T \rightarrow \sim T \vdash \sim T$$

Proof of validity:

1	(1)	$T \rightarrow \sim T$	A
2	(2)	T	PA
1,2	(3)	$\sim T$	1,2 $\rightarrow$O
1,2	(4)	$T \& \sim T$	2,3 &I
1	(5)	$\sim T$	2-4 $\sim$ I

In constructing this proof, I employed the *Tilde In strategy*:

> When you aim to derive a negated statement such as '$\sim T$' (and a more direct route is not apparent), make a provisional assumption of 'T' and try to derive a standard contradiction.

One feature of the proof of the "truth" argument deserves special comment. The conclusion of the argument is reached twice, at lines 3 and 5. It might seem, therefore, that the proof could have been concluded on line 3. A glance at the assumption-dependence column shows why this is not so. Line 3 does not depend solely on the original assumption; it also depends on the provisional assumption on line 2. This assumption is removed by the Tilde In step at line 5.

One summer, a student asked me whether the course on Continental Rationalism would be offered in the fall. Recalling that British Empiricism was included in the fall class schedule, I reached the answer to his question with a simple inference:

> The department won't offer both courses in the fall. EMPIRICISM will be taught. So, RATIONALISM is not being offered.

[3]Bernard Bolzano, *Theory of Science*, ed. and trans. by Rolf George (Berkeley and Los Angeles: University of California Press, 1972), p. 39.

In symbols:

$$\sim (E \;\&\; R), E \vdash \sim R$$

The pattern exhibited by the "Rationalism" inference is called *conjunctive argument*. Any argument exhibiting this pattern has two premises. The first premise is a negated conjunction, and the second is one of the conjuncts of that negated conjunction. The conclusion is the negation of the other conjunct.

The "Rationalism" argument is valid, as this proof demonstrates:

1	(1)	$\sim (E \;\&\; R)$	A
2	(2)	E	A
3	(3)	R	PA
2,3	(4)	E & R	2,3 & I
1,2,3	(5)	$(E \;\&\; R)\;\&\; \sim (E \;\&\; R)$	4,1 & I
1,2	(6)	$\sim R$	3-5 $\sim$ I

In devising a Tilde In (or Tilde Out) proof where one line is a negated compound statement (like line 1), it is smart to aim for a standard contradiction whose right conjunct is that negated compound statement.

Does the following argument exhibit the conjunctive-argument pattern?

> The department won't offer both KANT and HEGEL in the fall. The Kant seminar will not be held. Consequently, the Hegel seminar is being offered.

Symbolized:

$$\sim (K \;\&\; H), \sim K \vdash H$$

The "Kant" example exhibits a distinct pattern that we may call the *fallacy of denying a conjunct*. Compare the following patterns:

conjunctive argument:	$\sim (\mathcal{P} \;\&\; \mathcal{Q}), \mathcal{P} \vdash \sim \mathcal{Q}$ *(valid)*
denying a conjunct:	$\sim (\mathcal{P} \;\&\; \mathcal{Q}), \sim \mathcal{P} \vdash \mathcal{Q}$ *(invalid)*

It would be instructive to attempt a "proof" of the "Kant" argument. If you try, you will discover that the "proof" can be completed only by misapplying one or more rules.

5.3
Tilde Out

Consider this extremely simple argument:

> It is false that Rationalism won't be offered. So, it will be offered.

In symbols:

$$\sim \sim R \vdash R$$

Clearly, the conclusion of this argument follows from its premise. But we are not yet in a position to construct a proof of validity. We require a companion for the Tilde In Rule.

> *The Tilde Out Rule*: If from a negative assumption statement (and perhaps other assumptions) a standard contradiction can be derived, then derive the constituent of the negative assumption.

The rule restated:

> From the derivation of $\mathcal{B}$ & $\sim \mathcal{B}$ from assumption $\sim \mathcal{A}$ (and perhaps other assumptions) derive $\mathcal{A}$.

The assumption-dependence principle for this rule parallels the one for the Tilde In Rule.

With the help of the Tilde Out Rule we can construct a proof of validity for the above argument.

1	(1)	$\sim \sim R$	A
2	(2)	$\sim R$	PA
1,2	(3)	$\sim R$ & $\sim \sim R$	2,1 & I
1	(4)	R	2-3 $\sim$ O

Not only does '$\sim \sim R$' entail 'R' (as we have just established), but 'R' entails '$\sim \sim R$'. Thus, the two statements are logically equivalent.

In his *Autobiography*, Bertrand Russell writes:

> *I had had from the first a dark suspicion that the invitation [to lecture in China] might be a practical joke, and in order to test its genuineness I had got the Chinese to pay my passage money before I started. I thought that few people would spend £125 on a joke. . . .*[4]

Russell employed this argument (whose pattern resembles *modus tollens*):

> If the invitation is not GENUINE, the persons who extended it will not SPEND 125 pounds for my passage. Since they are spending it, the invitation must be genuine.

In symbols:

$$\sim G \rightarrow \sim S, S \vdash G$$

[4](Boston: Little, Brown, 1968), II; 172.

Proof:

$$
\begin{array}{lll}
1 & (1) & \sim G \to \sim S & A \\
2 & (2) & S & A \\
3 & (3) & \sim G & PA \\
1,3 & (4) & \sim S & 1,3 \to O \\
1,2,3 & (5) & S \, \& \sim S & 2,4 \, \& \, I \\
1,2 & (6) & G & 3\text{-}5 \sim O \\
\end{array}
$$

The *Tilde Out strategy* is simple:

> When you are seeking to derive some statement such as 'G'
> (and you do not see a more direct route to 'G'), make a provi-
> sional assumption of '~G' and try to derive a standard contra-
> diction.

When is the Tilde Out strategy likely to be useful? When the following three features are all present the chances are good that the strategy should be employed:

1.   The goal (or subgoal) is affirmative.
2.   The premise lines contain one or more tildes.
3.   No more direct path from premises to goal is obvious.

It may be helpful to view Tilde Out (as well as Tilde In) proofs as involving subproofs. The subproof begins with the provisional assumption and concludes with the standard contradiction. I illustrate by repeating the proof of the "Russell" argument:

$$
\begin{array}{lll}
1 & (1) & \sim G \to \sim S & A \\
2 & (2) & S & A \\
3 & (3) & \boxed{\sim G} & PA \\
1,3 & (4) & \sim S & 1,3 \to O \quad \leftarrow\text{subproof} \\
1,2,3 & (5) & S \, \& \sim S & 2,4 \, \& \, I \\
1,2 & (6) & G & 3\text{-}5 \sim O \\
\end{array}
$$

The first and last lines of the subproof are identified by the numbers in the justification entry of the Tilde Out step (line 6). The subproof shows that (with the help of assumptions 1 and 2) one can derive line 5 from the assumption on line 3. The completion of the subproof justifies the Tilde Out step on line 6. If the assumption of '~ G' leads us into a contradiction, then we are justified in concluding its opposite, 'G'. Viewing Tilde Out (and Tilde In) steps in terms of subproofs may help make sense out of proofs containing more than one provisional assumption (such as the proof displayed in the next paragraph).

In argument eight in section 4.1 it was claimed that S2 and S4 are logically equivalent statements.

(S2) If Lane is a MEMBER of the PBA, then he is WHITE.

(S4) If Lane is not white, then he is not a member of the PBA.

These two statements are equivalent if and only if each entails the other. We prove now that S4 entails S2. (Exercise 54 at the end of the chapter concerns the other entailment.)

1	(1)	$\sim W \rightarrow \sim M$	A	[1]
2	(2)	M	PA	[3]
3	(3)	$\sim W$	PA	[5]
1,3	(4)	$\sim M$	$1,3 \rightarrow O$	[6]
1,2,3	(5)	M & $\sim$ M	2,4 &I	[7]
1,2	(6)	W	3-5 $\sim O$	[4]
1	(7)	M $\rightarrow$ W	2-6 $\rightarrow$ I	[2]

This proof involves both Arrow In and Tilde Out strategies. The column of bracketed numbers on the right indicates the order of proof discovery.

I conclude the chapter with some comments which apply to both Tilde rules. The type of reasoning these rules sanction has traditionally been known as the *Reductio ad Absurdum* method of proof. One reduces some assumption to absurdity (by deriving a contradiction from it) and then concludes its denial. A logical justification of this method is provided by the following argument:

> Argument X is VALID if and only if it is LOGICALLY impossible for its premises to be true and its conclusion false. It is logically impossible for X's premises to be true and its conclusion false if and only if it is logically impossible for its premises and the DENIAL of its conclusion all to be true. If a CONTRADICTION can be derived from the premises of X and the denial of its conclusion, then it is logically impossible for the premises and the denial of the conclusion all to be true. Therefore, the derivation of a contradiction from the premises of X and the denial of its conclusion is a sufficient condition for the validity of X.

We shall prove the validity of this argument in the next chapter.

If you derive a standard contradiction in the course of constructing a proof, are you warranted in concluding by Tilde In the negation of *any* statement occurring earlier in the proof? (A parallel question regarding Tilde Out can be raised.) No; an examination of the rule shows that two conditions must be met: (1) The earlier statement must be an assumption. (2) The standard contradiction must be derived from that assumption (and perhaps other assumptions).[5]

---

[5]These conditions are implied by the particular formulation of the Tilde In and Tilde Out Rules presented in this book. There are other logically sound formulations of these rules that do not imply these conditions.

EXERCISES

42. Symbolize each statement using the suggested notation.

~T

(a)   (*Billy Graham*) "The New Testament does not mention TELEVISION."

1 pr eo.

w & ~ V

~F → S

(b & c)   (*Note on box of Triscuit Wafers*) "This package is sold by WEIGHT, not by VOLUME. If it does not appear FULL when opened, it is because contents have SETTLED during shipping."

~~B

(d)   (*Newspaper*) "Notre Dame is not unbeatable." (Let B abbreviate 'Notre Dame is beatable'.)

~f & ~W

(e)   (*James Watt*) "I don't like to PADDLE and I don't like to WALK."

~C → ~J

(f)   "If you're not CONFUSED, you're not well INFORMED."

the small society

IF YOU'RE NOT CONFUSED, YOU'RE NOT WELL INFORMED —

BRICKMAN

King Features Syndicate, Inc.

(~C & ~W) & ~F

(g)   (*Sartre's* Nausea) "The CASHIER was not there, nor the WAITER — nor M. FASQUELLE."

~D → E

(h)   (*Hans Christian Andersen*) "Now we shall have duck EGGS, unless it's a DRAKE."

~M → ~P

*(i)   (*Headline*) "Hamilton can't PRESIDE without MOVING to city."

~(R & ~M)

(~R → T) & (R → F)

(j)   (*Conversation*) "The May Day program will be THURSDAY afternoon — unless it RAINS, in which case it will be FRIDAY morning."

[C & ~(D & B)] → A

[C & (~D & ~B)] → A

*(k)   (*Student newspaper*) "If tomorrow's audience is COOPERATIVE, and there are no obvious signs of DRUGS and BOOZE, the administration will ALLOW more concerts to be held."

D = There are obvious signs of drugs
B = There are obvious signs of booze

if not both; both must obtain

$-(\sim S \& \sim H) \to \sim B$ $-(S \Delta H) \to \sim B$

(l)   (*Dickens dialogue*) "Unless I SEE it with my own eyes, and HEAR it with my own ears, I never will BELIEVE it."

$\sim(M \& G) \to E$

*(m)   (*Hitler*) "If I do not get the oil of MAIKOP and GROZNY, then I must END this war."

(n)   (*Police Benevolent Association bulletin*) "If you don't TAKE your money now and you let it ACCRUE to retirement, then our attorney has not HELPED you and you will not be asked to PAY a legal fee."

$\sim T \& A) \to (\sim H \& \sim P)$

43. Translate each formula into an English sentence using this "dictionary":

D = Justice O'Connor is a Democrat
R = Justice O'Connor is a Republican

(a) $\sim \sim R$
(b) $\sim D \& R$
*(c) $\sim (D \& R)$
(d) $\sim D \& \sim R$

44. Complete the following proofs. Every assumption has been identified.

(a)   1   (1) $\sim A \to B$ A   *A*
       2   (2) $\sim A \to \sim B$ A
       3   (3) $\sim A$ PA
             (4) B
             (5)   2,3 $\to$ O
    1,2,3   (6) B & $\sim$ B
    1,2   (7) A   3-6 $\sim$ O

(b)   1   (1) C & D   A
       1   (2) C
       1   (3) D
       4   (4) $\sim$ D   PA
    1,4   (5) D & $\sim$ D
       1   (6) $\sim \sim$ D
       1   (7) C & $\sim \sim$ D

*(c)   (1) E $\to$ F   A
             (2) $\sim$ (E & F)   A
             (3) E   PA
             (4)
             (5)
             (6) (E & F) & $\sim$ (E & F)
    1,2   (7)   3-6 $\sim$ I

(d)   (1) $\sim G \to H$ A
             (2) $\sim H$ PA
             (3) $\sim G$ PA
             (4)
             (5)

$$\begin{array}{llll} 1,2 & (6) & & 3\text{-}5 \;\sim O \\ 1 & (7) & \sim H \to G & 2\text{-}6 \to I \end{array}$$

Instructions for exercises 45 through 56: Symbolize the arguments and construct proofs.

45. Lucy's argument:

> Beethoven never played hockey. Proof: if he had PLAYED hockey, he would have written some hockey MUSIC. However, he wrote no hockey music.

May 16, 1981. ©1981 United Feature Syndicate, Inc.

46. The lawyer in the cartoon presents this argument:

> If I didn't have an AIRTIGHT case, I wouldn't be THUMBING my nose at you. Therefore, since I am thumbing my nose, I must have an airtight case.

"I ask you—would I be doing this to you if I didn't have an airtight case?"

47. A high-school chemistry text contains this discussion of the motion of electrons:

We recall that the nucleus has a positive charge due to its protons, and that a neutral atom contains an equal number of protons and negatively charged electrons. Thus we might expect electrons to be held in an atom by the attraction between oppositely charged particles. This is similar to the orbiting of a satellite about the earth. But instead of gravitational attraction which holds a satellite in orbit, the attraction of oppositely charged particles might be assumed to hold an electron in its path.

However, scientists have observed that electrically charged particles moving in curved paths give off energy. If an electron moving about a nucleus continually gave off energy, it should slow down, move nearer to the nucleus and eventually fall into it. This is like the slowing down of a satellite by friction with the earth's upper atmosphere. As this occurs the satellite falls toward the earth, and eventually burns up in the earth's atmosphere. We know that atoms do not collapse, electrons do not fall into the nucleus. Thus, while the attraction of oppositely charged particles may partly explain how electrons are held by the nucleus of an atom, it is not satisfactory for explaining the motion of electrons about the nucleus.[6]

The argument seems to be:

If the ATTRACTION between oppositely charged particles explains the motion of electrons around the nucleus, then electrons continually give off ENERGY. If they continually emit energy they should SLOW down, and if they slow down they should eventually FALL into the nucleus. [We know that] electrons do not fall into the nucleus. Thus, the attraction between oppositely charged particles does not explain the motion of electrons around the nucleus.

48. Ethicist Burton Leiser writes:

Liberty for the restaurant owners [to serve whom they chose] was incompatible with liberty for black travelers [to eat where they wished]. The latter could acquire the liberty to eat along the highway in Georgia only if Lester Maddox and other restaurant owners were deprived of their liberty to refuse to serve them.[7]

$\sim (R \text{ or } T)$

$T \to \sim R$

Prove that the first sentence follows logically from the second. Use these abbreviations: $R \to \sim T$ follows from

T = Black travelers are free to eat along the highway $T \to \sim R$
R = Restaurant owners are free to refuse to serve black travelers

[6]H. Clarke Metcalfe, John E. Williams, and Joseph F. Castka, *Modern Chemistry*, 4th ed. (New York: Holt, Rinehart & Winston, Inc., 1970), p. 61.

[7]Burton M. Leiser, ed., *Liberty, Justice, and Morals*, 2nd ed. (New York: Macmillan, 1979), p. 1.

*49. In the "Phaedo" Plato argues in the following way for the doctrine of immortality:

> *Besides, Socrates, rejoined Cebes, there is that theory which you have often described to us — that what we call learning is really just recollection. If that is true, then surely what we recollect now we must have learned at some time before, which is impossible unless our souls existed somewhere before they entered this human shape. So in that way too it seems likely that the soul is immortal.*[8]

The argument restated:

> Learning is actually RECOLLECTION. If that is true, then what we recollect now must have been learned before BIRTH. It is impossible that what we recollect was learned before birth unless the soul is immortal. So, the soul is immortal.

(Let *M* abbreviate 'The soul is mortal'.)

50. News story:

> *A rape charge against Jockey Henry Moreno has been dropped by the Broward State Attorney's office following medical tests which established that Moreno could not have been the attacker of a Fort Lauderdale waitress. . . .*
>
> *Broward authorities said that tests had established that the rapist had "O" type blood and that Moreno's test yesterday classified his blood as the "AB" type.*[9]

The following argument paraphrases the reasoning:

> The rapist has "O" blood. If this is so, then Moreno is the rapist only if he has "O" blood. But Moreno does not have "O" blood. Hence, it is false that he is the rapist.

Use these symbols:

> *A* = The rapist has "O" blood
> *B* = Moreno is the rapist
> *C* = Moreno has "O" blood

51. Joseph Heller's famous Catch-22:

> *There was only one catch and that was Catch-22, which specified that a concern for one's own safety in the face of dangers that were real and immediate was the process of a rational mind. Orr was crazy and could be grounded. All he had to*

[8]72e-73a. Hugh Tredennick, trans., "Phaedo," in *The Collected Dialogues of Plato*, ed. by Edith Hamilton and Huntington Cairns (Princeton, N.J.: Princeton University Press, 1961), p. 55.

[9]"Rape Charge against Jockey Moreno Dropped," *Miami News* (January 20, 1971), p. 7-A.

*do was ask; and as soon as he did, he would no longer be crazy and would have
to fly more missions. Orr would be crazy to fly more missions and sane if he
didn't, but if he was sane he had to fly them. If he flew them he was crazy and
didn't have to; but if he didn't want to he was sane and had to. Yossarian was
moved very deeply by the absolute simplicity of this clause of Catch-22 and let out
a respectful whistle.*

"That's some catch, that Catch-22," he observed.

"It's the best there is," Doc Daneeka agreed. [10]

One analysis of the argument contained in this passage:

Orr's ASKING to be grounded would be proof of his SANITY.
Asking to be grounded is a necessary condition for being
GROUNDED. If Orr is sane, then he cannot be grounded. All
of which shows that Orr cannot be grounded.

52. Prove the validity of argument 52 on page 43. Use these abbreviations:

D = S3 is equivalent to S5
E = S1 is equivalent to S3
F = S1 is equivalent to S5
A = The word 'only' in S1 affects the meaning of S1

53. News story:

*TALLAHASSEE—At least three votes cast during Thursday's debate in the
House on the governor's environmental agency bill were illegal. . . .*

*House rules provide that members must be present to vote on any motion,
amendment or bill.*

*Jacksonville Rep. Jon Forbes was recorded as voting for the bill creating the
new Department of Environmental Affairs.*

Forbes, however, was in Jacksonville when the vote was taken. [11]

The reporter reasoned:

Rep. Forbes voted LEGALLY only if he was in TALLA-
HASSEE when the vote was taken. However, since he was
in JACKSONVILLE at the time, he did not vote legally. Obviously, he was not in both cities when the vote was taken.

54. It was shown in section 5.3 that S4 entails S2.

(S2) If Lane is a MEMBER of the PBA, then he is WHITE.
(S4) If Lane is not white, then he is not a member of the PBA.

Now show that S2 entails S4 (thereby establishing logical equivalence).

[10]*Catch-22* (New York: Dell Pub. Co., Inc., 1961), p. 47.

[11]Rick Eyerdam, "3 Illegal Votes Cast during House Debate," *Miami News* (March 4, 1972), p. 1-A.

*55. The ontological argument for the existence of God was advanced by St. Anselm in the eleventh century.[12] He presented at least two versions of the argument, one of which may be paraphrased as follows:

> God exists in REALITY. The proof: God is a being a GREATER than which cannot be conceived. We understand the TERM 'God'. If we understand this term, then God exists in the UNDERSTANDING. If God exists in the understanding but not in reality, then [because we could conceive of a being who is like God except that he exists both in the understanding and in reality] God is *not* a being a greater than which cannot be conceived. Q.E.D.

G abbreviates 'God is a being a greater than which cannot be conceived'. Don't symbolize the bracketed material in premise four.

56. The philosopher John Hick writes:

> *As a challenge to theism, the problem of evil has traditionally been posed in the form of a dilemma: if God is perfectly LOVING, he must WISH to abolish evil; and if he is all-POWERFUL, he must be ABLE to abolish evil. But evil EXISTS; therefore God cannot be both omnipotent and perfectly loving.*[13]

Add this obviously true suppressed premise:

> If God wishes to abolish evil and is able to do so, then evil does not exist.

57. Solve the puzzle.

1	2	3		4	5	6
7			■	8		
9			10			
■		11			■	■
12	13				14	15
16			■	17		
18						

[12]See his *Proslogion*, the relevant part of which is reprinted in John Hick, ed., *The Existence of God* (New York: Macmillan, 1964), pp. 25-27.

[13]*Philosophy of Religion* (Englewood Cliffs, N.J.: Prentice-Hall, 1963), p. 40. Hick examines this argument but does not subscribe to it.

ACROSS

1. '~ ~ N' _____ from 14 d.
7. He is an OHIOAN since he lives in AKRON.
8. Follows from 'O → U' and 'O'.
9. Tacks on a tilde.
11. Entailed by '~ R → ~ I'.
12. Premise word.
16. Logically equivalent to '~ (U & ~ A)'.
17. From 'T & L' in three steps.
18. In a mood.

DOWN

1. Rooter.
2. She's OLD, *ergo* ELIGIBLE.
3. Denying the antecedent is not _____.
4. Rids a connective.
5. WASHINGTON and EVERS are black mayors.
6. Conclusion words.
10. If she's ABSENT, she's absent.
12. Conjunction word.
13. Only if he's OLD is he ELIGIBLE.
14. SUFFICIENT conditions are antecedents; NECESSARY conditions are consequents.
15. French conjunctions.

208. (CHALLENGE) Symbolize each statement using the suggested notation.

(a) (*Comic strip dialogue*) "Not only did Mrs. Viking TREAT me with contempt — but you IGNORED me."

(b) (*Time*) "If both Mao and Chiang claimed to rule all of China, only one could be right."

> A = Mao claims to rule all of China
> B = Chiang claims to rule all of China
> C = Mao's claim to rule all of China is correct
> D = Chiang's claim to rule all of China is correct

(c) (*Joe Namath*) "I'll REPORT to camp, but I won't PLAY in an exhibition game without a signed CONTRACT."

(d) (*Newspaper*) "The DONATION of the Virginia Key property, [Goode said,] should be made only if the university will USE the land only to expand the Marine and Atmospheric Sciences school and if the land will REVERT to Metro if CONSTRUCTION has not begun within three years from the date of transfer of title."

> D = Metro should donate the Virginia Key property
> U = The university uses the land only to expand the Marine and Atmospheric Sciences school

209. (CHALLENGE) Symbolize each statement using only capitals, grouping symbols, tildes, and ampersands.

$\sim (A \lor B) = \sim A \& \sim B$

   (a)   It is not the case that either AL or BETH will quit.
   (b)   Al and/or Beth will quit. $\sim(A \& \sim B)$
   (c)   Either Al or Beth will quit, but not both.

$\sim(A \& B \sim B) \& \sim(A \& B)$

Instructions for exercises 210 through 214: Symbolize the concrete arguments; construct proofs for all arguments.

210. (SEMICHALLENGE)

   (a) $\sim (R\ \&\ T) \vdash T \rightarrow\ \sim R$

What can you infer from the fact that arguments 48 (p. 77) and 210 are both valid?

   (b)   In what logical relation do these two formulas stand:

$\sim (R\ \&\ \sim T)$
$R \rightarrow T$

Demonstrate the correctness of your answer.

211. (CHALLENGE) In Rudyard Kipling's short story, "Rikki-Tikki-Tavi," Nagaina, the recently widowed King Cobra, seeks vengeance:

"Son of the big man that killed Nag," she hissed, "stay still. I am not ready yet. Wait a little. Keep very still. . . . If you move I strike, and if you do not move I strike." [14]

Demonstrate that her last statement entails 'I STRIKE'. Let *M* abbreviate 'You move'.

212. (CHALLENGE)

   $A\ \&\ \sim A \vdash B$

This peculiar argument is discussed in section 13.1. A five-line proof is possible. Remember the second restriction on the Tilde Rules.

213. (CHALLENGE)

   $\sim C \vdash C \rightarrow D$

An eight-line proof is possible.
   This argument is the mate of argument 206 (chapter four). Argument 213 is demonstrably valid, but some English arguments that seem to have this form are of questionable validity. An example:

[14] *The Jungle Book* (Garden City, N.Y.: Doubleday, 1964), p. 146.

Jane Fonda does not have two husbands. Hence, if she has two husbands she is monogamous.

Arguments 206 and 213 are commonly referred to as the "paradoxes of material implication." These paradoxes are discussed in appendix one.

214. (CHALLENGE) A newspaper editorial advocating taxing land instead of buildings contains these sentences:

> *Taxing buildings discourages the construction of housing, which increases rents and unemployment. Not taxing land enough causes inflated land prices, one of the major causes of inflation.* [15]

The passage suggests this argument:

Taxing BUILDINGS results in more UNEMPLOYMENT. Not taxing LAND leads to increased INFLATION. It follows that we can avoid both higher unemployment and greater inflation only if land is taxed but buildings are not.

---

[15]"The Tax Bite," *Springfield (Ohio) News & Sun* (January 16, 1979).

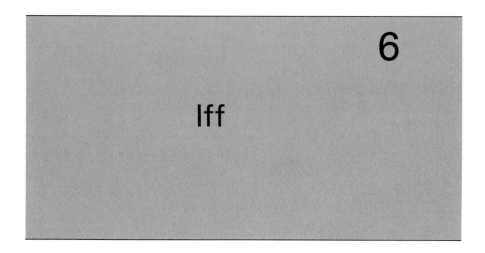

6

Iff

6.1
Symbolizing Biconditionals

A statement consisting of two constituent statements joined by the connective 'if and only if' is called a *biconditional*. An example:

> (S1) Norma will do GRADUATE work if and only if she receives a FELLOWSHIP.

A biconditional is equivalent to the conjunction of a pair of conditionals. Thus, S1 is logically equivalent to S2.

> (S2) Norma will do graduate work if she receives a fellowship, and she will do graduate work only if she receives a fellowship.

S2 is, of course, symbolized by F2:

> (F2) $(F \rightarrow G) \mathbin{\&} (G \rightarrow F)$

We could employ F2 as a symbolization of S1 and dispense with a special symbol for the locution 'if and only if'. However, because the locution is common in logical discourse, it will prove convenient to adopt the *double arrow* ('↔') as an abbreviation of it. We symbolize S1 with F1:

(F1)   G ↔ F

F1 is read "*G* if and only if *F*" or "*G* double arrow *F*." The expressions 'is a necessary and sufficient condition for' and 'just in case' are approximately synonymous with 'if and only if' and are also abbreviated by the double arrow.

The conventions for punctuating formulas containing arrows and ampersands also apply to formulas containing double arrows. For example, F3 represents a biconditional whose left constituent is a conjunction, and F4 symbolizes a conjunction whose right conjunct is a biconditional.

(F3)   (A & B) ↔ C
(F4)   A & (B ↔ C)

Although biconditionals occur regularly in logical and philosophical language, they occur only infrequently in many other areas of discourse. I suspect that this infrequent usage is due in part to the cumbersomeness of the pentasyllabic expression 'if and only if'. Some logicians have, in recent years, coined the shorter term 'iff' to remedy this difficulty; I will use this expression for the remainder of the book. (A defect of this expression is that it is phonetically indistinguishable from 'if'. Perhaps in the future a short biconditional connective will evolve in our natural language.) The logician Bas Van Fraassen saves one syllable with his expression 'exactly if'.

In the absence of such a convenient term, people will sometimes employ 'if' when they mean 'if and only if'. Thus, someone may utter S5 intending to claim S6.

(S5)   I will make the flight if I rush.
(S6)   I will make the flight if and only if I rush.

We need to distinguish between what a *person* means to claim and what the uttered *sentence* means. Strictly speaking, S5 expresses only a conditional.

6.2
Double Arrow In and Out

Examine this simple argument:

Norma MOVES to Chapel Hill iff she does GRADUATE work. So, she does graduate work iff she moves to Chapel Hill.

In symbols:

$$M \leftrightarrow G \vdash G \leftrightarrow M$$

This is a valid argument. (The double arrow is commutative.) We can prove the validity of this argument with the help of a pair of inference rules governing the double arrow.

> *The Double Arrow In Rule:* From $\mathcal{A} \rightarrow \mathcal{B}$ and $\mathcal{B} \rightarrow \mathcal{A}$ derive $\mathcal{A} \leftrightarrow \mathcal{B}$.
>
> *The Double Arrow Out Rule:* From $\mathcal{A} \leftrightarrow \mathcal{B}$ derive either $\mathcal{A} \rightarrow \mathcal{B}$ or $\mathcal{B} \rightarrow \mathcal{A}$.

Note that the Double Arrow In Rule sanctions a move from two premises, whereas the Double Arrow Out Rule sanctions a move from one premise. The standard assumption-dependence principle applies to both rules.

A proof for the "Chapel Hill" argument:

$$
\begin{array}{lll}
(1) & M \leftrightarrow G & A \\
(2) & M \rightarrow G & 1 \leftrightarrow O \\
(3) & G \rightarrow M & 1 \leftrightarrow O \\
(4) & G \leftrightarrow M & 3,2 \leftrightarrow I \\
\end{array}
$$

In the justification entry for a statement derived by the Double Arrow In Rule, I cite first the premise whose antecedent is identical with the biconditional's left constituent. However, you need not adopt this practice.

I shall illustrate the application of these two rules by constructing proofs for three other arguments. The first is suggested by an editorial in the *Huntington (West Virginia) Herald-Dispatch:*

> *Since the First Amendment to the Constitution forbids government from restraining the publication of news, it clearly follows that the government is equally powerless to compel the publication of news or opinion.* [1]

The argument formalized and symbolized:

> The government may RESTRAIN the publication of news iff it may COMPEL the publication of news. Since government may not restrain publication, it clearly follows that it also is not permitted to compel the publication of news.
>
> $R \leftrightarrow C, \sim R \vdash \sim C$

---

[1] Reprinted in *Miami News* (September 3, 1973), p. 12-A.

The proof:

1	(1)	R ↔ C	A
2	(2)	~R	A
3	(3)	C	PA
1	(4)	C → R	1 ↔ O
1,3	(5)	R	4,3 → O
1,2,3	(6)	R & ~R	5,2 & I
1,2	(7)	~C	3-6 ~I

At the end of section 5.3 I provided a justification for the Tilde In and Tilde Out Rules. This justification was formulated as an argument that is symbolized:

$$V ↔ \sim L, \sim L ↔ \sim D, C → \sim D \vdash C → V$$

Proof:

1	(1)	V ↔ ~L	A
2	(2)	~L ↔ ~D	A
3	(3)	C → ~D	A
4	(4)	C	PA
3,4	(5)	~D	3,4 → O
2	(6)	~D → ~L	2 ↔ O
2,3,4	(7)	~L	6,5 → O
1	(8)	~L → V	1 ↔ O
1,2,3,4	(9)	V	8,7 → O
1,2,3	(10)	C → V	4-9 → I

The third sample argument:

> Norma MOVES to Chapel Hill iff she does GRADUATE work. She does graduate work iff she receives a FELLOWSHIP. Hence, Norma moves to Chapel Hill just in case she gets a fellowship.

(This resembles the *chain* "VW" argument of section 4.2.) In symbols:

$$M ↔ G, G ↔ F \vdash M ↔ F$$

Proof:

1	(1)	M ↔ G	A	[1]
2	(2)	G ↔ F	A	[2]
3	(3)	M	PA	[6]

1	(4)	M → G	1 ↔ O	[8]
1,3	(5)	G	4,3 → O	[9]
2	(6)	G → F	2 ↔ O	[10]
1,2,3	(7)	F	6,5 → O	[7]
1,2	(8)	M → F	3-7 → I	[4]
9	(9)	F	PA	[11]
2	(10)	F → G	2 ↔ O	[13]
2,9	(11)	G	10,9 → O	[14]
1	(12)	G → M	1 ↔ O	[15]
1,2,9	(13)	M	12,11 → O	[12]
1,2	(14)	F → M	9-13 → I	[5]
1,2	(15)	M ↔ F	8,14 ↔ I	[3]

Note the proof-discovery numbers.

Both Double Arrow rules are "choice" rules. This is obvious in the case of Double Arrow Out, but not so evident for Double Arrow In. When Double Arrow In is applied to a pair of conditionals, either of two biconditionals may be deduced. The following proof illustrates:

(1)	D → E	A
(2)	E → D	A
(3)	D ↔ E	1,2 ↔ I
(4)	E ↔ D	2,1 ↔ I
(5)	(D ↔ E) & (E ↔ D)	3,4 & I

Strategic suggestions for the Double Arrow rules:

DOUBLE ARROW IN: If one of the goal lines is a biconditional, search the premise lines for the two associated conditionals (that is, the conditionals with the same constituent statements). If you find both conditionals, apply Double Arrow In. If you find only one of the associated conditionals, add the other as a goal line. If you find neither conditional among the premise lines, add both as goal lines.

DOUBLE ARROW OUT: If one of the premise lines is a biconditional, apply Double Arrow Out (once or twice).

EXERCISES

58. Symbolize each statement using the suggested notation.

(a)   *(College memo)* "We can emphasize these APPLIED areas most effectively if, and only if, we emphasize also the FUNDAMENTAL areas of research."

A ↔ F

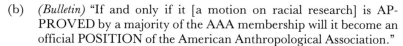

$A \leftrightarrow P$

(b) *(Bulletin)* "If and only if it [a motion on racial research] is AP-PROVED by a majority of the AAA membership will it become an official POSITION of the American Anthropological Association."

(c) *(Newspaper)* "North Vietnam will MEET with U.S. negotiator Henry Kissinger Monday but only if the U.S. will AGREE to sign the peace agreement Tuesday on schedule." $M \to A$

(d) *(Section 5.3)* "These two statements [S2 and S4] are EQUIVA-LENT if and only if each entails the other."

$E \leftrightarrow (A \wedge B)$

A = S2 entails S4
B = S4 entails S2

$(M \leftrightarrow W) \, \& \, (\sim M \to S)$

(e) *(Minutes)* "The assistantship will be offered to McGRAW if and only if she does not get a tuition WAIVER; and it will be offered to SPIEGELMAN if not offered to McGraw."

*(f) *(Logician Geoffrey Hunter)* "A set C is a *PROPER* subset of a set D iff there is no member of C that is not a member of D but there is a member of D that is not a member of C." $P \leftrightarrow (\sim A \, \& \, B)$

A = There is a member of C that is not a member of D
B = There is a member of D that is not a member of C

*(g) *(Student newspaper)* "This is Tate's LAST year on his contract and RENEWAL of it depends on two things: a WINNING team, and an EXCITING team." $L \, \& \, [R \to (W \, \& \, E)]$

(h) *(Insurance premium notice)* "No receipt will be FURNISHED except by WRITTEN request." $F \to W$

59. Translate each formula into an English sentence using this "diction-ary":

B = Smith wins the batting crown
S = Smith makes an out
H = Smith gets a hit
J = Jones makes an out

(a) $B \leftrightarrow \sim S$ *Smith wins batting crown iff he doesn't make an out.*
(b) $B \leftrightarrow (H \, \& \, J)$ " *if he gets a hit and Jones makes an out.*
*(c) $(B \leftrightarrow H) \, \& \, J$ *Smith wins... gets a hit; J. makes an out.*
(d) $H \to (B \leftrightarrow J)$ *If S. gets a hit then he wins be. iff Jones makes out.*

60. Complete the following proofs. Every assumption has been iden-tified.

(a)

	(1)	$A \leftrightarrow B$	A
2	(2)	$C \leftrightarrow B$	A

3	(3)	A	PA
1	(4)	A → B	1 ↔ O
1,3	(5)	B	3,4 → O
2	(6)	B → C	2 ↔ O
1,2,3	(7)	B C	5,6 → O
1,2	(8)	A → C	3-7 → I

(b)

(1)	D ↔ E	A
(2)	(E → D) → (G → F)	A
(3)	(D → E) → (F → G)	A
(4)	E → D	
(5)	G → F	
(6)		
(7)		
(8)	F ↔ G	

*(c)

	(1)	H ↔ (I & J)	A
	(2)	I → H	A
	(3)	H	PA
	(4)		1 ↔ O
	(5)		
	(6)		
	(7)		3-6 → I
1,2	(8)	H ↔ I	7,2 ↔ I

Instructions for exercises 61 through 72: Symbolize the arguments and construct proofs.

61. A group of black golfers provides a scholarship at the University of Miami for "a promising black golfer who can qualify academically."[2] Though admiring their generosity, I have reservations about the terms of the scholarship. This argument expresses my objection:

> A scholarship restricted to BLACK golfers is racially discriminatory if and only if a scholarship restricted to WHITE golfers is discriminatory. Clearly, a scholarship for which only white golfers are eligible is discriminatory. Therefore, a scholarship for which only black golfers are eligible is discriminatory as well.

62. Philosopher John Locke writes:

> ... *He that will consider that the same fire that, at one distance produces in us the sensation of warmth, does, at a nearer approach, produce in us the far different sensation of pain, ought to bethink himself what reason he has to say —*

[2]Charlie Nobles, "Black Golfers on a Treadmill," *Miami News* (February 18, 1972), p. 4-B.

that this idea of warmth, which was produced in him by the fire, is actually in the fire; *and his idea of pain, which the same fire produced in him the same way, is* not *in the fire.* [3]

Locke is arguing:

> The WARMTH is a quality of the fire exactly if the PAIN is a quality of the fire. Since the pain is not a quality of the fire, neither is the warmth.

63. Mrs. Lockhorn appears to reason as follows:

> If ignorance is BLISS, then Lockhorn is the HAPPIEST man in the world just in case he is the most IGNORANT. He *is* the most ignorant. Therefore, if ignorance is bliss, he's got to be the happiest man in the world.

"IF IGNORANCE IS BLISS, HE'S GOT TO BE THE HAPPIEST MAN IN THE WORLD."

July 11, 1974. © King Features Syndicate, World rights reserved. 1974.

64. The logicians Hughes and Cresswell write:

> *It should be noted that whenever we have a thesis of the form* Cab *we can always use TR3 to obtain* ⊢ LCab, *and hence, by Def F,* ⊢ Fab. *Moreover, whenever we have* ⊢ Fab *we can, by Def F, substitution of* Cab *for p in A5, and Modus Ponens, obtain* ⊢ Cab. *I.e. whenever* Cab *is a thesis, so is* Fab, *and vice versa.* [4]

---

[3]John Locke, *An Essay Concerning Human Understanding*, 2 vols. (New York: Dover, 1959), I: 174.

[4]G. E. Hughes and M. J. Cresswell, *An Introduction to Modal Logic* (London: Methuen, 1968), p. 31. I have replaced their notation by one that is more readily printed.

Their reasoning may be paraphrased:

> If *Cab* is a theorem, then *LCab* is also, and if *LCab* is a theorem, then *Fab* is a theorem. Moreover, if *Fab* is a theorem, then *Cab* is too. This proves that *Cab* is a theorem iff *Fab* is a theorem.

Adopt these abbreviations:

$$C = Cab \text{ is a theorem}$$
$$L = LCab \text{ is a theorem}$$
$$F = Fab \text{ is a theorem}$$

*65. Argument 65 on page 43 deals with the meaning of 'only if'. Prove that it is valid. Use these symbols:

$$A = \text{S1 is equivalent to S3}$$
$$B = \text{S1 is compatible with S6}$$
$$C = \text{S3 is compatible with S6}$$

66. The philosopher Norman Malcolm[5] is critical of the view that brain phenomena and mental phenomena are identical. I have paraphrased one of his arguments as follows:

> If brain phenomena are IDENTICAL with mental phenomena, then the former's having spatial location constitutes a necessary and sufficient condition for the latter's having spatial location. BRAIN phenomena can be located spatially. Provided that MENTAL phenomena are spatially locatable, it will be meaningful to assign spatial location to a THOUGHT. It is not meaningful to do this. So, it is false that brain phenomena and mental phenomena are identical.

67. This argument provides the rationale for wiring backup lights through the transmission.

> Backup lights are NEEDED only if the car is in REVERSE. [Because they are connected to the transmission] they are ON iff the car is in reverse. If they are on only if the car is in reverse, then they use very LITTLE power. Therefore, the backup lights are on if needed, yet they use very little power.

[5]See "[Abstract of] Scientific Materialism and the Identity Theory," *Journal of Philosophy*, LX (October 24, 1963), 662–63.

68. The "TUMOR" argument [see section 1.1] is symbolized in propositional logic as 'A, N ⊢ B'. If propositional logic yields this symbolization, then provided that this branch of logic is ADEQUATE for evaluating the argument, the ENGLISH argument is valid iff the SYMBOLIZED version is valid. The English argument is valid, but the symbolization isn't. It follows that propositional logic is inadequate for evaluating the "tumor" argument.

69. A news story about a meeting of the Coral Gables City Commission contains this passage:

> *Politics has taken up residence in the old Biltmore Hotel. ...*
>
> *The issue is whether the city wants to try to obtain the 19.8-acres from the federal government. ...*
>
> *After a series of confusing votes Friday, the commission's answer depends on your political viewpoint.*
>
> *"Yes," commissioners said, "the city wants the property if voters agree." On the other hand commissioners said "no, the city doesn't want it, unless voters say they do."* [6]

There is the implication in this story that the two views expressed in the final paragraph are unclear or perhaps inconsistent. Yet, the two views taken together (see S1) are logically equivalent to S2, a perfectly straightforward biconditional.

(S1)   The CITY wants the property if the VOTERS want it, and the city doesn't want it unless the voters want it.

(S2)   The city wants the property iff the voters want it.

Prove that S1 entails S2.

70. Prove that S2 in the preceding exercise entails S1. These two proofs establish the logical equivalence of S1 and S2.

*71. In a *Star Trek* show, the crew of the starship *Enterprise* is held captive by a powerful computer. The crew escapes after one of them says to the computer, "I am lying to you." This inference blew the computer's fuses:

He SAYS that he is lying. If he says that he is lying and he *is* LYING, then he isn't lying. But also, if he says that he is lying and he *isn't* lying, then he is lying. This proves that he is lying iff he isn't lying.

[6]Louis Salome, "Biltmore: Yes, the City Wants it; No, it Doesn't ... Unless the Voters Do," *Miami News* (March 16, 1971), p. 5-A.

72. There are people who believe that at some time after their death God will re-create their bodies. Would the re-creation of, say, Billy Graham be Billy or merely a *replica* of Billy? The realization that it is logically possible that God produce two re-creations of Graham (label them *A* and *B*) may count against the view that either re-creation would be Graham. Argument 72 pursues this point.

    A is Billy just in case B is Billy. It is not true that Both A and B are Billy. Therefore, A is not Billy and neither is B.

    (A = A is Billy, B = B is Billy)

215. (CHALLENGE) I can symbolize the following sentence with a formula consisting of eighteen symbols (connectives, letters, and grouping symbols). Can you provide an equally short (or shorter) symbolization?

    Exactly one of these three people will be hired: SOSA, KHATCHADOURIAN, and LEHRER.

Instructions for exercises 216 through 218: Symbolize the concrete arguments; construct proofs for all arguments.

216. (CHALLENGE)

    Norma's receiving a FELLOWSHIP is a necessary and sufficient condition for her doing GRADUATE work. Consequently, her not receiving a fellowship is a necessary and sufficient condition for her not doing graduate work.

217. (CHALLENGE)

    $\sim D \leftrightarrow E \vdash \sim (D \leftrightarrow E)$

218. (CHALLENGE) If you invent an expression, you are entitled to assign a meaning to it. Suppose someone coined the sentence 'Blubs grub' and assigned it this meaning: "If the statement 'Blubs grub' is true, then God exists." The person would then be in a position to advance the following argument for the existence of God:

    [By definition] BLUBS grub iff, if the statement 'Blubs grub' is TRUE then GOD exists. The statement 'Blubs grub' is true iff blubs do grub. It follows that God exists.

    Prove that this argument has a valid logical form. Of course, there is something wrong with the argument's content. What is it?

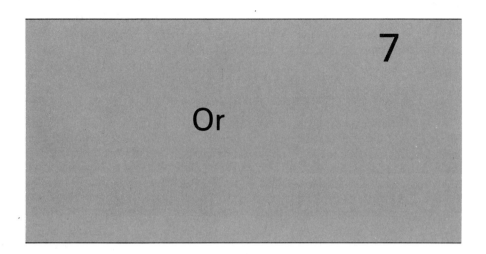

7

Or

7.1
Symbolizing Disjunctions

A statement consisting of two constituent statements joined by the connective 'or' is called a disjunction; the component statements are called *disjuncts*. Often, the first disjunct is preceded by the word 'either'. A sample disjunction:

> Either one of the CHILDREN is up or there is an INTRUDER in the house.

We introduce the *wedge* ('v') as an abbreviation for the connective 'or'. Accordingly, the above disjunction is symbolized:

> C v I

This formula is read "*C* or *I*" or "*C* wedge *I*." We adopt the conventions concerning the use of parentheses that we developed for the other dyadic connectives.

Very often, when we assert a disjunction we intend to admit the possibility that both disjuncts are true. For example, the disjunction above would not be proved false by the discovery that one of the children was up *and* there was an intruder in the house. In such a case 'or' is said to be used in the *inclusive* sense. When we wish to make it quite clear that we are including the possibility that both disjuncts are true, we may use one of these locutions:

> A *or* B *or both.*
> A *and/or* B.

Sometimes when we utter an "or" sentence for the purpose of telling people what they *should* do or what they are *permitted* to do, we intend to rule out the case where both disjuncts are true. A mother who says "You may have an ice-cream sandwich or a Popsicle" is very likely excluding the case where the child gets both. In such a sentence 'or' is said to be used in the *exclusive* sense. When we wish to be explicit about excluding the case where both disjuncts are true, we employ this expression:

> A *or* B *but not both.*

To sum up, when S1 means the same as S2, the 'or' in S1 has the inclusive sense; when S1 means the same as S3, the 'or' in S1 has the exclusive sense.

> (S1)   A or B.
> (S2)   A or B or both.
> (S3)   A or B but not both.

What shall we say about this disjunction?

> Erma is in Seattle or Dallas.

Is the 'or' being used in the inclusive or the exclusive sense? The answer is that there is no satisfactory way to tell in which sense it is being used. The two disjuncts, because of their content, cannot both be true. Inasmuch as (independently of the way in which 'or' is being used here) they rule each other out, it is impossible to determine that, in addition, the 'or' is being used in a "strong" sense that excludes their both being true.

Logic cannot tolerate ambiguity. We must decide whether the wedge abbreviates the inclusive 'or' or the exclusive 'or'. The decision is easily reached. Most (all?) clear-cut cases of an exclusive 'or' involve regulative language (that is, command-giving language) and not descriptive language. The logic we are piecing together is a logic of descriptive language, in which 'or' is generally used in the inclusive sense. Hence, we ascribe that sense to the wedge and adopt the following convention:

Disjunctions shall be treated as exclusive iff they contain the expression 'but not both' (or a similar locution).

How shall we symbolize exclusive disjunctions (for example, the following sentence)?

> Either the CASHIER or the MANAGER will be fired, but not both.

F4 is the literal translation, but F5 and F6 are equally acceptable.

> (F4)   (C v M) & ~ (C & M)
> (F5)   C ↔ ~ M
> (F6)   ~ C ↔ M

(We shall prove the logical equivalence of F4 and F5 in section 13.2.)

How shall we symbolize this sentence?

> Either the SUSPECT or the WITNESS or the DETECTIVE lied.

Three possibilities:

> (F7)   S v W v D
> (F8)   S v (W v D)
> (F9)   (S v W) v D

We exclude F7 because accepting it would complicate the statement of the wedge inference rules (and a technique developed later in the book). F8 and F9 are logically equivalent (the wedge is associative), and, hence, both are satisfactory symbolizations of S2. Exercise 221 involves half the task of showing that the wedge is associative.

7.2
Wedge In

Consider this argument:

> If Norma is offered either a FELLOWSHIP or a teaching ASSISTANTSHIP, she will do GRADUATE work. Therefore, she will do graduate work if she is offered a fellowship.

In symbols:

> $(F \lor A) \to G \vdash F \to G$

The validity of this argument is quite obvious. In order to construct a proof for the argument, we need to adopt a rule for deriving disjunctions.

> *The Wedge In Rule:* From a statement derive a disjunction which has that statement as one disjunct and any statement as the other disjunct.

The rule restated:

> From $\mathcal{A}$ derive either $\mathcal{A} \vee \mathcal{B}$ or $\mathcal{B} \vee \mathcal{A}$.

This is a *choice* rule with a vengeance; it offers the proof constructor *two* choices: (1) The premise of a Wedge In step must reappear as one of the disjuncts of the statement derived, but it may be either the left or the right disjunct. (2) The other disjunct of the statement derived may be any statement whatever. We use the standard assumption-dependence principle with this rule.

Now we can construct a proof for the "fellowship" argument:

1	(1)	(F ∨ A) → G	A
2	(2)	F	PA
2	(3)	F ∨ A	2 ∨I
1,2	(4)	G	1,3 → O
1	(5)	F → G	2-4 → I

The *Wedge In proof strategy* is obvious:

> If one of the goal lines is a disjunction, search the premise lines for one of the disjuncts. If you find such a premise, apply Wedge In.

When people first study the Wedge In Rule, they often regard it as being excessively liberal. "You mean you can introduce any statement—even one that does not appear elsewhere in the proof—as the other disjunct?" We will attempt to justify the rule with an argument:

> An inclusive disjunction is TRUE whenever even one of its disjuncts is true. If so, then WHENEVER the premise of a Wedge In inference is true the conclusion is also. The Wedge In Rule is "SAFE" if whenever the premise of an inference made according to it is true the conclusion is also true. Hence, Wedge In is a "safe" rule.

Is this argument valid?

One explanation of the skeptical attitude people often assume when first exposed to the Wedge In Rule is that it sanctions an inference pattern that we are not accustomed to employing. We rarely reason in this way because having learned the truth of a certain statement, we are not concerned with demonstrating that the disjunction of that statement and some other statement is also a truth. The disjunctive statement is less specific and, therefore, less informative than the statement already established. Nevertheless, we do occasionally reason in this way. My fourteen-year-old brother-in-law was bugging his father for a lightweight Honda motorcycle. My father-in-law told him, "I will either buy you the most powerful Honda made or no Honda at all." Had my father-in-law been asked to justify his statement, I'm confident he would have replied, "I'm not buying him a Honda." The argument 'I'm not buying him a Honda; therefore, I'll either buy him the most powerful Honda or no Honda' is, of course, an inference sanctioned by the Wedge In Rule.

A logic text that I have used contains this abstract argument:

$$P \& Q \vdash P \vee Q$$

Many of my students constructed the following "proof" for the argument:

(1) P & Q   A
(2) P   1 &O
(3) Q   1 &O
(4) P ∨ Q   2,3 vI (ERROR!)

The error lies in treating Wedge In as a two-premised inference. These two proofs of the argument are correct:

(1) P & Q   A
(2) P   1 &O
(3) P ∨ Q   2 vI

(1) P & Q   A
(2) Q   1 &O
(3) P ∨ Q   2 vI

Of course, the quickest way to repair the above incorrect "proof" would be to delete one line number from the justification of the fourth line. The resulting proof would be disorganized (because there would be a pointless line) but correct.

How should we symbolize S1 (quoted from a newspaper article)?

(S1)   The Orange Bowl is neither ORANGE nor a BOWL.

As 'neither O nor B' is a contraction of 'not either O or B', the literal symbolization is F1:

(F1)   ~(O ∨ B)

F1 is logically equivalent to F2.

(F2)   ~O & ~B

Thus, both of these formulas are correct symbolizations of S1. F3 and F4, on the other hand, are not equivalent to F1 and F2 and are not acceptable symbolizations of S1.

(F3) ~(O & B)

(F4) ~O v ~B

Can you explain why F3 and F4 do not correctly symbolize S1?

We can show that F1 and F2 are logically equivalent by demonstrating that each entails the other. I prove now that F1 entails F2; in chapter ten I will prove that F2 entails F1.

1	(1)	~(O v B)	A	[1]
2	(2)	O	PA	[5]
2	(3)	O v B	2 vI	[6]
1,2	(4)	(O v B) & ~(O v B)	3,1 &I	[7]
1	(5)	~O	2-4 ~I	[3]
6	(6)	B	PA	[8]
6	(7)	O v B	6 vI	[9]
1,6	(8)	(O v B) & ~(O v B)	7,1 &I	[10]
1	(9)	~B	6-8 ~I	[4]
1	(10)	~O & ~B	5,9 &I	[2]

Note the proof-discovery numbers.

7.3
Wedge Out

In his speech to the Athenian jury that sentenced him to death (as recounted in Plato's "Apology"), Socrates argues that death is not something to be feared, but rather is a benefit:

> ... *Death is one of two things. Either it is annihilation, and the dead have no consciousness of anything, or, as we are told, it is really a change—a migration of the soul from this place to another. Now if there is no consciousness but only a dreamless sleep, death must be a marvelous gain. ... If death is like this, then, I call it a gain, because the whole of time, if you look at it in this way, can be regarded as no more than one single night. If on the other hand death is a removal from here to some other place, and if what we are told is true, that all the dead are there, what greater blessing could there be than this, gentlemen? ... Put it in this way. How much would one of you give to meet Orpheus and Musaeus, Hesiod and Homer?*[1]

---

[1]40c–41a. Hugh Tredennick, trans., "Apology," in *The Collected Dialogues of Plato*, ed. by Edith Hamilton and Huntington Cairns (Princeton, N.J.: Princeton University Press, 1961), p. 25.

Socrates' argument expressed simply:

> Death is either ANNIHILATION or MIGRATION. If death is annihilation it is a BENEFIT. If, on the other hand, it is migration it is still a benefit. So, death is a benefit.

In symbols:

$$A \vee M, A \rightarrow B, M \rightarrow B \vdash B$$

The pattern of inference exhibited by this argument is one form of the *dilemma*. Two characteristics shared by all dilemmas are (1) a disjunctive premise and (2) two conditional premises. Logicians recognize several species of dilemma; the two most common forms:

simple constructive: $\mathcal{P} \vee \mathcal{Q}, \mathcal{P} \rightarrow \mathcal{R}, \mathcal{Q} \rightarrow \mathcal{R} \vdash \mathcal{R}$

complex constructive: $\mathcal{P} \vee \mathcal{Q}, \mathcal{P} \rightarrow \mathcal{R}, \mathcal{Q} \rightarrow \mathcal{S} \vdash \mathcal{R} \vee \mathcal{S}$

Socrates advanced a simple constructive dilemma. Examples of each type will be found in the exercises at the end of this chapter.

We can base our Wedge Out Rule on the obviously sound simple constructive dilemma.

The Wedge Out Rule: From $\mathcal{A} \vee \mathcal{B}$, $\mathcal{A} \rightarrow \mathcal{C}$, and $\mathcal{B} \rightarrow \mathcal{C}$ derive $\mathcal{C}$.

I will illustrate the employment of the rule by constructing four proofs, beginning with a proof of Socrates' argument:

(1)	A ∨ M	A
(2)	A → B	A
(3)	M → B	A
(4)	B	1,2,3 ∨O

The Wedge Out Rule is applicable because the statement on line 4 matches the consequent of both conditionals and the antecedents of those conditionals match the disjuncts in line 1. The justification entry for any Wedge Out step will include three line numbers. I cite first the disjunctive premise, and second the conditional whose antecedent matches the left disjunct of the disjunctive premise.

The second proof concerns this simple argument:

> Death is either ANNIHILATION or MIGRATION. Thus, it is either migration or annihilation.

In symbols:

$$A \vee M \vdash M \vee A$$

The argument is valid; the wedge is commutative. The proof for this argument is going to involve both the Wedge Out Rule (because of the disjunctive premise) and the Wedge In Rule (because of the disjunctive conclusion). The dominant pattern in the proof is Wedge Out. In order to apply the Wedge Out Rule at the conclusion of the proof, we will need (in addition to the disjunctive premise) two conditional statements. We can tell exactly what those conditionals will be:

$$A \rightarrow (M \vee A)$$
$$M \rightarrow (M \vee A)$$

The antecedent of the first conditional will match the left disjunct of the disjunctive premise and the antecedent of the second will match the right disjunct. Both conditionals will have a consequent that matches the conclusion to be reached by Wedge Out. The two conditionals will be derived by means of the Arrow In Rule. The proof goes as follows:

1	(1)	$A \vee M$	A
2	(2)	A	PA
2	(3)	$M \vee A$	2 vI
	(4)	$A \rightarrow (M \vee A)$	2-3 $\rightarrow$I
5	(5)	M	PA
5	(6)	$M \vee A$	5 vI
	(7)	$M \rightarrow (M \vee A)$	5-6 $\rightarrow$I
1	(8)	$M \vee A$	1,4,7 vO

Note that lines 4 and 7 depend on *no* assumptions. Line 4, for example, depends upon whatever line 3 depends on (namely, 2) less line 2; that is, nothing. This phenomenon is discussed in section 12.1 below. The standard assumption-dependence principle applies to the Wedge Out Rule. Line 8 depends on all of the assumptions on which lines 1, 4, and 7 depend. A peculiar feature of the proof above (and of many Wedge Out proofs) is that the same statement occurs on three lines (3, 6, and 8). However, the lines differ in assumption dependence, and only line 8 is free of dependence on a provisional assumption.

The *Wedge Out strategy* may be summarized as follows:

If one of the premise lines is a disjunction, search the other premise lines for two conditionals whose antecedents match the disjuncts and whose consequents (both) match some goal line. If you find both conditionals, apply Wedge Out. If you find only one of the two conditionals, add the other as a goal line. If you find neither conditional among the premise lines, add both as goal lines.

The Wedge Out strategy will be further illustrated in a third proof which establishes the validity of a complex constructive dilemma. A newspaper story revealed that the full-time director of a federal scholarship program was working at his own veterinary clinic in Miami. The situation was further complicated by the fact that he was the only licensed veterinarian at the clinic. Florida law requires the presence of a licensed vet. The article notes:

> *Both Dr. González-Mayo and his wife realized that he was caught in a serious dilemma: If he said he was working at the federal program, then his clinic was being tended by veterinarians who were unlicensed; if he said he was at the clinic supervising them, then he was not fulfilling his role as director of the scholarship program.*[2]

There is a connection between the ordinary meaning of 'dilemma' (a situation involving a choice between equally unsatisfactory alternatives) and the logician's meaning. The unfortunate situation can be expressed by a dilemma (argument), as for example:

> Dr. González-Mayo is working at the federal PROGRAM or at his veterinary CLINIC. If the former, then the clinic is not operating LEGALLY. If the latter, then he is not working full-time as project DIRECTOR. Therefore, either his clinic is operating illegally or he is not working full-time as project director.

The dilemma symbolized:

$$P \lor C, P \rightarrow \sim L, C \rightarrow \sim D \vdash \sim L \lor \sim D$$

This argument is a *complex*, rather than a *simple*, dilemma. Note that the consequents of the conditionals do not match; instead, each consequent matches one of the disjuncts of the conclusion. In order to complete a Wedge Out proof for this argument, it will be necessary to deduce two conditionals (lines 7 and 11 in the proof below) whose consequents match the argument's conclusion.

1	(1)	$P \lor C$	A
2	(2)	$P \rightarrow \sim L$	A
3	(3)	$C \rightarrow \sim D$	A
4	(4)	P	PA
2,4	(5)	$\sim L$	2,4 $\rightarrow$O
2,4	(6)	$\sim L \lor \sim D$	5 vI
2	(7)	$P \rightarrow (\sim L \lor \sim D)$	4-6 $\rightarrow$I
8	(8)	C	PA
3,8	(9)	$\sim D$	3,8 $\rightarrow$O
3,8	(10)	$\sim L \lor \sim D$	9 vI
3	(11)	$C \rightarrow (\sim L \lor \sim D)$	8-10 $\rightarrow$I
1,2,3	(12)	$\sim L \lor \sim D$	1,7,11 vO

---

[2]Louis Salome and Hilda Inclan, "Aid Chief Runs Own Clinic While on U.S. Payroll," *Miami News* (October 4, 1976), p. 4-A.

The fourth proof shows that formula F1 entails F2.

(F1)   A & (B v C)

(F2)   (A & B) v (A & C)

F2 also entails F1 (exercise 86 at the end of the chapter), and, so, the two formulas are logically equivalent. Their equivalence constitutes one of the two main cases of a principle known as *distribution*. The other main case of distribution involves formulas like F3 and F4.

(F3)   D v (E & F)

(F4)   (D v E) & (D v F)

The equivalence of F3 and F4 is discussed in chapter thirteen. The proof that F1 entails F2:

1	(1)	A & (B v C)	A	[1]
1	(2)	A	1 &O	[3]
1	(3)	B v C	1 &O	[4]
4	(4)	B	PA	[7]
1,4	(5)	A & B	2,4 &I	[9]
1,4	(6)	(A & B) v (A & C)	5 vI	[8]
1	(7)	B → [(A & B) v (A & C)]	4-6 →I	[5]
8	(8)	C	PA	[10]
1,8	(9)	A & C	2,8 &I	[12]
1,8	(10)	(A & B) v (A & C)	9 vI	[11]
1	(11)	C → [(A & B) v (A & C)]	8-10 →I	[6]
1	(12)	(A & B) v (A & C)	3,7,11 vO	[2]

Note the proof-discovery numbers.

I conclude this section with a cautionary note. Many Wedge Out proofs will incorporate two Arrow In subproofs; the last three proofs have been of this sort. In constructing the second subproof, one must avoid incurring dependence on the provisional assumption that begins the first subproof. If this does occur, then the statement derived by Wedge Out will depend on the first provisional assumption and the proof will not be complete.

EXERCISES

73. Symbolize each statement using the suggested notation.

(a)   *(Plautus dialogue)* "This woman must be either MAD or DRUNK."

(b) *(Forensic pathologist)* "Either the eyewitnesses are mistaken or this is not the body of Nathaniel Cater."

  E = The eyewitnesses are correct
  N = This is the body of Nathaniel Cater

*(c) *(John Volpe)* "The whole [railroad] system will wind up BROKE and/or NATIONALIZED."

(d) *(Dust jacket ad)* "Webster's New Collegiate does not begin with 'A' or end with 'Z'."

  A = *Webster's New Collegiate* begins with 'A'
  Z = *Webster's New Collegiate* ends with 'Z'

(e) *(Advertisement)* "If our TV repairman SAYS he'll be there Thursday he'll BE there Thursday or the cost of the LABOR is on us."

(f) *(Student newspaper)* "Nottage will DIE if he does not CONTINUE the dialysis treatment or UNDERGO the kidney transplant."

(g) *(Newspaper)* "Shula will have to trade or waive either Ron Sellers or Bo Rather, or both."

  C = Shula trades Ron Sellers
  D = Shula waives Ron Sellers
  E = Shula trades Bo Rather
  F = Shula waives Bo Rather

(h) *(Judicial decision)* "While the tenant has been unchaste, she is neither DISORDERLY nor a PROSTITUTE."

  C = The tenant is chaste
  D = The tenant is disorderly

*(i) *(Section 10.1)* "If either S2 or S3 or both are false, then S1 is false."

  A = S2 is true
  B = S3 is true
  C = S1 is true

(j) We will hire RACHELS or ALLISON but not both.

(k) *(Rasputin to Empress Alexandra)* "If I DIE or YOU desert me, you will lose your SON and your CROWN within six months."

  S = You lose your son within six months
  C = You lose your crown within six months

$\left(\sim R \ \& \ \sim A \right) \rightarrow H$

(l)   *(Arabian Nights)* "Your head shall answer for my son's life, unless he returns safe, or unless I hear that he is alive."

       H = I shall cut your head off
       R = My son returns safely
       A = I hear that my son is alive

*(m)   *(Newspaper)* "If it becomes necessary to PULL equipment off the line for repairs or if an ACCIDENT saps generating capacity, the company could be forced to REDUCE power to all areas or BLACK out some sections of the Gold Coast."

(n)   *(NBC Sports president)* "The only way we won't COVER the games is if RUSSIA tells us we can't, or if the UNITED STATES doesn't send a team."

       R = Russia tells NBC it cannot cover the games

74.   Translate each formula into an English sentence using this "dictionary":

       E = Zero is even
       O = Zero is odd
       P = Zero is positive
       N = Zero is negative
       C = Zero is a cardinal number

    (a) $\sim E \vee \sim O$
    (b) $\sim (P \vee N)$
    (c) $C \rightarrow (E \vee O)$
  *(d) $E \vee \sim (E \vee O)$

75.   Complete the following proofs. Every assumption has been identified.

(a)

	(1)	$\sim (A \vee B)$	A
	(2)	A & B	PA
	(3)	A	
	(4)	A ∨ B	
	(5)	$(A \vee B) \ \& \sim (A \vee B)$	
1	(6)	$\sim (A \ \& \ B)$	

(b)

	(1)	$(C \rightarrow D) \ \& \ (E \rightarrow D)$	A
	(2)	$C \rightarrow D$	
	(3)		1 &O
	(4)		PA
	(5)		4,2,3 ∨O
1	(6)	$(C \vee E) \rightarrow D$	4-5 →I

*(c)

	(1)	(C v E) → D	A
	(2)	C	PA
	(3)	C v E	
	(4)	D	
	(5)	C → D	
	(6)		PA
	(7)	C v E	
	(8)	D	
	(9)	E → D	
1	(10)	(C → D) & (E → D)	

(d)

	(1)	F v (G & H)	A
	(2)	F	PA
	(3)	F v G	2 vI
	(4)	F → (F v G)	2-3 →I
	(5)	G & H	PA
	(6)	G	5 &O
	(7)	F v G	6 vI
	(8)	(G & H) → (F v G)	5-7 →I
1	(9)	F v G	1,4,8 vO

(handwritten:) E → (F v G)   (G&H) →

76. The argument 'A ⊢ B' is clearly not valid. Therefore, the "proof" below must contain some error. Find it.

1	(1)	A	A
1	(2)	B v A	1 vI
3	(3)	B	PA
1,3	(4)	A & B	1,3 &I
1,3	(5)	B	4 &O
1	(6)	B → B	3-5 →I
7	(7)	A	PA
1,3,7	(8)	A & B	7,5 &I
1,3,7	(9)	B	8 &O
1,3	(10)	A → B	7-9 →I
1	(11)	B	2,6,10 vO

Instructions for exercises 77 through 86: Symbolize the concrete arguments; construct proofs for all arguments.

77. Billy Hayes, author of *Midnight Express*, told a college audience of his decision to escape from the Turkish prison in which he had been confined for five years:

> *My thoughts were that if I made it, I would be free. If they shot and killed me I would also be free.* [3]

[3]Bill Kaczaraba, "No More 'Crazy House' for Hayes," *Miami Hurricane* (October 31, 1978), p. 1.

Hayes was advancing a simple constructive dilemma:

If I ESCAPE, I will be FREE. If they KILL me, I will also be free. Either I escape or they kill me. So, I will be free.

78. $A \vdash (B \lor A) \lor C$

79. Letter to the Editor of *Life*:

> *Sirs:*
> Ed Cox [husband of Tricia Nixon Cox] is considered a very intelligent man. He is also a good friend of Nader.
> There is a picture of Ed and Tricia sitting in a car. Neither of them is wearing a seat belt. If he were so intelligent he would be wearing his seat belt. If he were such a good friend of Nader he would wear his seat belt. Nader is trying to get everybody to wear seat belts.
> I am ten years old and I don't like to be in a car that has no seat belts.
> *Yolande Ruess*[4]

Yolande's argument can be formulated in this way:

It is false that Ed Cox is either INTELLIGENT or a good FRIEND of Nader's, for these reasons: Ed is not wearing a SEAT belt. If he were intelligent he would be wearing one. And if he were a good friend of Nader's he would be wearing one.

*80. $\sim (D \lor E) \vdash \sim D$

81. A news story concerns one Willie Dennis who, in exchange for a reduction of charges against him from murder to manslaughter, agreed to testify in the trial of a second man. However, the testimony Dennis gave in the trial of the other man differed from what he had previously told the state attorney; whereupon the judge ordered Dennis's manslaughter conviction vacated and directed the state to indict him for murder. The newspaper account quotes the judge as giving the following justification of his action:

> "His [Dennis's] in-court statement was a confession to first-degree murder and contradicted his story to the state attorney," Sepe said. "He reneged and lied—either to the state attorney or to the jury."
> "He did not cooperate with the state, an essential condition to his plea to the lesser charge of manslaughter."[5]

Judge Sepe's reasoning may be paraphrased with this argument:

Dennis's in-court statement CONTRADICTED the story he told the state attorney. If this is so, then he lied

[4]July 9, 1971, p. 20A.
[5]"Murder Suspect-Witness Stripped of Lesser Plea," *Miami News* (October 7, 1971), p. 5-A.

either to the JURY or to the state ATTORNEY or perhaps both. Provided that he lied to the jury, he did not
cooperate with the STATE. And if he lied to the state
attorney, he also did not cooperate with the state.
Since Dennis's cooperating with the state was a necessary condition for dropping the charge of MURDER, the
state will charge him with murder.

82. A complex constructive dilemma underlies this "Andy Capp" comic
strip. Flo Capp reasons:

If Andy's OUT I don't NEED an excuse. If he's IN I don't
get a CHANCE to use an excuse. He's either out or in.
Therefore, I either don't need an excuse or don't get a
chance to use one.

"Andy Capp" by Reggie Smythe. ©1968 Daily Mirror
Newspapers Ltd. Dist. Field Newspaper Syndicate.

*83. In a newspaper interview the chairman of Days Inns, Richard
Kessler, explains why his firm has chosen to own instead of lease
many of the properties in its chain of motels:

"We've hedged our bet," Kessler observed. "If inflation continues at a high rate,
our assets will continue to appreciate because of our ownership in the properties.
Thus, we are able to keep up with inflation.

"But if inflation subsides, more people will be able to travel and we will
profit from a higher operating income."[6]

Kessler's reasoning:

If INFLATION continues at a high rate, our assets will
APPRECIATE. But if inflation subsides more people will
TRAVEL, and if more folks travel our OPERATING in-
come will rise. Obviously, inflation will continue at a

[6]Nick Poulos, "Days Inns' Chairman Sees Real-Estate Investment as Key to Suc-
cess," *Atlanta Constitution* (July 6, 1981), p. 6-C.

high rate or else subside. Consequently, either our assets will appreciate or our operating income will rise.

84. Flo's problem:

If I talk about OTHERS Andy thinks I'm a GOSSIP, and if I talk about MYSELF he thinks I'm a BORE. If I talk to ANDY I talk either about others or about myself. Hence, if I talk to Andy he thinks I'm a gossip or a bore.

"Andy Capp" by Reggie Smythe. ©1968 Daily Mirror Newspapers Ltd. Dist. Field Newspaper Syndicate.

85. Because the author of *Alice in Wonderland*, Lewis Carroll, was a logician, it is not surprising to find Alice employing deductive arguments:

Soon her eye fell on a little glass box that was lying under the table: she opened it, and found in it a very small cake, on which the words "EAT ME" were beautifully marked in currants. "Well, I'll eat it," said Alice, "and if it makes me larger, I can reach the key; and if it makes me smaller, I can creep under the door; so either way I'll get into the garden, and I don't care which happens!"[7]

Alice's argument:

The cake will make me either LARGER or SMALLER. If it makes me larger, I can reach the KEY; and if it makes me smaller, I can CREEP under the door. If I reach the key, I'll get into the GARDEN; and if I creep under the door, I'll get into the garden. So [either way] I'll get into the garden.

86. Prove that F2 entails F1.

(F1)   A & (B v C)

(F2)   (A & B) v (A & C)

[7] Lewis Carroll, *Alice in Wonderland* (London: Dent, 1961), pp. 8–9.

219. (CHALLENGE) Symbolize each statement using the suggested notation.

(a) *(Newspaper)* "Neither father nor son is named in the indictment as a defendant or co-conspirator."

A = The father is named as a defendant
B = The son is named as a defendant
C = The father is named as a co-conspirator
D = The son is named as a co-conspirator

(b) Exactly one of these two men will be hired: RACHELS and ALLISON.

R = Rachels is hired
A = Allison is hired

(c) More than one of these three men will be hired: SOSA, KHATCHADOURIAN, and LEHRER.

(d) *(Parental lecture)* "A 'no' from one of us means a 'no' from both of us."

M = Mother says "no"
F = Father says "no"

(e) *(Around the World in Eighty Days)* "If then — for there were 'ifs' still — the SEA did not become too boisterous, if the wind did not VEER round to the east, if no accident happened to the BOAT or its MACHINERY, the *Henrietta* might CROSS the three thousand miles from New York to Liverpool in the nine days, between the 12th and the 21st of December."

(f) *(Edmund Burke)* "The only thing necessary for the triumph of evil is for good men to do nothing."

T = Evil triumphs
N = Good men do nothing

(g) *(Umpire to Cleveland and Detroit managers)* "If either pitcher throws at anyone again, both the pitcher and the manager will be out of the game."

A = The Cleveland pitcher throws at someone again
B = The Cleveland pitcher is out of the game
C = The Cleveland manager is out of the game
D = The Detroit pitcher throws at someone again

E = The Detroit pitcher is out of the game
F = The Detroit manager is out of the game

(h) *(Newspaper)* "If the [LSU] Tigers lose (or tie) either the Tulane game or the Mississippi game, the Orange Bowl will try to shift to the Texas-Arkansas loser, providing it is Arkansas."

C = LSU loses the Tulane game
D = LSU ties the Tulane game
E = LSU loses the Mississippi game
F = LSU ties the Mississippi game
O = The Orange Bowl tries to shift to the Texas-Arkansas loser
A = Arkansas loses to Texas

(i) *(Sports columnist Robert Lipsyte)* "The LAKERS win when CHAMBERLAIN or BAYLOR or WEST gets hot, or any two of the three do well."

D = Chamberlain does well
E = Baylor does well
F = West does well

220. (CHALLENGE) Construct two four-line proofs for exercise 207 (chapter four). In one proof use a Wedge Rule; in the other employ a Tilde Rule.

Instructions for exercises 221 through 225: Symbolize the concrete arguments; construct proofs for all arguments.

221. (CHALLENGE)

$$S \vee (W \vee D) \vdash (S \vee W) \vee D$$

Proving the validity of this argument constitutes half the demonstration that the wedge is associative.

222. (CHALLENGE) A newspaper article begins, "Saudi Arabia is threatening to raise its oil prices if Congress does not approve a windfall profits tax." Later in the story Treasury Secretary G. William Miller states the Saudi position as, "Either you put in a windfall profits tax or we're going to be raising prices."[8] Prove the logical equivalence of these two statements by establishing the validity of 222 and 223.

---

[8]"Saudis Put Pressure upon U.S. to Enact Windfall Profits Tax," *Miami Herald* (November 25, 1979), p. 1-A.

Saudi Arabia will RAISE its oil prices if CONGRESS does not approve a windfall profits tax. So, either Congress approves a windfall profits tax or Saudi Arabia will raise its oil prices.

223. (CHALLENGE)

Either Congress approves a windfall profits tax or Saudi Arabia will raise its oil prices. Thus, Saudi Arabia will raise its oil prices if Congress does not approve a windfall profits tax.

224. (CHALLENGE)
(a) A *simple destructive dilemma*:

$$F \rightarrow G, F \rightarrow H, \sim G \vee \sim H \vdash \sim F$$

(b) A *complex destructive dilemma*:

$$I \rightarrow J, K \rightarrow L, \sim J \vee \sim L \vdash \sim I \vee \sim K$$

225. (CHALLENGE) I received a birthday card with the following message:

Some Philosophy for Your Birthday: WHY WORRY??? There are only two things to worry about, either you're healthy or you're sick. If you're healthy, there's nothing to worry about and if you're sick ... there are two things to worry about ... either you'll get well or you won't. If you get well there is nothing to worry about, but if you don't, you'll have two things to worry about ... either you'll go to heaven or to hell. If you go to heaven you have nothing to worry about and if you go to hell you'll be so busy shaking hands with all of us that you'll have no time to worry.

This is an argument whose unstated conclusion is 'Either you have nothing to worry about or you'll have no time to worry'. Use these abbreviations:

H = You are healthy
S = You are sick
W = You have something to worry about
A = You will get well
B = You will go to heaven
C = You will go to hell
T = You will have time to worry

Résumé

8.1
Summary of Inference Rules

In the preceding six chapters eleven proof rules have been introduced. Ten of these rules sanction deductions and may be called *inference rules*. (The Rule of Assumptions will be considered a proof rule but not an inference rule.) For each of the five statement connectives there is an inference rule that sanctions a move *to* a formula containing that connective; these are the five "In" rules. And for each of the connectives there is a rule that sanctions a move *from* a formula that contains the connective; these, of course, are the five "Out" rules. The ten inference rules are summarized in the following table. We call the rules "primitive" (original, primary) in order to distinguish them from additional rules introduced in the next chapter.

Recall that each of these inference rules applies to *whole* lines but not to *parts* of lines. This abstract argument is invalid:

$$A \to B \vdash (A \vee C) \to B$$

Can you show it to be invalid?[1] By applying one of the inference rules to a part of a line, we can construct a "proof" of the argument.

(1) $A \to B$ A
(2) $(A \vee C) \to B$ 1 vI (ERROR!)

[1]Try constructing a concrete argument exhibiting the same form that has a true premise and a false conclusion.

114

The Ten Primitive Inference Rules

	IN	OUT
→	From the derivation of B from assumption A (and perhaps other assumptions) derive $A \rightarrow B$.	From $A \rightarrow B$ and A derive B.
&	From A and B derive $A \& B$.	From $A \& B$ derive either A or B.
∨	From A derive either $A \vee B$ or $B \vee A$.	From $A \vee B$, $A \rightarrow C$, and $B \rightarrow C$ derive C.
↔	From $A \rightarrow B$ and $B \rightarrow A$ derive $A \leftrightarrow B$.	From $A \leftrightarrow B$ derive either $A \rightarrow B$ or $B \rightarrow A$.
~	From the derivation of $B \& \sim B$ from assumption A (and perhaps other assumptions) derive $\sim A$.	From the derivation of $B \& \sim B$ from assumption $\sim A$ (and perhaps other assumptions) derive A.

For each of the ten inference rules a principle has been provided for determining the assumption dependence of any formula introduced into a proof by that rule. These principles are listed in the following table. (The "standard" principle mentioned in the table is that the statement derived depends on all of the assumptions on which the premise(s) of the step depend(s).)

Assumption-Dependence Principles for the Ten Primitive Inference Rules

	IN	OUT
→	$A \rightarrow B$ depends on whatever assumptions B depends on (less A).	Standard
&	Standard	Standard
∨	Standard	Standard
↔	Standard	Standard
~	$\sim A$ depends on whatever assumptions $B \& \sim B$ depends on (less A).	A depends on whatever assumptions $B \& \sim B$ depends on (less $\sim A$).

In working the exercises for the preceding chapters, you have constructed proofs for a large number of valid propositional arguments. The following question may have occurred to you:

Just how powerful *is the proof procedure (the set of eleven proof rules) we have developed? What proportion of the total collection of valid propositional arguments can be demonstrated by this procedure? Thirty percent? Perhaps sixty percent?*

The answer, surprisingly, is that our set of eleven rules has maximum power; it is sufficient to demonstrate the validity of *every* valid propositional argument.[2] In logicians' terminology, our set of rules is *complete*. This answer seems more surprising when you realize that the number of possible distinct valid propositional arguments is infinite.

A second question:

How safe *is our set of proof rules? Can we by correctly applying these rules construct "proofs" for some invalid propositional arguments?*

The answer is that our rule set is completely safe. In logicians' terms our set of rules is *consistent*. If the set were inconsistent, it would not provide a means of establishing the validity of arguments and, hence, would be of no value to us.

The demonstration that our rule set is complete is lengthy and complicated; the same is true of the demonstration that the set is consistent. Furthermore, these proofs belong to *pure* logic, whereas this book is oriented toward *applied* logic. For these reasons I will not offer either demonstration. References are provided for those who wish to explore these intriguing matters.[3]

A third question:

Is the set of proof rules presented here the only one that is both complete and consistent?

The answer is that there are a great many such rule sets. The set given here, however, is an especially attractive one. It is more compact than most rule sets; it is especially suited to exercising a proof-builder's ingenuity and developing ability to plot strategy; and it is highly symmetrical (with one "In" rule and one "Out" rule for each connective).

[2]Of course, this does not mean that a given individual will be able to complete a proof for any valid propositional argument. It means that for each such argument a proof is in principle possible.

[3]For a general treatment of the completeness and consistency of propositional logic see parts one and two of Geoffrey Hunter, *Metalogic* (Berkeley and Los Angeles: University of California Press, 1971). E. J. Lemmon, in *Beginning Logic* (London: Thomas Nelson and Sons Ltd., 1965), develops a rule set quite similar to the one presented here. Lemmon established the consistency and completeness of his set in sections four and five of chapter two of his text.

8.2
Proof Strategy

As you have discovered, devising proofs requires insight and ingenuity; it is not a mechanical enterprise. Herein lies the challenge of constructing proofs. Proofs exercise our creative abilities. Because proof construction is essentially creative, I cannot provide a set of directions that when mechanically applied will enable you to devise a proof for any valid propositional argument. I can, however, offer some suggestions that should help you plot proof strategy. I begin by displaying in one place the suggestions made in earlier chapters—one suggestion for each rule of inference. I don't recommend committing this table to memory; I do recommend studying the suggestions until you fully understand them, and also referring back to the table when a proof has you stumped.

Some of the strategies suggested in this table should be given precedence over others because employing them usually gives an overall structure to the proof. I have in mind the strategies for Arrow In, Tilde In, and Wedge Out. The Tilde Out strategy also gives an overall structure to a proof, but it is often used as a last resort when other approaches fail.

I will illustrate how some of these strategies can be applied by constructing a proof for an argument advanced by Bertrand Russell:

> *There can be no permanent peace unless there is only one Air Force in the world, —with the degree of international government that that implies.*[4]

Supplying the unstated conclusion, this argument emerges:

> There can be no permanent PEACE unless there is only one AIR Force in the world. There will be one air force only if there is an INTERNATIONAL government. Therefore, the existence of an international government is a necessary condition for permanent peace.

Symbolized:

$$\sim A \rightarrow \sim P, A \rightarrow I \vdash P \rightarrow I$$

Simple proofs can be constructed "top-to-bottom." The premises of the argument are recorded at the top of the proof; then statements are derived from others higher in the list until the conclusion of the argument is reached. Some proofs are best done "backwards." First, you put the conclusion at the bottom of a sheet. Then, on the next line up, you put the statement that enables you to deduce the conclusion. You repeat this procedure until you reach the premises at the top of the proof. Of course,

---

[4] *The Autobiography of Bertrand Russell* (Boston: Little, Brown, 1968), II: 365.

Strategic Suggestions for the Ten Primitive Inference Rules

→I	If a goal line is a conditional, make a provisional assumption of the antecedent and add the consequent as a goal line.
→O	If a premise line is a conditional, search the other premise lines for the antecedent. If you find it, apply Arrow Out. If you do not find the antecedent among the premise lines, add it as a goal line.
&I	If a goal line is a conjunction, search the premise lines for the two conjuncts. If you find both conjuncts, apply Ampersand In. If you find only one conjunct, add the other as a goal line. If you find neither conjunct among the premise lines, add both as goal lines.
&O	If a premise line is a conjunction, apply Ampersand Out (once or twice).
vI	If a goal line is a disjunction, search the premise lines for one of the disjuncts. If you find such a premise, apply Wedge In.
vO	If a premise line is a disjunction, search the other premise lines for two conditionals whose antecedents match the disjuncts and whose consequents (both) match some goal line. If you find both conditionals, apply Wedge Out. If you find only one of the two conditionals, add the other as a goal line. If you find neither conditional among the premise lines, add both as goal lines.
↔I	If a goal line is a biconditional, search the premise lines for the two associated conditionals (that is, the conditionals with the same constituent statements). If you find both conditionals, apply Double Arrow In. If you find only one of the associated conditionals, add the other as a goal line. If you find neither conditional among the premise lines, add both as goal lines.
↔O	If a premise line is a biconditional, apply Double Arrow Out (once or twice).
~I	If a goal line is a negation (and a more direct way of reaching it is not apparent), make a provisional assumption of the statement less its initial tilde and try to derive a standard contradiction.
~O	If a goal line is affirmative (and a more direct way of reaching it is not apparent), make a provisional assumption of its negation and try to derive a standard contradiction.

when you employ this method you are not making deductions but setting subgoals; and after reaching the top of the proof you have to turn around and descend, filling in the justification column indicating how the statements are to be deduced.

Many proofs are best done by combining the forward and backward approaches. The premises of the argument are recorded at the top and the conclusion at the bottom; then the gap in the middle is reduced by alternately making deductions and provisional assumptions (above the gap) and setting subgoals (below the gap). The aim in this approach is to eliminate the gap in the middle. The proof of Russell's argument is best done in this fashion. To understand my strategy, read the bracketed comments in the right-hand column in numerical order.

(1)	$\sim A \rightarrow \sim P$	A	
(2)	$A \rightarrow I$	A	
(3)	P	PA	[1. In accordance with the Arrow In strategy I provisionally assume 'P' on line 3 and set down 'I' as the first subgoal.]
(4)	$\sim A$	PA	[3. Seeing no more direct route for the proof, I fall back on the Tilde Out strategy and provisionally assume the negation of my highest subgoal, 'A'. I keep in mind the need to reach a standard contradiction.]
(5)	$\sim P$	$1,4 \rightarrow O$	[4. The Arrow Out strategy dictates this deduction.]
(6)	$P \& \sim P$	$3,5 \&I$	[5. My subgoal of deducing a standard contradiction, combined with the Ampersand In strategy, leads to the deduction of line 6. Now the gap in the middle of the proof has been eliminated, since I can reach 'A' by Tilde Out.]
	A		[2. Normally, the Arrow In provisional assumption makes some deduction immediately possible, but that is not true in this proof. I notice that the subgoal 'I' matches the consequent of line 2, which leads me to apply the Arrow Out strategy to line 2 and set down 'A' as another subgoal.]
	I		
	$P \rightarrow I$		

Having successfully closed the gap between premise lines and goal lines, all that I have to do now is add the remaining line numbers and justification entries and fill in the assumption-dependence column:

1	(1)	~A → ~P	A
2	(2)	A → I	A
3	(3)	P	PA
4	(4)	~A	PA
1,4	(5)	~P	1,4 →O
1,3,4	(6)	P & ~P	3,5 &I
1,3	(7)	A	4-6 ~O
1,2,3	(8)	I	2,7 →O
1,2	(9)	P → I	3-8 →I

8.3
Definitions

Since chapter two we have been operating with the concept of "formula," but I have nowhere provided a definition of it. I shall now turn to this task. To make the definition brief, I will first define the terms 'capital', 'connective', 'grouper', and 'symbol'. In stating these definitions, I abbreviate 'equals by definition' as ' = $_{df}$'.

capital	= $_{df}$	an upper-case letter of the English alphabet
connective	= $_{df}$	an arrow, ampersand, double arrow, wedge, or tilde
grouper	= $_{df}$	a parenthesis, bracket, or brace
symbol	= $_{df}$	a capital, connective, or grouper

Now we are able to define 'formula'.

formula	= $_{df}$	a symbol or a horizontal string of symbols

According to this definition, F1 through F3 are formulas.

(F1) I → (J → K)
(F2) I → J → K
(F3) I → → JK)(

In our past usage of the term 'formula' we would be inclined to say that F1 is a "proper" formula, F2 an incorrectly punctuated formula, and F3 no formula at all but, rather, a jumble of symbols. It will prove convenient to use the term 'formula' with the broader meaning assigned above and to introduce a second term, 'well-formed formula', to distinguish F1 from

F2 and F3. The expression 'well-formed formula' (abbreviated 'wff'[5]) will correspond closely to the term 'formula' as we used it in earlier chapters. To facilitate defining 'wff', I will define the expressions 'left-hand grouper', 'matching right-hand grouper', and 'dyadic connective'.

left-hand grouper $=_{df}$ either the mark '(' or '[' or '{'

matching right-hand grouper $=_{df}$ the mirror image of a left-hand grouper

dyadic connective $=_{df}$ connective other than the tilde

The term 'wff' is defined by the following set of statements:

1. Any capital is a wff.
2. A tilde followed by a wff is a wff.
3. A left-hand grouper followed by a wff followed by a dyadic connective followed by another wff followed by a matching right-hand grouper is a wff.
4. No formula is a wff unless its being so follows from clauses one through three.

This definition belongs to a special type called *recursive definitions*, found mainly in logic and mathematics. The principal feature of a recursive definition is that one must often apply the various clauses in the definition again and again in order to discover whether some object falls within the scope of the term defined. Let's illustrate this, using the definition of 'wff' just given. Is F4 a wff by that definition?

(F4)   ~(L → ~M)
(F5)   L
(F6)   M
(F7)   ~M
(F8)   (L → ~M)

By clause one of the definition, F5 and F6 are wffs. Since F6 is a wff, by clause two F7 is also a wff. Since F5 and F7 are wffs, by clause three F8 is a wff. And since F8 is a wff, by clause two F4 is one too. Is F9 a wff by our recursive definition?

(F9)   (N~ → O)
(F10)   N~

F10 is not a wff by any of the first three clauses of the definition; hence, by virtue of clause four it is not a wff. Neither of the first two clauses applies to F9; therefore, it is a wff (by the third clause) iff F10 is a wff. But

[5] 'Wff' rhymes with 'hoof'.

we already established that F10 is not a wff; it follows that F9 is not a wff. In a similar manner you can decide whether any formula—no matter how long—is a wff or not.

You may have noticed that according to the definition proposed, F11 is a wff, whereas F12 is not.

(F11)   (P → Q)

(F12)   P → Q

This does not agree with our practice in earlier chapters, according to which we would say that F12 is a proper formula but that F11 contains a superfluous pair of parentheses. The justification for making this change is that by doing so we greatly simplified the definition of 'wff'. If you doubt that this is so, try to formulate an alternative definition. As a test of correctness for your definition, be sure that it includes F1 and excludes F2 (see above). It must be admitted that the parentheses in F11 do no work (preclude no ambiguity), so in practice we will omit any pair of groupers that begin and end a wff.

There is one other unusual result stemming from our definition. In addition to F13, F14 and F15 count as wffs.

(F13)   ~[(R & S) → T]

(F14)   ~((R & S) → T)

(F15)   ~[[R & S] → T]

There is no harm in this; none of the formulas are ambiguous. The justification for this change is the same as the one given in the previous paragraph; it simplified the definition of 'wff'. Experimenting with the definition will convince you that this is so. Again, in practice we will conform to our old ways, which in this case means preferring F13 over the other two formulas.

With the exception of the two matters just discussed, the definition of 'wff' agrees completely with the punctuation principles adopted in chapters two through seven. For example, it excludes F16 and F17.

(F16)   (U & V → W)

(F17)   (X & Y & Z)

F16 is viciously, and F17 benignly, ambiguous. You should study the definition until you see how they are excluded.

An examination of the definitions of 'formula' and 'wff' will reveal that wffs are a species of formula. Specifically, wffs are formulas that are structured in accordance with the formation rules of our logic. The formation rules are contained in the definition of 'wff'. The notion of a "wff" in logic is analogous to the concept of a "grammatical sentence" in a natural language.

With 'wff' defined, we are now able to define 'symbolized argument'.

> symbolized argument = _{df} a wff, or a string of wffs separated by commas, followed by a turnstile followed by a wff

The following obvious definitions will prove useful in a moment:

> premise of symbolized argument S = _{df} a wff of S that precedes the turnstile
>
> conclusion of symbolized argument S = _{df} the wff of S that follows the turnstile

In section 2.3 I provided a rough account of the concept of "formal proof." Now we can give a precise definition.

> formal proof of symbolized argument S = _{df} a list of wffs such that:
>
> (i) each wff either is an assumption or is deduced from wffs (or derivations of wffs) above it in the list by one of the stated rules of inference,
>
> (ii) the last wff is the conclusion of S,
>
> (iii) every assumption on which the last wff depends is a premise of S

EXERCISES

87. On the basis of the definition of 'wff' provided in section 8.3, determine for each of the following formulas whether it is a wff. (This is the only exercise in the book in which the outermost groupers are included.)

(a) $(\sim A \rightarrow B)$

(b) $\sim (C \rightarrow \sim \sim \sim D)$

(c) $(E \sim F)$

*(d) $(G \rightarrow H \& I)$

(e) $\{ J \lor \sim [(K \lor \sim L) \leftrightarrow M] \}$

(f) $N O$

(g) $\leftrightarrow P$

88. Complete the following proofs. Every assumption has been identified.

(a)

1	(1)	D v (E & F)	A
2	(2)	D	PA
2	(3)		2 vI
2	(4)		2 vI
2	(5)		3,4 &I
	(6)		2-5 →I
7	(7)	E & F	PA
7	(8)		7 &O
7	(9)		8 vI
7	(10)		7 &O
7	(11)		10 vI
7	(12)		9,11 &I
	(13)		7-12 →I
1	(14)	(D v E) & (D v F)	1,6,13 vO

*(b)

	(1)	T v P	A
	(2)	~P	A
	(3)	T	PA
	(4)	T & ~P	
	(5)	T	
	(6)	T → T	
	(7)	P	PA
	(8)	~T	PA
	(9)	P & ~P	
	(10)	(P & ~P) & ~T	
	(11)	P & ~P	
	(12)	T	
	(13)	P → T	
1,2	(14)	T	

Instructions for exercises 89 through 98: Symbolize the arguments and construct proofs.

89. A newspaper article begins:

Only the rains of a very wet hurricane ... can save South Florida from a spring drought of near catastrophic proportions, say the nation's weather scientists.
And the chance of such a natural blessing is extremely remote because the storm season in the tropics is in its dying days. [6]

[6]"Catastrophic Drought Foreseen," *Miami News* (October 16, 1971), p. 14-A.

The argument contained in these paragraphs may be formulated:

➥ South Florida will avoid a spring DROUGHT only if a wet HURRICANE passes through the area. So, there will be a drought this spring in South Florida, since there will not be a wet hurricane in the area.

90. An ancient Chinese paradox:[7]

If the world is DISORDERED, it cannot be REFORMED unless a SAGE appears. But no sage can appear if the world is disordered. It follows that the world cannot be reformed if it is disordered.

91. A passage from *The Long Winter* by Laura Ingalls Wilder:

Laura looked at the four pounds of beef. She thought of the few potatoes left and she saw the partly filled sack of wheat standing in the corner....
Laura could not help asking, "Pa, you couldn't shoot a rabbit?"
Pa ... did not answer Laura's question. She knew what the answer was. There was not a rabbit left in all that country. They must have gone south when the birds went. Pa never took his gun with him when he was hauling hay, and he would have taken it if he had ever seen so much as one rabbit's track.[8]

Laura inferred the answer to her question with this argument:

Pa did not take his GUN with him. Pa would have taken it if he had seen rabbit TRACKS. Had there been RAB-BITS in the area, he would have seen their tracks. Hence, there was not a rabbit left in all that country.

92. The political cartoon suggests this argument:

If AUSTRIA attacks Serbia, RUSSIA will attack Austria. Provided that Russia attacks Austria, GERMANY will attack Russia. And if Germany attacks Russia, both FRANCE and ENGLAND will attack Germany. There-fore, ''if Austria attacks Serbia, Russia will fall upon Austria, Germany upon Russia, and France and England upon Germany.''

[7]See Arthur Waley, *Three Ways of Thought in Ancient China* (Garden City, N.Y.: Doubleday, 1956), p. 10, n. 1.
[8](New York: Harper & Row, Pub., 1953), pp. 214–15.

"A Chain of Friendship"—"If Austria attacks Serbia, Russia will fall upon Austria, Germany upon Russia, and France and England upon Germany." (*The Brooklyn Eagle*, 1914. Professor Oron J. Hale provided the cartoon.)

93.   One version of the "pragmatic" justification of induction:[9]

> If INDUCTION does not work, then no METHOD of inference about the future will work; for these reasons: If there are UNIFORMITIES in nature, induction will work. And if there is a method of inference about the future which works, then there are uniformities in nature.

*94.   A newspaper sports story:

> *BALTIMORE, July 20—Earl Weaver, the Baltimore Oriole manager, thinks he has finally found a foolproof protest.*
>
> *Last week in Oakland, Weaver was arguing about a hit-batsman call and the umpires refused to allow his pitcher, Sam Stewart, to warm up during the argument. He protested the game, contending there was no such rule in the book. That protest is pending.*
>
> *Last night, when Manager Jim Fregosi of California was arguing in the same situation, the umpires allowed Dave LaRoche, the Angel pitcher, to continue warming up. Weaver again protested the game.*
>
> *"I want to see how he gets out of this one," said Weaver, referring to Lee*

---

[9]Wesley C. Salmon discusses this argument in *The Foundations of Scientific Inference* (Pittsburgh: University of Pittsburgh Press, 1967), pp. 52–54.

MacPhail, the American League president. "There is no chance of losing both protests. If they don't allow at least one of them, we'll have a rule-book-burning promotion night." [10]

Weaver's argument may be phrased as follows:

We will win the FIRST protest exactly if we do not win the SECOND. So, we will not lose both protests.

95. In a letter to the editor of the *Proceedings and Addresses of the American Philosophical Association*, Professor Philip Devine protests the association's passing resolutions on matters of public policy:

The argument takes the form of a dilemma. Either the issue in question is amenable to philosophical argument, and the passing of resolutions prejudices philosophical discussion. Or it is not, and philosophers as such have no competence to decide it. [11]

Devine's argument (applied to a specific issue of public policy):

Either the issue is AMENABLE to philosophical argument and passing a resolution PREJUDICES philosophical discussion, or it is not amenable and philosophers have no special COMPETENCE to decide it. It follows that either passing a resolution prejudices philosophical discussion of the issue or philosophers have no special competence to decide the issue.

96. In William Harvey's day it was generally accepted that blood is created in the heart and flows from that organ only in an outward direction. Harvey's main attack on that theory is summarized by this argument: [12]

In an hour, a human heart THROWS out more blood than the human's own weight. If this is so and if blood flows only OUTWARD from the heart, then the heart creates MORE blood in an hour than the weight of a human. But the heart cannot do this. If the blood does not flow only out of the heart, then it must CIRCULATE through the body and REENTER the heart. Thus, the view that blood flows only out of the heart is false, and the view that blood circulates through the body and reenters the heart is true.

[10] "Weaver Sets up an Umpire Trap," *New York Times* (July 21, 1979), p. 15.
[11] LIII (1980), 501.
[12] See Herbert Butterfield, *The Origins of Modern Science* (New York: Free Press, 1957), pp. 64–65.

*97. In the "Peanuts" strip, Shermy reasons:

> If there is a SANTA Claus, then it does not MATTER how I act. And if there isn't any Santa Claus, then it still doesn't matter how I act. So, it does not matter how I act.

©1961 United Feature Syndicate, Inc.

98. A paraphrase of St. Thomas Aquinas's third cosmological argument for the existence of God:[13]

> There is a NECESSARY being who has created some contingent beings. Proof: There have been contingent beings for either a FINITE or an INFINITE period of time. If the former, then provided that no contingent beings have created themselves, there must be a necessary being which has created some contingent beings. No contingent beings have created themselves. On the other hand, if there have been contingent beings for an infinite period of time, then all the POSSIBLE combinations of the existence and nonexistence of contingent beings have been realized. If all the possible combinations have been realized, then there was a TIME in the past when no contingent being existed. If there was such a time in the past and if no contingent beings have created themselves, then there are contingent BEINGS today only if there is a necessary being who has created some contingent beings. Of course, there are contingent beings today.

Use these symbols:

N = There is a necessary being who has created some contingent beings

F = There have been contingent beings for a finite period of time

[13]See the selection from *Summa Theologica* in John Hick, ed., *The Existence of God* (New York: Macmillan, 1964), p. 84.

I = There have been contingent beings for an infinite period of time

D = Some contingent beings have created themselves

P = All the possible combinations of the existence and nonexistence of contingent beings have been realized

T = There was a time in the past when no contingent being existed

B = There are contingent beings today

This exercise exemplifies the utility and power of the logical system we have presented. The argument is so complex that, for most of us, it falls outside the range of logical intuition. Although symbolizing and proving the argument involve some time, neither procedure is particularly difficult. And in symbolizing and constructing a proof, one gains an insight into the structure of the English argument.

226. (CHALLENGE) Symbolize this newspaper sports story (excluding the first paragraph). Select capitals to abbreviate simple statements, indicating which statement each capital abbreviates.

With two weeks remaining in the pro football regular season, here's how the American Football Conference playoff situation stands:

... Miami leads Baltimore by a half-game in the East and Kansas City leads Oakland by a half-game in the West. A Miami victory over the Colts Saturday and a Kansas City victory over Oakland Sunday would wrap up the conference titles for both teams and would allow the Colts to secure the fourth playoff spot with a victory over Boston closing day.

... The Dolphins could qualify by losing twice, providing the Chiefs or Raiders sustain one loss.

One Miami victory or tie would put the Dolphins in the playoffs as either the East champion or runner-up team.... In the event of a Miami-Baltimore tie and a Miami win over the Packers, the Colts would automatically qualify with a victory over New England with the second-place team in the West eliminated.

Miami can be eliminated if it should lose to the Colts and Packers and the Chiefs and Raiders tie and then win closing day. An Oakland-Kansas City tie is not far-fetched. A tie would benefit the Chiefs, making it only necessary they defeat Buffalo on closing day to win their division. A tie would give Oakland a chance at the playoffs should the Raiders beat Denver on the 19th and Miami lose twice.

Baltimore can be eliminated with losses to Miami and New England, providing neither the Chiefs nor Raiders sustain two defeats. One Colt victory and one defeat would require that neither the Chiefs nor the Raiders sustain a defeat if the Colts are to be eliminated. [14]

[14]"Dolphins in Strong Playoff Spot," *Miami News* (December 7, 1971), p. 1-B.

Instructions for exercises 227 through 229: Symbolize the arguments and construct proofs.

227. (CHALLENGE) Jules Verne writes in *Around the World in Eighty Days*:

    The situation, in any event, was a terrible one, and might be thus stated: if Phileas Fogg was honest he was ruined; and if he was a knave, he was caught.[15]

    Show that the statement following the colon entails:

    Phileas Fogg was either RUINED or CAUGHT.

    Let *H* abbreviate 'Phileas Fogg was honest'.

228. (CHALLENGE) A variation on exercise 94:

    We will win the FIRST protest exactly if we do not win the SECOND. So, we will win at least one of them.

229. (CHALLENGE) (a) In a story about an NCAA regional baseball tournament, a sports reporter writes:

    By then, either Florida State or Florida must have at least one defeat in this double-elimination affair, since the Seminoles and Gators meet in Round 1.[16]

    The reporter may be viewed as drawing this simple inference:

    It is not the case that both Florida STATE and UNIVERSITY of Florida will win in the first round of the tournament [since they play each other]. Thus, either Florida State or University of Florida will lose in the first round.

    As tied games are not permitted in tournaments, '*X* loses' is equivalent to '*X* does not win'.

    (b) Show that the conclusion entails the premise (thereby demonstrating logical equivalence).

230. (CHALLENGE) Symbolize and construct proofs for the arguments in these exercises following chapter nine:

    (a)   Exercise 104
    (b)   Exercise 110

---

[15] *The Jules Verne Omnibus* (Philadelphia: Lippincott, n.d.), p. 472.

[16] Mike Smith, "Luck of the Draw Makes Miami the Heavy Favorite," *Miami News* (May 21, 1981), p. 4-C.

(c) Exercise 106
(d) Exercise 112
(e) Exercise 111

231. (SUPERCHALLENGE) Construct a proof for this argument:

~ (D ↔ E) ⊢ ~D ↔ E

This is the second hardest proof problem in the book. My proof has 28 lines. Compare 231 with 217 (chapter six).

9

Derived Rules

9.1
Eight Additional Rules

A newspaper story describes the difficulties of a married couple:

> *About a year ago, their troubles began. Mrs. Mathias was having medical problems and went to a doctor who told her "she either had a tumor or was pregnant," Mathias said.*
>
> *"We were scared because she couldn't be pregnant and we thought it had to be a tumor," he said.* [1]

The couple believed that the wife could not be pregnant since she had undergone a sterilization operation. They employed this simple argument to reach a terrifying conclusion:

> Mrs. Mathias either has a TUMOR or she is PREGNANT.
> But she can't be pregnant. Thus, she has a tumor.

[1]Bill Gjebre, "Unplanned Birth Nearly Cost Marriage," *Miami News* (February 2, 1976), p. 1-A.

In symbols:

T v P, ~P ⊢ T

The inference pattern exhibited here is known as *disjunctive argument*. Any argument embodying this pattern has two premises. The first is a disjunction, and the second is the negation of one of the disjuncts of the first premise; the conclusion is the other disjunct. This argument pattern is obviously valid, yet the conclusion of the argument was false—Mrs. Mathias did not have a tumor. Whenever a valid argument has a false conclusion, at least one premise is also false. In the present case the second premise was false; the sterilization had failed and the woman was pregnant.

Compare this argument with a superficially similar but invalid inference:

> Mrs. Mathias either has a tumor or she is pregnant. She is pregnant. Thus, she does not have a tumor.

T v P, P ⊢ ~T

This argument is invalid because it is possible for both its premises to be true although its conclusion is false—she could have a tumor *and* be pregnant. Look again at the first argument and note that it could *not* have two true premises and a false conclusion. We term the pattern exhibited by the second argument the *fallacy of affirming a disjunct*. Compare these patterns:

> disjunctive argument: $\mathcal{P} \vee \mathcal{Q}, \sim \mathcal{Q} \vdash \mathcal{P}$ (*valid*)
> affirming a disjunct: $\mathcal{P} \vee \mathcal{Q}, \mathcal{Q} \vdash \sim \mathcal{P}$ (*invalid*)

In spite of the simplicity of the valid "tumor" argument, it is quite difficult to prove using only primitive proof rules. The following proof is the simplest proof we can construct. (You have already encountered this proof as exercise 88(b) in the last chapter.)

1	(1)	T v P	A
2	(2)	~P	A
3	(3)	T	PA
2,3	(4)	T & ~P	3,2 &I
2,3	(5)	T	4 &O
2	(6)	T → T	3-5 →I
7	(7)	P	PA
8	(8)	~T	PA
2,7	(9)	P & ~P	7,2 &I
2,7,8	(10)	(P & ~P) & ~T	9,8 &I

2,7,8	(11)	P & ~P	10 &O
2,7	(12)	T	8-11 ~O
2	(13)	P → T	7-12 →I
1,2	(14)	T	1,6,13 vO

What is the point of the maneuver performed on lines 4 and 5?[2] Why are lines 10 and 11 required?[3]

It is of interest to show that a proof employing just primitive rules can be constructed for the "tumor" argument. But you would not want to travel that tortuous path whenever you encountered an argument that exhibits this pattern. For this reason I propose that we add to our stock of rules one which will sanction a direct move from lines 1 and 2 to line 14, in the above proof.

> *The Disjunctive Argument Rule:* From a disjunction and the negation of one of the disjuncts derive the other disjunct.

The rule restated:

From $\mathcal{A}$ v $\mathcal{B}$ and ~$\mathcal{A}$ derive $\mathcal{B}$. From $\mathcal{A}$ v $\mathcal{B}$ and ~$\mathcal{B}$ derive $\mathcal{A}$.

With the help of this rule (which we abbreviate 'DA'), the proof of the "tumor" argument becomes suitably simple:

(1)	T v P	A
(2)	~P	A
(3)	T	1,2 DA

We may speak of Disjunctive Argument as a *derived* inference rule, in contrast with the *primitive* inference rules summarized in chapter eight. It is a derived rule in the sense that it sanctions deductions that could be made without its help by employing only primitive rules. In any proof that involves a Disjunctive Argument step, that step could be omitted at the cost of increasing the length of the proof by 11 lines. The first proof of the "tumor" argument provides us with a "recipe" for constructing the lengthened proof. It follows that if the eleven primitive proof rules are "safe," then the Rule of Disjunctive Argument must also be "safe."

Having added one derived rule to our stockpile, we must decide whether to add others. In principle, we could add an infinite number of derived rules because there is an infinite number of distinct argument patterns whose validity can be established with the primitive rules. In practice, however, it is desirable to keep the set of rules compact. With this in mind, I propose the following table of derived rules. Another logician would probably submit a different (though equally defensible) set.

---

[2]to satisfy the second restriction on the Arrow In Rule (applied on line 6)
[3]because of the second restriction on the Tilde Out Rule (applied on line 12)

You will need to commit to memory these derived rules of inference. This is probably best done gradually (with little conscious effort), while practicing proof construction.

The Eight Derived Inference Rules

Modus Tollens (MT)	From $\mathcal{A} \rightarrow \mathcal{B}$ and $\sim\mathcal{B}$ derive $\sim\mathcal{A}$.	**I**
Disjunctive Argument (DA)	From $\mathcal{A} \vee \mathcal{B}$ and $\sim\mathcal{A}$ derive $\mathcal{B}$. From $\mathcal{A} \vee \mathcal{B}$ and $\sim\mathcal{B}$ derive $\mathcal{A}$.	
Conjunctive Argument (CA)	From $\sim(\mathcal{A} \& \mathcal{B})$ and $\mathcal{A}$ derive $\sim\mathcal{B}$. From $\sim(\mathcal{A} \& \mathcal{B})$ and $\mathcal{B}$ derive $\sim\mathcal{A}$.	
Chain Argument (CH)	From $\mathcal{A} \rightarrow \mathcal{B}$ and $\mathcal{B} \rightarrow \mathcal{C}$ derive $\mathcal{A} \rightarrow \mathcal{C}$.	
Double Negation (DN)	From $\mathcal{A}$ derive $\sim\sim\mathcal{A}$ and vice versa.	**II**
DeMorgan's Law (DM)	From $\mathcal{A} \& \mathcal{B}$ derive $\sim(\sim\mathcal{A} \vee \sim\mathcal{B})$ and vice versa. From $\sim(\mathcal{A} \& \mathcal{B})$ derive $\sim\mathcal{A} \vee \sim\mathcal{B}$ and vice versa. From $\sim\mathcal{A} \& \sim\mathcal{B}$ derive $\sim(\mathcal{A} \vee \mathcal{B})$ and vice versa. From $\sim(\sim\mathcal{A} \& \sim\mathcal{B})$ derive $\mathcal{A} \vee \mathcal{B}$ and vice versa.	
Arrow (AR)	From $\mathcal{A} \rightarrow \mathcal{B}$ derive $\sim\mathcal{A} \vee \mathcal{B}$ and vice versa. From $\sim\mathcal{A} \rightarrow \mathcal{B}$ derive $\mathcal{A} \vee \mathcal{B}$ and vice versa. From $\mathcal{A} \rightarrow \mathcal{B}$ derive $\sim(\mathcal{A} \& \sim\mathcal{B})$ and vice versa. From $\sim(\mathcal{A} \rightarrow \mathcal{B})$ derive $\mathcal{A} \& \sim\mathcal{B}$ and vice versa.	
Contraposition (CN)	From $\mathcal{A} \rightarrow \mathcal{B}$ derive $\sim\mathcal{B} \rightarrow \sim\mathcal{A}$ and vice versa. From $\mathcal{A} \rightarrow \sim\mathcal{B}$ derive $\mathcal{B} \rightarrow \sim\mathcal{A}$. From $\sim\mathcal{A} \rightarrow \mathcal{B}$ derive $\sim\mathcal{B} \rightarrow \mathcal{A}$.	

We will apply these eight rules to whole lines only.[4] The standard assumption-dependence principle applies to each rule. The rules in group I involve two premises,[5] and those in group II, one premise. Whereas the rules in the first group are "one-way" rules, the rules in the second operate in both directions.[6] Thus, for example, the Rule of Double Negation not

[4]It is a logical mistake to apply the four rules in group I to parts of lines. The rules in group II can be safely used with parts of lines, but for the sake of uniformity I have decided to use these four inference rules (like the other fourteen) on whole lines only. The opposite decision is defensible, and your instructor may direct you to apply the rules in group II to parts of lines as well as to whole lines.

[5]Although "chain" arguments (described in section 4.2) may have more than two premises, the *Rule of Chain Argument*, as I have formulated it, applies only to *pairs* of premises.

[6]Why have I omitted the expression 'and vice versa' from the last two versions of Contraposition?

only sanctions prefixing a wff with two tildes, it also allows dropping two tildes at the beginning of a wff.

These eight derived rules comprise twenty-eight subrules. Each of the twenty-eight can be shown sound by constructing a proof that incorporates only the primitive rules. Six of these proofs have been presented above. The student who has worked all the exercises so far (including the challenges) has constructed nine more of these proofs.

I will illustrate the use of these derived rules by constructing several proofs. In section 7.3 I discussed an argument contained in Plato's "Apology"; here is another passage from that source:

> *If it is a fact that I [Socrates] am in process of corrupting some of the young, and have succeeded already in corrupting others, and if it were a fact that some of the latter, being now grown up, had discovered that I had ever given them bad advice when they were young, surely they ought now to be coming forward to denounce and punish me. And if they did not like to do it themselves, you would expect some of their families — their fathers and brothers and other near relations — to remember it now, if their own flesh and blood have suffered any harm from me.* [7]

Socrates' defense:

> If I have CORRUPTED the young, then either they or their RELATIVES will accuse me. But my young FOLLOWERS do not accuse me, and neither do their relatives. It follows that I have not corrupted the young.

The argument is symbolized:

$$C \rightarrow (Y \vee R), \sim Y \& \sim R \vdash \sim C$$

A proof of validity for this argument that employs just primitive rules of inference is 19 lines in length. The use of derived rules shortens the proof by 15 lines:

(1)	$C \rightarrow (Y \vee R)$	A
(2)	$\sim Y \& \sim R$	A
(3)	$\sim (Y \vee R)$	2 DM
(4)	$\sim C$	1,3 MT

A second advantage of this proof over the primitive-rules proof is that the assumption-dependence column is eliminated. The DeMorgan's Law Rule comprises eight subrules; the subrule used in deducing line 3 is the "left-to-right" half of the third line of the rule.

---

[7] 33c–33d. Hugh Tredennick, trans., "Apology," in *The Collected Dialogues of Plato*, ed. by Edith Hamilton and Huntington Cairns (Princeton, N.J.: Princeton University Press, 1961), p. 19.

Officials of the Memphis Housing Authority told Mable Moore, an elderly widow, to get rid of her pet dog or get out of her public housing apartment.[8] She insisted that if the poodle were evicted she would go with him. Mable's dilemma expressed in argument form:

> Either the POODLE leaves or MABLE leaves. If the poodle leaves, Mable leaves. So, Mable leaves.

$P \lor M, P \to M \vdash M$

The proof uses the Tilde Out strategy:

1	(1)	$P \lor M$	A
2	(2)	$P \to M$	A
3	(3)	$\sim M$	PA
1,3	(4)	P	1,3 DA
1,2,3	(5)	M	2,4 $\to$O
1,2,3	(6)	$M \,\&\, \sim M$	5,3 &I
1,2	(7)	M	3-6 $\sim$O

When derived rules are used the number of proof options tends to increase. For instance, the middle section of this proof could have gone differently:

2,3	(4)	$\sim P$	2,3 MT
1,2,3	(5)	M	1,4 DA

Several proofs that further illustrate the application of these eight derived rules will be constructed in the next two sections of this chapter.

9.2
Proof Strategy

Proof construction is a skilled activity, and as with most skills, proficiency is developed through practice. I can make some general observations that may help you build proofs that involve the derived rules. I shall start by providing a strategic hint for each derived rule. Study the following table until you understand the hints, but don't attempt to memorize them.

In most cases a proof line is "used" only once; that is, only one deduction is made from the line. (Conjunctions and biconditionals are often exceptions.) So, it may be helpful to "check off" the used lines in a partially completed proof. (You may prefer to mark the used lines in

---

[8]"If Poodle Goes, I Go, Widow Says," *Miami News* (May 13, 1975), p. 2-A.

Strategic Suggestions for the Eight Derived Inference Rules

MT	If a premise line is a conditional and the negation of its antecedent is a goal line, search the other premise lines for the negation of the consequent. If you find it, apply Modus Tollens. If you do not find the negation of the consequent among the premise lines, add it as a goal line.
DA	If a premise line is a disjunction and one of its disjuncts is a goal line, search the other premise lines for the negation of the other disjunct. If you find it, apply Disjunctive Argument. If you do not find the negation of the other disjunct among the premise lines, add it as a goal line.
CA	If a premise line is the negation of a conjunction and the negation of one of the conjuncts is a goal line, search the other premise lines for the other conjunct. If you find it, apply Conjunctive Argument. If you do not find the other conjunct among the premise lines, add it as a goal line.
CH	If the consequent of one conditional premise line matches the antecedent of another, apply Chain Argument.
DN	If a premise or goal line is a double negation, consider using Double Negation.
DM	If a premise or goal line is a negated conjunction or a negated disjunction, consider using DeMorgan's Law.
AR	If a conditional premise line and a disjunctive goal line (or vice versa) have identical components except for an initial tilde, apply Arrow to the premise line. If a premise or goal line is a negated conditional, consider using Arrow.
CN	If a conditional premise or goal line has (one or two) negated constituents, consider using Contraposition.

some other way such as circling the line number.) This procedure allows you to ignore lines that are unlikely to be used in future deductions and to concentrate attention on the remaining "unchecked" lines. In most proofs each line but the last will be involved as a premise line in some deduction,[9] so it makes good sense to attend to previously unused premise lines.

I will illustrate the "checking" procedure as well as some of the suggestions in the table above by constructing a proof for an argument by the philosopher Ludwig Wittgenstein.[10] Wittgenstein attacked the view that the meaning of a proper name is the individual who bears the name; let's call this view the "Bearer Theory." His refutation of the Bearer Theory:

---

[9]The exceptions will be (1) proofs for arguments having superfluous premises (these are rare), and (2) inelegant proofs that contain pointless deductions.

[10]See *Philosophical Investigations*, 3rd ed. (New York: Macmillan, 1958), p. 20.

If the BEARER Theory is correct and John Jones is DEAD, then the NAME 'John Jones' has no meaning. But if that name has no meaning, then the SENTENCE 'John Jones is dead' also has no meaning. Obviously, the sentence 'John Jones is dead' is meaningful although John Jones is dead. Therefore, the Bearer Theory is mistaken.

$$(B \& D) \rightarrow \sim N, \sim N \rightarrow \sim S, S \& D \vdash \sim B$$

I shall interject comments as I build the proof for this argument. I use the strategy suggestion for Chain Argument to deduce line 4 and then I place check marks before lines 1 and 2.

✓(1)	$(B \& D) \rightarrow \sim N$	A
✓(2)	$\sim N \rightarrow \sim S$	A
(3)	$S \& D$	A
(4)	$(B \& D) \rightarrow \sim S$	1,2 CH

Concentrating on the unchecked lines (3 and 4), I decide to apply Ampersand Out (twice) to line 3 — then I check line 3.

✓(3)	$S \& D$	A
(4)	$(B \& D) \rightarrow \sim S$	1,2 CH
(5)	S	3 &O
(6)	D	3 &O

Using the strategic hint for Contraposition, I deduce line 7 from line 4 — and check 4. I use the second line of the rule.

✓(4)	$(B \& D) \rightarrow \sim S$	1,2 CH
(5)	S	3 &O
(6)	D	3 &O
(7)	$S \rightarrow \sim(B \& D)$	4 CN

Looking only at the unchecked lines (5 through 7), I spot an opportunity to use Arrow Out. When I make the deduction, I check lines 5 and 7.

✓(5)	S	3 &O
(6)	D	3 &O
✓(7)	$S \rightarrow \sim(B \& D)$	4 CN
(8)	$\sim(B \& D)$	7,5 →O

Studying the two remaining unchecked lines (6 and 8), I realize that I can deduce the argument's conclusion from them by Conjunctive Argument (second version).

(9) ~ B   8,6 CA

It is definitely not a good idea to claim in mail advertisements that the magazines you sell are pornographic, as this news story makes clear:

George Smith, 61, of Baldwin, Long Island, has been arrested by the Nassau County district attorney for selling porno magazines that aren't porno and, for that matter, aren't magazines. Smith's mail-order "sex magazines" cost $21.50 for a set and were about the size of postcards and showed no more cleavage than Mary Poppins. "If it had turned out to be hard-core pornography, he would have been in violation of obscenity laws," said D.A. Denis Dillon. "As it is, he's in violation of fraud statutes." [11]

The district attorney knew he could "nail" Smith even before he examined the magazines, as this argument makes clear:

> If the "magazines" are PORNOGRAPHIC, Smith is violating OBSCENITY laws. And if they aren't porno, Smith is violating FRAUD statutes. Hence, he is violating either obscenity or fraud laws.
>
> $P \rightarrow O$, $\sim P \rightarrow F \vdash O \vee F$

This is a simple argument whose validity is obvious. The proofs for it, however, are not simple — not even when derived rules are made available. As a general rule, proofs for arguments with disjunctive conclusions tend to be tough. For this reason it will be useful to have a plan for devising such proofs. I will suggest two strategies.

One of these may be called the *Tilde Out–DeMorgan's Law strategy*. It consists in making a provisional assumption of the negation of the conclusion (anticipating a later Tilde Out move) and transforming this assumption into a conjunction by DeMorgan's Law. The conjunction, of course, yields its ingredients through applications of Ampersand Out. The following proof for the "porno" argument illustrates this strategy:

1	(1)	$P \rightarrow O$	A
2	(2)	$\sim P \rightarrow F$	A
3	(3)	$\sim(O \vee F)$	PA
3	(4)	$\sim O \,\&\, \sim F$	3 DM
3	(5)	$\sim O$	4 &O
1,3	(6)	$\sim P$	1,5 MT
1,2,3	(7)	F	2,6 →O
3	(8)	$\sim F$	4 &O
1,2,3	(9)	$F \,\&\, \sim F$	7,8 &I
1,2	(10)	$O \vee F$	3-9 ~O

[11]"Hustler," *Miami News* (October 13, 1980), p. 1-A.

plan for proving arguments with disjunctive conclusions may b.   the *Arrow strategy*. The idea here is to set as a subgoal a conditio,   s.atement that can be converted by the Arrow Rule into the disjunctive conclusion. Notice that the antecedent of the conditional will contain one more or one less tilde than the left disjunct of the disjunction. The rationale of the Arrow strategy is that it is usually easier to derive a conditional than a disjunction. Conditionals can be derived by applying Arrow In or Chain Argument (among other rules). The following two proofs of the "porno" argument employ the Arrow strategy:

1	(1)	P → O	A	(1)	P → O	A
2	(2)	~P → F	A	(2)	~P → F	A
3	(3)	~O	PA	(3)	~O → ~P	1 CN
1,3	(4)	~P	1,3 MT			
1,2,3	(5)	F	2,4 →O			
1,2	(6)	~O → F	3-5 →I	(4)	~O → F	3,2 CH
1,2	(7)	O v F	6 AR	(5)	O v F	4 AR

The Tilde Out–DeMorgan's Law strategy is probably easier for beginners to employ; however, I prefer the Arrow strategy because it usually leads to shorter proofs. Also, the former strategy always requires a provisional assumption (and therefore an assumption-dependence column), but with the Arrow strategy you can often avoid provisional assumptions.

9.3
Substitution Instance

In the cartoon on page 142 one of the youngsters reasons:

> The child-labor laws have no TEETH. Proof: If they had teeth I wouldn't have to clean my ROOM. However, I do have to clean it.
>
> T → ~R, R ⊢ ~T

A putative proof for this argument:

(1)	T → ~R	A
(2)	R	A
(3)	~T	1,2 MT (ERROR!)

The inference from lines 1 and 2 to line 3 may appear to be sanctioned by the Rule of Modus Tollens, but in fact it is not. The second premise of a deduction sanctioned by that rule consists of a tilde followed by the consequent of the first (conditional) premise. Clearly, line 2 of the above "proof" does not fit this description because it contains no tilde at all.

"THE CHILD-LABOR LAWS HAVE NO TEETH IN THEM.
I STILL HAVE TO CLEAN MY ROOM."

© 1979 McCall's Magazine, reprinted by permission of Orlando Busino.

"But," someone is sure to say, "anyone can *see* that the step on line 3 amounts to the same thing as Modus Tollens; so why not accept the proof?" A person who makes this remark has forgotten that we have developed a procedure of *formal* proof. The procedure is formal in two respects: (1) every step made is explicitly sanctioned by a rule that refers only to the *forms* of statements, and (2) references to logical intuition ("I *see* that they amount to the same thing") are not permitted as justifications. Why this rejection of logical intuition? Because though usually reliable, it is not always reliable; and because the method of proofs should be an *objective* instrument. That is, a completed proof should convince not only the deviser of the proof, but any knowledgeable inspector of the proof. Inasmuch as I may not share your logical intuitions, a proof of yours that relies on your intuitions may not convince me.

To make it clearer that the step on line 3 of the above putative proof is not sanctioned by the Modus Tollens Rule, we introduce the notions of "argument-form" and "substitution instance." An *argument-form* is a string of symbols that differs from a symbolized argument in only one respect: the capitals occurring in it are script letters. Actually, we have been using argument-forms to represent patterns of inference since chapter one. There is an argument-form corresponding to each derived inference rule. For example, this argument-form corresponds to the Rule of Modus Tollens:

$$\mathcal{Q} \rightarrow \mathcal{B}, \sim\mathcal{B} \vdash \sim\mathcal{Q}$$

Every argument-form represents many arguments, which are called *substitution instances* of the argument-form. A definition of 'substitution instance':

> A symbolized argument is a substitution instance of an argument-form iff the argument can be generated from the argument-form by replacing each (script) capital in the argument-form by a wff.

We require *uniform substitution*; that is, if a (script) capital appears more than once in the argument-form, all occurrences of that capital must be replaced by the same wff. Some sample substitution instances:

Substitution Instances of $\mathcal{Q} \rightarrow \mathcal{B}, \sim\mathcal{B} \vdash \sim\mathcal{Q}$

(1) A → B, ~B ⊢ ~A
(2) (C & D) → (E ∨ F), ~(E ∨ F) ⊢ ~(C & D)
(3) G → ~H, ~ ~H ⊢ ~G
(4) ~I → ~J, ~ ~J ⊢ ~ ~I
(5) K → K, ~K ⊢ ~K

In argument 3, the wff '~H' is substituted (twice) for the script capital $\mathcal{B}$. In argument 4, what wff has been substituted for the script capital $\mathcal{Q}$? Has this substitution been carried out uniformly? Argument 5 may appear to violate the uniform-substitution requirement; however, if you examine that requirement carefully, you will see that the fifth argument conforms. Additional examples:

Not Substitution Instances of $\mathcal{Q} \rightarrow \mathcal{B}, \sim\mathcal{B} \vdash \sim\mathcal{Q}$

(6) L → M, ~L ⊢ ~M
(7) N → O, ~P ⊢ ~N
(8) G → ~H, H ⊢ ~G
(9) ~I → ~J, J ⊢ I

Arguments 6 and 7 are not substitution instances of the argument-form in question because they do not satisfy the requirement of uniform substitution. Arguments 8 and 9 would not be substitution instances of that argument-form even if we waived the uniform-substitution condition. If this is not clear, review the definition of 'substitution instance'.[12]

Now we are in a position to state precisely the conditions that must be satisfied if the Rule of Modus Tollens is applicable. The rule may be

---

[12]Because the second premise of argument 8 (9) has no tilde, it cannot be generated from the second premise of the argument-form. A similar remark applies to the conclusion of argument 9.

applied to two wffs in a proof iff they are the premises of a substitution instance of the argument-form corresponding to the rule. The wff that may be derived, of course, is the conclusion of that substitution instance. Let us return to the putative proof of the "child labor" argument:

$$
\begin{array}{lll}
(1) & T \rightarrow \sim R & A \\
(2) & R & A \\
(3) & \sim T & 1,2 \text{ MT (ERROR!)}
\end{array}
$$

Lines 1 and 2 are not the premises of a substitution instance of the argument-form '$\mathcal{A} \rightarrow \mathcal{B}, \sim \mathcal{B} \vdash \sim \mathcal{A}$'. Questions about the legitimacy of the application of any derived rule of inference can be answered by employing the notion of "substitution instance." Such questions most commonly arise concerning (in addition to Modus Tollens) Disjunctive Argument, Conjunctive Argument, DeMorgan's Law, and Arrow. The concept of "substitution instance" helps us see, for example, that wff F2 can be derived from F1 by DeMorgan's Law (using the right-to-left half of the third line of the rule), while the move from F1 to F3 is not covered by our formulation of that rule.

$$
\begin{array}{ll}
(F1) & \sim (K \vee \sim L) \\
(F2) & \sim K \,\&\, \sim \sim L \\
(F3) & \sim K \,\&\, L
\end{array}
$$

How can we establish the validity of the "child labor" argument? Here are two correct proofs:

$$
\begin{array}{lllllll}
(1) & T \rightarrow \sim R & A & & & & \\
(2) & R & A & & & & \\
(3) & \sim \sim R & 2 \text{ DN} & & (3) & R \rightarrow \sim T & 1 \text{ CN} \\
(4) & \sim T & 1,3 \text{ MT} & & (4) & \sim T & 3,2 \rightarrow O
\end{array}
$$

Every substitution instance of a valid argument-form is itself valid. (This principle provides part of the justification of the method of formal proofs.) But some substitution instances of an invalid argument-form are invalid and others are valid! Consider these examples:

Substitution Instances of $\mathcal{A} \rightarrow \mathcal{B}, \mathcal{B} \vdash \mathcal{A}$

$$
\begin{array}{l}
Q \rightarrow R, R \vdash Q \, (invalid) \\
S \rightarrow (T \,\&\, S), T \,\&\, S \vdash S \, (valid)
\end{array}
$$

EXERCISES

99. Complete the justification column for each proof. Each line requiring justification is a derived line (not an assumption).

(a) (1) A v ~ B   A
     (2) B   A
     (3) ~ ~ B
     (4) A

(b) (1) C → D   A
     (2) ~ D   A
     (3) ~ C
     (4) ~ ~ ~ C

*(c) (1) E → ~ F   A
     (2) G → F   A
     (3) F → ~ E
     (4) G → ~ E
     (5) ~ (G & ~ ~ E)

(d) (1) ~ [(H & ~ I) & J]   A
     (2) J   A
     (3) ~ (H & ~ I)
     (4) ~ H v ~ ~ I
     (5) H → ~ ~ I

100. Identify and explain the errors committed in the following putative
     proofs:

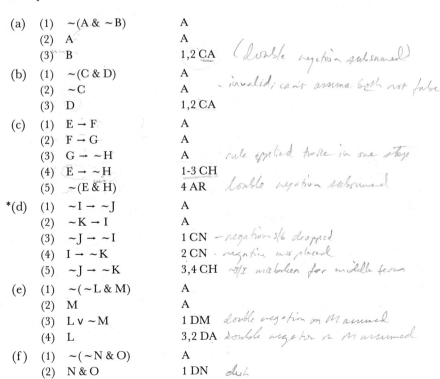

(a) (1) ~ (A & ~ B)   A
     (2) A   A
     (3) B   1,2 CA   (double negation subsumed)

(b) (1) ~ (C & D)   A   — invalid; can't assume both not false
     (2) ~ C   A
     (3) D   1,2 CA

(c) (1) E → F   A
     (2) F → G   A
     (3) G → ~ H   A   rule applied twice in one step
     (4) E → ~ H   1-3 CH
     (5) ~ (E & H)   4 AR   double negation subsumed

*(d) (1) ~ I → ~ J   A
     (2) ~ K → I   A
     (3) ~ J → ~ I   1 CN   — negation s/b dropped
     (4) I → ~ K   2 CN   — negation misplaced
     (5) ~ J → ~ K   3,4 CH   ~J/I mistaken for middle term

(e) (1) ~ (~ L & M)   A
     (2) M   A
     (3) L v ~ M   1 DM   double negation on M assumed
     (4) L   3,2 DA   double negation on M assumed

(f) (1) ~ (~ N & O)   A
     (2) N & O   1 DN   duh

(g)   (1)   P → Q   A
        (2)   P & R   A
        (3)   ~P & ~R   2 DN *duh*
        (4)   ~P   3 &O ✓
        (5)   ~Q   1,4 MT *reversed (denying antecedent)*

Instructions for exercises 101 through 112: Symbolize the arguments not previously symbolized; construct proofs for all arguments. In each proof employ at least one derived rule.

101.   Construct proofs for the arguments in these exercises from earlier chapters:

       (a)   Exercise 50 (chapter five)
     *(b)   Exercise 89 (chapter eight)
       (c)   Exercise 91 (chapter eight)
       (d)   Exercise 46 (chapter five)
       (e)   Exercise 53 (chapter five)

102.   In the fourth and fifth panels of the "Hi and Lois" strip the youth recites his parents' argument. We may express the argument's conclusion: 'If I don't get good MARKS, I won't have a good LIFE.' Use these abbreviations:

$$C \; = \; \text{I get into a good college}$$
$$J \; = \; \text{I get a good job}$$

The argument has three premises.

October 14, 1979, © King Features Syndicate, Inc.

103. A young paraplegic teacher who lost her job due to a budget cut despaired of finding another one. In an interview she said,

It is no secret that handicapped persons face prejudice in the job market or there would be no slogan like "Hire the Handicapped." [13]

This is an argument with an unstated premise and an unstated conclusion. Supply these missing elements. Use these abbreviations:

P = Handicapped persons face prejudice in the job market
S = There is a slogan "Hire the Handicapped"

*104. A news report includes these paragraphs:

Beach police theorized the trio of robbers who invaded the Tepper residence at 4830 Pine Tree Dr. about 9:15 a.m. yesterday arrived by boat. They got away with $5,000 in jewelry and currency.
  A crew of linemen in the street outside the home saw no cars arrive or leave during the robbery. But the rear of the house has a dock on Indian Creek. [14]

The police theory and the data supporting it are contained in this argument:

The robbers entered the house either from the FRONT or from the REAR. Had they entered from the front, the line crew would have SEEN their car. But the linemen did not see their car. If the robbers entered the house from the rear, they must have arrived by BOAT. This proves that the robbers came by boat.

105. When I asked Mike and Amy to pick up leaves in the yard, I received this reply from Amy (then aged four):

We are not going to pick them up, because I won't do it without Mike and he won't do it.

This is an explanation cast as an argument. Use these symbols:

A = Amy picks up leaves
M = Mike picks up leaves

[13] "Cutback Costs Paralyzed Mom Teaching Job," *Miami News* (June 6, 1975), p. 11-A.

[14] Milt Sosin, "Doctor Gets Call from Thief: 'You'd Better Go Home,'" *Miami News* (April 25, 1972), p. 5-A.

'Amy won't pick up without Mike' amounts to 'It is false that Amy does pick up while Mike does not'.

106. The philosopher G. E. Moore writes:

> *I do know that this pencil exists; but I could not know this, if Hume's principles were true; therefore, Hume's principles, one or both of them, are false.*[15]

Use these abbreviations:

K = I know that this pencil exists
A = Hume's first principle is true
B = Hume's second principle is true

107. Construct proofs for the arguments in these exercises from earlier chapters:

(a)   Exercise 93 (chapter eight)
(b)   Exercise 96 (chapter eight)
(c)   Exercise 52 (chapter five)
(d)   Exercise 79 (chapter seven)
*(e)   Exercise 48 (chapter five)

108. Newspapers employed deductive reasoning to predict the resignation of Israel's prime minister:

> *TEL AVIV—Prime Minister Menachem Begin ... will resign next week, setting up elections as soon as this summer, Israeli newspapers predicted today.*
>
> *Begin will quit unless a compromise is reached on salary demands by the nation's 58,000 teachers, and both Finance Minister Yigael Hurvitz and Education Minister Zevulun Hammer decide to stay in office, the papers said.*
>
> *Hurvitz, seeking to cap an inflationary spiral that left Israel with the world's highest inflation rate—131 percent—last year, has threatened to quit if the Begin government gives in to the teachers' demands for higher pay. Hammer says he will resign if the teachers don't get salary hikes.*[16]

The argument formalized:

If the teachers get RAISES, the FINANCE Minister will resign. And the EDUCATION Minister will resign *unless* they get raises. Since the PRIME Minister will resign if

---

[15]*Some Main Problems of Philosophy* (London: Allen & Unwin, 1953), pp. 119–20.

[16]"Begin Will Quit Next Week, Israeli Newspapers Predict," *Miami News* (January 8, 1981), p. 4-A.

either of these ministers resigns, it follows that he will
resign.

109. A newspaper sports story begins:

> *Last week Roy Wilfork insisted that Jackson High's track team would have to
> win all three relay events to win the Class AAAA state meet in Winter Park
> over the weekend.*
>
> *The Jackson coach was wrong. But he was not disappointed.*
>
> *The Generals won two of the relays Saturday night — the sprint medley and
> the 880 — and won the state championship.* [17]

The reporter's argument:

> The Generals did not win all the RELAY events but they
> won the state CHAMPIONSHIP anyway. Hence, it is
> false that their winning all the relays was a necessary
> condition for taking the state championship.

*110. Huckleberry Finn reports a conversation with his raft companion
Jim:

> *He said that when I went in the texas and he crawled back to get on the raft and
> found her gone he nearly died, because he judged it was all up with him
> anyway it could be fixed; for if he didn't get saved he would get drownded; and
> if he did get saved, whoever saved him would send him back home so as to get
> the reward, and then Miss Watson would sell him South, sure.* [18]

Jim reasoned:

> If I'm not SAVED I'll DROWN, and if I am saved I'll be
> sent HOME. If I'm sent home, then I'll BE sold South.
> So, I'll either drown or be sold South.

111. In the ABC television miniseries *Masada*, Eleazar ben Yair tells his
followers that the Roman soldiers will soon enter their mountaintop
fortress, and recommends mass suicide:

> *You can choose to fight them in the morning — they'll kill you or enslave you.
> You can choose to hide from them — they'll find you. Or you can take their vic-
> tory from them. They will remember you.*

---

[17] "Coach Wrong; but Jackson's Still a Runaway," *Miami News* (May 15, 1972), p.
2-B.

[18] Mark Twain, *The Adventures of Huckleberry Finn* (New York: Collier Books, 1962),
p. 87.

One analysis of ben Yair's reasoning:

> If we FIGHT, they will KILL or ENSLAVE us. If we HIDE they WILL find us, and if they find us they will kill us or enslave us. We either fight, hide, or commit SUICIDE. Thus, committing suicide is the only way we can avoid being killed or enslaved by the Romans.

112. A neighbor of mine was faced with a difficult decision in 1943 when his P-38 developed engine trouble over New Guinea.

> If I BAIL out, I'll land in ENEMY territory. Unless I bail out, I'll CRASH. Therefore, I'll either bail out and land in enemy territory or crash.

He chose to ride the plane down, thereby fracturing his skull and breaking his back.

113. Solve the puzzle.

ACROSS	DOWN

ACROSS

1. To '~I → W' by derived rule.
4. Logically equivalent to 'B & T'.
7. From '~ ~(F & F)' by derived rule.
8. Entailed by 'U'.
9. From 'F → F' and 'F → F' by ↔I.
10. Not a well-formed formula.
11. Try this when all strategies fail.
13. Double choice.
15. Derived rule.
16. A valid argument may have all _____ premises.
17. Letter addition.
18. Derived rule.
19. Cult.
21. 'v' homophone.
23. Diamond stat.
26. From 'U → A' and 'A → R' by derived rule.
27. She's from URUGUAY but he's NICARAGUAN.
28. Poetic contraction.
29. Measures.

DOWN

1. If and only if.
2. The commutative connectives.
3. 'P' and '~P' are, but '↔P' and 'P & Q v R' aren't.
4. Conclusion word.
5. The key connectives in the variations of DM.
6. Conjunction word.
12. Troublesome terms.
14. Antecedent introducers.
15. Winged pest.
19. Makes a mistake.
20. A valid argument may have a _____ conclusion.
21. Word with black and cook.
22. From '~I → ~A' by derived rule.
24. From '~(~B v ~N)' by derived rule.
25. Election winners.

232. (SEMICHALLENGE) Construct proofs for the arguments in these exercises from earlier chapters:

(a) Exercise 211 (chapter five)
(b) Exercise 213 (chapter five)
(c) Exercise 206 (chapter four)
(d) Exercise 94 (chapter eight)
(e) Exercise 212 (chapter five)

In each proof employ at least one derived rule. The length of my proofs: (a) eight lines, (b) three, (c) three, (d) five, and (e) five.

233. (CHALLENGE) Of the twenty-eight derived subrules, six were justified by proofs in the text and nine relate to earlier exercises. Of the remaining thirteen subrules, twelve can be warranted by proofs similar to those presented in the text or assigned in exercises. Only the seventh version of the Arrow Rule offers a real challenge. Justify that subrule by constructing a proof for this abstract argument:

~(A → B) ⊢ A & ~B

Employ only primitive rules. A ten-line proof is possible.

152   Chapter 9

Instructions for exercises 234 and 235: Symbolize the concrete argument; construct proofs for both arguments. You may use derived rules.

234. (CHALLENGE)

Albert's thesis will be ACCEPTED iff at least two of these three committee members approve it: BROWN, CLARK, and DAVIS. Brown will approve the thesis iff both Clark and Davis approve it. It follows that if Clark and/or Davis fails to approve the thesis, it will not be accepted.

This is the first argument in the book that utilizes all five connectives. The proof can be made more challenging by substituting this conclusion: Therefore, if even one of these three committee members fails to approve the thesis, it will not be accepted.

235. (MAXICHALLENGE)

$$C \leftrightarrow (D \leftrightarrow E) \vdash (C \leftrightarrow D) \leftrightarrow E$$

Proving the validity of 235 constitutes half the demonstration that the double arrow is associative. This is the most difficult exercise in the book. A thirty-nine-line proof is possible.

10

Truth Tables

10.1
Constructing Truth Tables

In the preceding chapters we have developed an efficient and powerful instrument for demonstrating the validity of propositional arguments. However, this device has one major limitation: it does not demonstrate *in*validity. For example, consider the "Heller" argument, discussed in section 1.2:

> Joseph Heller is an AMERICAN. Therefore, he is an American and he is also a NOVELIST.

Symbolized:

> A ⊢ A & N

Intuitively, we know this argument to be invalid. We may also be certain that we cannot construct a formal proof for it. However, an individual's failure to construct a proof for an argument *does not* demonstrate the invalidity of the argument. For there is always at least a theoretical possibility that the failure to complete the proof results from the thickheadedness of the proof constructor rather than from the invalidity of the argument under evaluation.

A system of logic that has no method of demonstrating the invalidity of arguments is an inadequate tool for individuals who want to *apply* logic to the arguments they encounter. Some of the arguments that confront us in daily life are invalid, and we want to be able to establish their invalidity. For this reason, in the present chapter we supplement the method of formal proofs with the method of truth tables. In the remainder of this section, fundamentals of the latter are set forth. In the next section the method is applied to several arguments.

Every statement—simple or compound—has a *truth-value*; that is, every statement is either true or false. The truth-value of a conjunction (S1, for example) is determined by the truth-values of its conjuncts (S2 and S3).

> (S1) Heller is an American and he is a novelist.
> (S2) Heller is an American.
> (S3) Heller is a novelist.

If both S2 and S3 are true, then S1 is true. If either S2 or S3 or both are false, then S1 is false. The same can be said of F1 through F3, the symbolizations of these statements. The truth-value of F1 is entirely determined by the truth-values of F2 and F3.

> (F1) A & N
> (F2) A
> (F3) N

We will regard each of the five connective symbols as having this characteristic: the truth-value of a wff in which that symbol is the major connective is determined by the truth-values of the wff or wffs it connects. In logicians' jargon, the five connectives are *truth-functional*.[1] The specific ways in which the truth-values of wffs are determined by the truth-values of constituent wffs are shown in the following *basic truth table*:[2]

GUIDE COLUMNS		(1) $\sim P$	(2) $P \& Q$	(3) $P \vee Q$	(4) $P \to Q$	(5) $P \leftrightarrow Q$
	P \quad Q					
(a)	T \quad T	F	T	T	T	T
(b)	F \quad T	T	F	T	T	F
(c)	T \quad F		F	T	F	F
(d)	F \quad F		F	F	T	T

[1]Because the connectives studied in propositional logic are truth-functional, this branch of logic is often called *truth-functional logic*.

[2]One may wonder whether the five connective symbols as interpreted by this basic truth table are faithful translations of English connective expressions. This interesting and important question is discussed in appendix one.

Column 3 (to take an example) shows that a disjunctive wff is true when both disjuncts are true (row a), is also true when one disjunct is true (rows b and c), but is false when both disjuncts are false (row d). Column 1 (to take another example) indicates that a negative wff is false when the fragment following the tilde is true (row a) and is true when the negated constituent is false (row b).

One cannot employ the truth-table method without learning the information contained in the basic truth table. But, fortunately, this information can be reformulated in a way that is easier to retain. The entire content of the basic truth table is captured in these five principles:

(P1) A statement and its *negation* have opposite truth-values.

(P2) A *conjunction* is true iff both conjuncts are true.

(P3) A *disjunction* is false iff both disjuncts are false.[3]

(P4) A *conditional* is false iff its antecedent is true and its consequent is false.

(P5) A *biconditional* is true iff its two components have the same truth-value.

Satisfy yourself that these five principles accurately summarize the basic truth table. These principles should be memorized because you will employ them repeatedly in working exercises for this chapter and the next.

With the aid of these five principles we can determine the truth-value of *any* compound wff (belonging to propositional logic), provided that we know the truth-values of the simple wffs (capitals) it contains. I will illustrate with wff F4:

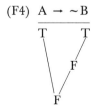

(F4)   A → ~B

Suppose in this case that the capitals abbreviate true statements. We indicate this by placing *T*'s beneath the capitals. By applying principle P1, we determine that the fragment ' ~ B' is false. Then, by applying P4, we learn that the entire wff is false. For a second example consider F5:

---

[3]P3 may also be stated: A *disjunction* is true iff at least one disjunct is true.

(F5)   ~ [(C & D) ↔ E]

We begin with the information that 'C' and 'E' are true and 'D' is false. By applying P2, P5, and P1 (in that order), we establish that F5 is true. Notice that we began with the truth-values of the smallest fragments of F5 (namely, the capitals) and then considered in turn larger and larger fragments until we reached the complete wff. It will soon prove important to economize on vertical space. We can do this by writing all the *T*'s and *F*'s on one row, as in the following:

(F5)   ~[(C & D) ↔ E]
_____
 T   TFF   F T

I have employed this convention: each *T* (*F*) is located under the major symbol in the fragment to which it applies. For example, the major symbol in 'C & D' is the ampersand; hence, the *F* located under the ampersand indicates that the conjunction is false.

We have seen how to determine the truth-value of a wff, given the actual truth-values of its simple constituents. We can also determine the truth-values that a wff *would* have for each of the *possible* assignments of truth-values to its simple constituents. The chart in which these possibilities are worked out is called a *truth table*. We return to wff F4 for an illustration. There are four possible assignments of truth-values to its simple constituents:

A	B
T	T
F	T
T	F
F	F

A convenient way of listing these combinations is to alternate *T*'s and *F*'s, singly in the first column and in pairs in the second column. These *guide columns* form the starting point for the truth table for F4. They are separated from the rest of the table by a pair of vertical lines.

A	B	A	→	~	B
T	T	T	F	F	T
F	T	F	T	F	T
T	F	T	T	T	F
F	F	F	T	T	F
			*		
[1]	[2]	[3]	[6]	[5]	[4]

The bracketed numbers at the bottoms of the columns are not part of the truth table. They are included to simplify making references and to indicate the order in which I filled in the columns.

The sixteen entries to the right of the double vertical line can be computed on a row-by-row basis by working from the top of the table to the bottom or by proceeding from one column to another. I will adopt the latter procedure because it is faster. Column 3 provides possible truth-values for the fragment 'A' and is copied from guide column 1. Column 4 is copied from column 2 in the same way. As column 3 is identical with column 1, 3 could be omitted from the table; column 4 could also be dropped. In the future I shall employ this shortcut. Column 5 gives possible truth-values for the fragment ' ~ B'. It is computed by applying principle P1 to column 4. Column 6, which covers the entire wff, is constructed by applying P4 to columns 3 and 5. (Column 3 gives values for the antecedent of F4, and column 5 gives values for the consequent.) Column 6 informs us that wff F4 is false iff both its simple constituents are true. The column that gives values for the whole wff is marked with an asterisk. (The asterisk is omitted when there is only one column.)

If a wff contains three simple constituents, there will be eight possible assignments to consider. This truth table for F5 illustrates:

C	D	E		~	[(C & D)	↦	E]
T	T	T		F	T		T
F	T	T		T	F		F
T	F	T		T	F		F
F	F	T		T	F		F
T	T	F		T	T		F
F	T	F		F	F		T
T	F	F		F	F		T
F	F	F		F	F		T
				*			
[1]	[2]	[3]		[6]	[4]		[5]

(I insert a horizontal line between the fourth and fifth rows of an eight-row truth table to help align the entries in the various columns. This practice is not essential.) The third guide column is constructed by alternating *T*'s and *F*'s in quartets. How many rows of truth-values would a truth table with four guide columns have? How would the fourth column be constructed (assuming we continue with the scheme I have been using)? How many rows are there in a truth table with one guide column?

You should realize that the pattern of truth-value assignments in the guide columns of the above table is only one of many feasible patterns. All that is essential is that each of the eight possible assignments to 'C', 'D', and 'E' be included. You should also realize that it is immaterial whether the first column is headed with 'C', 'D', or 'E'.

Column 4 of the truth table for F5 is computed by applying P2 to columns 1 and 2. Column 5 is constructed by using P5 on columns 4 and 3. Finally, column 6 is produced by applying P1 to column 5. Column 6 can be constructed only after column 5 has been completed, and the completion of 5 must await the construction of 4. Do you see why?

10.2
Testing Arguments

In the preceding section we learned how to construct truth tables for wffs. It is a simple matter to extend the technique to symbolized arguments. A truth table for the "Heller" argument looks like this:

A	N	A	⊢A & N
T	T	T	T
F	T	F	F
T	F	T	F
F	F	F	F

The wffs composing the argument are separated from one another by single vertical lines. A turnstile marks the conclusion.

By examining the truth table, we can determine whether the argument is valid or invalid. We employ this principle:

A propositional argument is invalid iff there is one or more rows on its truth table where all the premises are true and the conclusion is false.[4]

On the third row of the above truth table the premise is true and the conclusion is false; this establishes the invalidity of the "Heller" argument. A ring is drawn around the crucial pattern. The third row of the table indicates that (whatever the actual truth-values of the premise and conclusion of the "Heller" argument) it is *possible* that the premise is true and the conclusion is false. By definition, it is impossible for a (one-premised) valid argument to have a true premise and a false conclusion. Hence, the "Heller" argument is not valid.

In section 2.3 I promised to provide a justification of the inference pattern *modus ponens*; the time to fulfill that promise has arrived. A truth table for an abstract *modus ponens* argument:

F	G	F → G	F	⊢G
T	T	T	T	T
F	T	T	F	T
T	F	F	T	F
F	F	T	F	F

[4]In chapters ten and eleven (as earlier in the book) we concentrate on arguments that can be satisfactorily analyzed with the techniques of propositional logic. This restriction should be understood even though it is frequently unstated.

We search the table unsuccessfully for a row in which both premises are true and the conclusion is false. From the absence of such a row we conclude that this argument (and, by extension, any *modus ponens* argument) is valid. Why is it sound to conclude this? The table sets forth all the possible combinations of the truth-values of the premises and conclusion. These do not include an instance where there are true premises and a false conclusion. The table reveals that, due to the form of the argument alone, it is impossible that its premises are true and its conclusion is false. This is the defining characteristic of a valid argument.

By constructing truth tables, we can show the legitimacy of any of the inference rules that govern the deduction of statements from statements (these are the rules to which the standard assumption-dependence principle applies). Why can't we validate the other inference rules by constructing truth tables?

I also promised in section 2.3 to demonstrate formally the invalidity of the "revelation" argument, an instance of the fallacy of affirming the consequent.

R	W	R → W	W	⊢R
T	T	T	T	T
F	T	T	T	F
T	F	F	F	T
F	F	T	F	F

The critical pattern that establishes invalidity occurs on row 2.

In section 7.2 a formal proof was constructed to demonstrate that F1 entails F2.

(F1) ~(O v B)
(F2) ~O & ~B

I now establish by truth table that F2 also entails F1.

O	B	~ O	&	~ B	⊢ ~	(O v B)
T	T	F	F	F	F	T
F	T	T	F	F	F	T
T	F	F	F	T	F	T
F	F	T	T	T	T	F
			*		*	
[1]	[2]	[3]	[5]	[4]	[7]	[6]

The asterisks identify the principal columns. The critical pattern of a *T* in column 5 and an *F* in column 7 appears on no row; hence, F2 entails F1.

Notice how the truth-values in column 7 were calculated on the basis of a column (6) of values for the fragment 'O v B'. I have encountered the following faulty table devised by students.

O	B	~	(O	v	B)
T	T	F	F		F
F	T	T	T		F
T	F	F	F		T
F	F	T	T		T
				*	
[1]	[2]	[3]	[5]		[4]

Column 3 was constructed by applying P1 to column 1, and column 4 was built by applying the same principle to column 2. Then 5 was computed by using P3 with columns 3 and 4. A comparison of column 5 from this table with column 7 of the preceding table indicates that something has gone wrong. The mistaken truth table above rests on the false supposition that F1 is equivalent to F4.

(F1) ~ (O v B)
(F4) ~ O v ~ B

The following table establishes the invalidity of the "prime" argument, discussed in sections 3.3 and 4.2:

L	E	P	(L & E)	→ P	⊢L	→ P
T	T	T	T	T		T
F	T	T	F	T		T
T	F	T	F	T		T
F	F	T	F	T		T
T	T	F	T	F		F
F	T	F	F	T		T
T	F	F	F	T		F
F	F	F	F	T		T
				*		

Our final example is more complex. In a column on busing, newspaper editor Jim Fain writes:

> . . . *Without busing as one tool for integrating society, the near-total segregation of the major cities is almost guaranteed.*
> *Whites flee inner cities in order to place their children in all-white school systems more than for any other reason.* [5]

Fain's point is expressed by this argument:

> If school children are not BUSED, whites will MOVE to the suburbs. Provided that whites move to the suburbs and chil-

[5] "Two-Society America Will Not Endure," *Miami News* (August 3, 1974), p. 10-A.

dren are not bused, then schools will be SEGREGATED. It follows that the failure to bus school children will lead to segregated schools.

In symbols:

~ B → M, (M & ~ B) → S ⊢ ~ B → S

The truth table:

B M S	~ B → M	(M & ~ B) → S	⊢ ~ B → S
T T T	F T	F F T	F T
F T T	T T	T T T	T T
T F T	F T	F F T	F T
F F T	T F	F T T	T T
T T F	F T	F F T	F T
F T F	T T	T T F	T F
T F F	F T	F F T	F T
F F F	T F	F T T	T F
	*	*	*
[1] [2] [3]	[4] [5]	[7][6] [8]	[9] [10]

The critical pattern (*T*'s in columns 5 and 8 and *F* in 10) appears on no row; this shows the argument to be valid.

The truth-table and formal-proof techniques differ in several respects. The most obvious difference is that while truth tables demonstrate both validity and invalidity, formal proofs show only validity. Truth tables are an *effective* procedure—that is, a truth table will lead to a definite result in a finite number of steps. Formal proofs are not "effective." Also, truth tables are a *mechanical* procedure—that is, the method can be described by a completely explicit set of instructions that tell what step to take at every point in the procedure. The technique makes no demands on ingenuity or creativity. Formal proofs, of course, are not "mechanical."

Do the two methods yield consistent results? Yes. Every propositional argument for which a formal proof can be constructed will be assessed as valid by the truth-table test, and for every argument judged valid by this method a formal proof is possible.

EXERCISES

114. Complete each of the following truth tables. Indicate for each abstract argument whether it is valid or invalid.

(a)

A	A	⊢ ~ ~A
T		
F	F	F T
		*
[1]	[2]	[4][3]

(b)

B	C	B → C	⊢B ∨ ~ C
T	T	T	T F
F	T		
T	F		
F	F	T	T T
			*
[1]	[2]	[3]	[5] [4]

*(c)

D	E	F	D → E	E ∨ F	⊢(D ∨ F) → (E & F)
T	T	T	T	T	T T T
F	T	T			
T	F	T			
F	F	T			
T	T	F			
F	T	F			
T	F	F			
F	F	F	T	F	F T F
					*

(d)

G	H	I	(G & H) ↔ I	H	⊢~(G & ~ I)
T	T	T	T T	T	T F F
F	T	T			
T	F	T			
F	F	T			
T	T	F			
F	T	F			
T	F	F			
F	F	F	F T	F	T F T
			*		*

Instructions for exercises 115 through 126 (and 236-237): Symbolize each argument and test it by the truth-table method. Indicate whether it is valid or invalid.

115.   This argument was discussed in section 9.1:

Mrs. Mathias either has a TUMOR or she is PREGNANT.
She is pregnant. Thus, she does not have a tumor.

© 1980 by Nicole Hollander.

116. Evaluate the argument advanced in the middle panels of the "Sylvia" comic strip. Use these abbreviations:

    T = Women played team sports as children
    F = Women fit smoothly into the corporate world

*117. The philosopher Grover Maxwell summarizes a line of thought with this argument:

    Thus if "electron" is an OBSERVATION term, then it is not *an observation term. Therefore it is not an observation term.* [6]

118. From a philosophy midterm examination:

    The determinist says that if all actions are caused then no actions are free and no actions are free, therefore everything is caused.

    Use these abbreviations:

    C = All actions are caused
    F = Some actions are free

    Note that 'No actions are free' is equivalent to the negation of 'Some actions are free'.

119. Philosopher Carl Hempel examines—but does not endorse—this argument concerning the existence of theoretical entities:

    . . . When two alternative theories—such as the particle and wave theories of light before the "crucial experiments" of the nineteenth century—equally account for a given set of empirical phenomena, then, if "real existence" is granted to the

---

[6] "The Ontological Status of Theoretical Entities," in *Minnesota Studies in the Philosophy of Science*, III: 9-10, ed. Herbert Feigl and Grover Maxwell (Minneapolis: University of Minnesota Press, 1962). Maxwell examines the argument but does not subscribe to it.

theoretical entities assumed by one of them, it must be granted to the quite different entities assumed by the other; hence, the entities posited by none of the alternative theories can be held actually to exist. [7]

The argument reformulated:

The theoretical entities postulated by the PARTICLE theory of light exist iff those postulated by the WAVE theory exist. It is not the case that the theoretical entities postulated by both theories exist. Hence, it is not true that the entities posited by either theory exist.

120. One of my students in Introduction to Philosophy advanced this argument:

If God EXISTS, then he is all-POWERFUL. If he exists and is all-powerful, then the world hangs TOGETHER. This shows that God exists because the world does hang together.

This may be the first three-premised argument for which you have constructed a truth table. The critical pattern is $T\ T\ T\ F.$

121. An article in a religious newspaper claims that among the world's religions, Christianity (and only Christianity) incorporates significant or meaningful statements. The author writes:

Jesus Christ made statements significant only if He was something more than a man, and He proved He was by dying and rising again — a physical transmigration. . . .
He died and rose again to make His "game" meaningful and factually significant. [8]

He is advancing the following argument:

Jesus made SIGNIFICANT statements only if he was MORE than a man. If he ROSE from the dead, then he was more than a man. And he did rise from the dead. This proves that Jesus' statements are significant.

122. The television drama *Anne of Cleves* contains these words addressed to Anne by Thomas Cromwell.

If you fall I fall; if I fall you fall. And if both of us fall, the Church of England falls.

[7] *Philosophy of Natural Science* (Englewood Cliffs, N.J.: Prentice-Hall, 1966), p. 80.
[8] Bill Luck, "The Games People Play," *The Logos* (Miami, Fla.), September, 1970, p. 3.

Does it follow from Cromwell's remarks that the Church of EN-GLAND falls if either ANNE or CROMWELL falls?

123.   A Volkswagen ad features a photo of a street of identical houses. In front of each home (twenty-three in all) is parked a red and white Volkswagen bus. Under the photo is this message:

If the world looked like this, and you wanted to buy a car that sticks out a little, you . . . wouldn't buy a Volkswagen Station Wagon. But in case you haven't noticed, the world doesn't look like this. So if you've wanted to buy a car that sticks out a little you know just what to do.

The consequent of the conclusion may be paraphrased "you will buy a Volkswagen Station Wagon." Employ these abbreviations:

   W = The world looks like this
   S = You want a car that sticks out a little
   V = You will buy a Volkswagen Station Wagon

* 124.   Business administration educator Eugene F. Brigham writes:

If stocks were negatively correlated, or if there were zero correlation, then a properly constructed portfolio would have very little risk. However, stocks tend to be positively (but less than perfectly) correlated with one another, so all stock portfolios tend to be somewhat risky. [9]

Employ these abbreviations:

   N = Stocks are negatively correlated
   P = Stocks are positively correlated
   R = Stock portfolios involve significant risk

'Stocks have zero correlation' is equivalent to 'Stocks are neither positively nor negatively correlated'.

125.   After the California Angels suspended outfielder Alex Johnson without pay for "not showing the proper mental attitude" and fined him $3,750 for misconduct, an arbitration board ruled that his behavior was caused by emotional disturbance and ordered the club to pay Johnson $29,970 in back pay. However, the board upheld the disciplinary fines. A newspaper story gives this account of the reaction of an Angels official to the board's decision:

General Manager Dick Walsh called the ruling inconsistent and asked: If Johnson was not responsible for his actions, why allow the fines to stand? If he was, why not uphold the suspension?

---

[9] *Fundamentals of Financial Management* (Hinsdale, Ill.: Dryden Press, 1978), p. 107.

"Either Johnson was or was not responsible for his actions," Walsh said. "If he was responsible, then the suspension and fines were justified." [10]

We can formalize Walsh's criticism as follows:

The view [of the arbitration board] that the FINE was justified but the SUSPENSION was not is mistaken, for the following reasons: Either Johnson was or was not RESPONSIBLE for his actions. If he was, then the fine and the suspension were both justified. But if he wasn't responsible, then neither the fine nor the suspension was justified.

126.   The second paragraph of chapter four begins:

We can establish conclusively that S1 and S3 are not logically equivalent statements. If they were equivalent, they would have to agree as regards truth (or falsity). But though S1 is true, S3 is false.

The first premise may be paraphrased with 'If they are equivalent, then they are either both true or both false'. Use these abbreviations:

E = S1 and S3 are logically equivalent
A = S1 is true
B = S3 is true

236.   (CHALLENGE)

Providing any one of my three children [Mike, Amy, and Mark] is telling the truth, then the other two are not. It follows that one of them is telling the truth and the other two are not.

Employ these symbols:

B = Mike is telling the truth
A = Amy is telling the truth
C = Mark is telling the truth

237.   (CHALLENGE) The following puzzle appears in *101 Puzzles in Thought and Logic*, by C. R. Wylie, Jr.:

The personnel director of a firm in speaking of three men the company was thinking of hiring once said,

"We need Brown and if we need Jones then we need Smith, if and only if we need either Brown or Jones and don't need Smith."

[10]"Alex Wins, but ... ; Bunning Retires," *Miami News* (September 29, 1971), p.
4-B.

$[B \& (J \to S)] \leftrightarrow [(B \lor J) \& \sim S]$

If the company actually needed more than one of the men, which ones were they? [11]

(Read no further if you want to solve the puzzle on your own.) One proposed solution to the puzzle: 'The company needs Jones and Smith, but not Brown'. Discover whether this solution is correct by evaluating the argument that has it as the conclusion and that has as premises the personnel director's statement and the claim that the company needs more than one of the men. Use these abbreviations:

B = The company needs Brown
J = The company needs Jones
S = The company needs Smith

$(J \& S) \& \sim B$

238.   (CHALLENGE) The Univac version of the programming language BASIC contains all of the statement connectives used in this book plus two not employed in the book:

(1)   XOR (exclusive disjunction)
(2)   IF-THEN-ELSE

For a discussion of exclusive disjunction, see section 7.1. Let's symbolize 'P XOR Q' as 'P X Q' and 'IF R THEN S ELSE T' as '*R,S,T'. (The 'ELSE' in 'IF R THEN S ELSE T' is short for 'AND IF NOT R THEN'.)

1.   Define both connectives with the help of other propositional-logic connectives.
2.   Construct basic truth tables for both connectives.
3.   Formulate an "In" rule and an "Out" rule for each connective. Aim for consistency and completeness (as explained in section 8.1).

---

[11](New York: Dover, 1957), puzzle 42. Reprinted through permission of the publisher.

11

Brief
Truth Tables

11.1

Proving Invalidity

The truth-table method developed in the preceding chapter is an attractive test procedure. In the first place, it can establish invalidity as well as validity. Second, being a mechanical method that does not rely on the ingenuity of the tester, it does not fail when the tester's inventive powers fail. Finally, the method, when carried through, yields an evaluation of *any* argument within the province of propositional logic.[1]

The main defect in the method is a practical one. For arguments involving four or more simple statements the procedure consumes too much space and time. A complete truth table has 2^n rows, where n is the number of guide columns in the table. A truth table with four guide columns is 2^4, or 16 rows long; one with five guide columns has 32 rows, and so on. A truth table for exercise 98, with its seven simple statements,

[1]In view of these attractive features of the truth-table method, you may wonder why I bothered to develop the method of formal proofs in chapters two through nine. Here are two reasons: (1) Learning to construct formal proofs strengthens a person's logical powers to a greater extent than does learning to employ the truth-table test. (2) Truth tables have only limited use beyond propositional logic, whereas formal-proof procedures are important in every branch of deductive logic. Thus learning to construct proofs in propositional logic prepares you for study in other areas of logic.

would contain 128 rows. Constructing a 128-row table is a snap for a computer, but it is unreasonable to ask a human to perform this task. For practical reasons, then, the truth-table procedure should be supplemented by other methods. The present chapter is devoted to explaining two techniques which are abridgments of the truth-table test introduced in the last chapter; we call them *brief truth tables*. In this section I explain the brief-truth-table method of demonstrating invalidity; in the next section I cover the brief-table method of establishing validity.

In a full truth table for an argument, the existence of one row where the premises of the argument are assigned the value *T* and the conclusion is marked *F* establishes the invalidity of the argument. The other rows on the table may be ignored; in fact, they need never have been constructed. This is the idea behind the brief-table method of establishing invalidity. The table contains only one row, which is *the* row (or one of the rows) exhibiting the crucial pattern of true premises and false conclusion.

I'll illustrate this brief-table method by establishing the invalidity of the "Oh God!" argument discussed in section 5.2. In symbols:

$$S \rightarrow B, \sim S \vdash \sim B$$

The brief truth table:

S	B	S → B	~S	⊢ ~B
F	T	T	T	F
[4]	[5]	[1]	[2]	[3]

(The numbers enclosed by brackets indicate the order in which I inserted *T*'s and *F*'s; the numbers are not part of the truth table.) The portion of this table which lies above the horizontal line is completed as it would be for a full truth table. The crucial pattern (*T*'s under the premises and an *F* under the conclusion) is written in columns 1 through 3. Next I attempt to complete the row of truth values consistent with this critical pattern. The *T* in column 2 requires an *F* in guide column 4, and the *F* in column 3 requires a *T* in guide column 5. (Here, and throughout the chapter, I assume that you are fully familiar with principles P1 through P5, introduced in section 10.1.) I omit placing *F*'s under the occurrences of 'S' in the premises (and also omit placing *T*'s under the occurrences of 'B' in the first premise and conclusion) as a shortcut; they may, of course, be included. The guide-column entries were selected so that they would support the entries in columns 2 and 3 — but what of the entry in column 1? An application of principle P4 confirms the correctness of the entry in column 1. Thus, I have successfully extracted from a complete truth table that row which shows that it is possible for the premises of the argument to be true while the conclusion is false. I have produced the row that establishes invalidity without computing the insignificant rows.

We may summarize the brief-truth-table procedure for demonstrating invalidity as follows:

> **Make a goal assignment of *T* to each premise of the argument and *F* to the conclusion. If the remaining assignments are completed consistently, the argument is invalid.**

The "Kant" argument from section 5.2 provides a second example. Symbolized:

~ (K & H), ~K ⊢H

The brief truth table:

K	H	~(K & H)	~K	⊢H
F	F	T F	T	F
[5]	[4]	[1] [6]	[2]	[3]

(Recall that, as in the previous chapter, *T*'s and *F*'s are entered under the principal symbol of the wff or wff fragment to which they apply. So, for example, column 1 refers to the negation '~(K & H)', whereas column 6 applies to the conjunction 'K & H'.) The crucial pattern is entered in columns 1 through 3. The *F* entry in column 3 requires a similar entry in guide column 4, and the *T* in column 2 forces an *F* into guide column 5. Having completed the guide columns in a way that conforms to columns 2 and 3, we check to see whether the guide columns are also consistent with the entry of *T* in column 1. The guide-column entries require the placement of *F* in column 6, and that entry supports the *T* in column 1. So the invalidity of the "Kant" inference is established.

Why did I attend to the second premise and the conclusion before considering the first premise? Because they "force" additional truth-value assignments, whereas the first premise does not. The assignment of *T* to the first premise is compatible with several assignments in the guide columns. We adopt this procedural principle for the brief-truth-table technique:

> **Concentrate first on those statements in the argument whose truth-value assignments force additional assignments.**

For a third example of the brief-truth-table method of establishing invalidity, we evaluate this philosophical argument:

> Causal explanations of human acts are not SATISFACTORY unless such acts are CAUSED. This proves that human acts are uncaused, for it is known that causal explanations of human acts are unsatisfactory.

The symbolization:

~C → ~S, ~S ⊢~C

This brief truth table establishes the argument's invalidity:

C	S	~C	→	~S	~S	⊢~C
T	F	F	T	T	T	F
[5]	[4]	[7]	[1]	[6]	[2]	[3]

The *T* in column 2 forces an *F* into guide column 4. Similarly, the *F* in column 3 requires a *T* in guide column 5. The column 7 entry is copied from 3, and 6 is copied from 2. The entries in columns 7 and 6 substantiate the *T* in 1.

This abstract argument provides a final example:

A, (B → A) & (~C v B) ⊢C

The brief truth table:

A	B	C	A	(B	→	A)	&	(~C	v	B)	⊢ C
T	T	F	T		T		T	T	T		F
[4]	[9]	[5]	[1]		[6]		[2]	[7]	[8]		[3]

The goal entries in columns 1 and 3 force entries in guide columns 4 and 5. The *T* in 4 leads to a *T* in 6 (because conditionals with true consequents are true). The *F* in 5 results in a *T* in 7, which in turn forces a *T* into column 8. The *T*'s in 6 and 8 support the goal entry of *T* in column 2. This shows that regardless of what letter is inserted in guide column 9, it is possible for the premises to be true and the conclusion false. The invalidity of the argument is, therefore, established. To complete the table, I "flip a truth-value coin" and enter a *T* in column 9. This example shows that for some invalid arguments (a minority of those we are likely to encounter) more than one brief truth table is possible.

11.2
Proving Validity

The brief-truth-table method of establishing validity is nearly identical to the technique explained in the last section. I'll illustrate it by evaluating the "Pope Paul" argument from section 2.3. That argument is symbolized:

P → D, P ⊢D

We draw up a brief truth table and make goal assignments to the premises and conclusion.

P	D	P → D	P	⊢ D
		T	T	F

When we make the additional truth-value assignments that are forced by these initial assignments we land in a contradiction!

P	D	P → D	P	⊢ D
T	F	T	T	F
		F		
[4]	[5]	[1]	[2]	[3]

The *T* in column 2 is copied over in column 4 and the *F* in column 3 is recorded in 5. When we check the first premise against the guide columns, "trouble" emerges. The antecedent of the first premise has been assigned *T* and the consequent *F*; but in this case the premise itself must be false—which conflicts with the initial assignment of *T* to that premise. Note that every step taken after the initial goal assignment was forced upon us. Therefore, ending with a contradiction (both *T* and *F* assigned to the first premise) shows that the initial goal assignment was impossible. But if it is impossible for the premises to be true and the conclusion false, then the argument is valid.

Note that the contradiction could have "popped up" at other locations, for example:

P	D	P → D	P	⊢D
T	T	T	T	F
				T
[4]	[5]	[1]	[2]	[3]

The *T* in column 2 is transferred to 4. Given that a true conditional with a true antecedent must have a true consequent, the *T*'s in columns 1 and 4 dictate that the consequent of the first premise also be true, and that information is recorded in column 5. When the *T* in 5 is transferred to the conclusion a contradiction erupts in column 3. Wherever the contradiction emerges, it is proof of validity—providing only that each assignment made was required by earlier assignments (going all the way back to the initial goal assignments).

We have developed a brief-truth-table test of validity, which may be summarized:

> **Make a goal assignment of *T* to each premise of the argument and *F* to the conclusion. If this assignment forces a contradictory assignment, the argument is valid.**

For a second illustration of the method, I assess an argument of Albert Einstein's. Einstein said:

I am convinced that there is absolute truth. If there isn't an absolute truth, there cannot be a relative truth.

Einstein makes the (plausible) assumption that there is some sort of truth. His argument may be expressed as follows:

> There is ABSOLUTE truth. Proof: There is either absolute or RELATIVE truth. And if there isn't an absolute truth, there cannot be a relative truth.[2]

Symbolized:

$$A \vee R, \sim A \to \sim R \vdash A$$

The brief truth table:

A R	A ∨ R	~A → ~R	⊢ A
F T	T	T T F	F
		F	
[4] [6]	[1]	[5] [2][7]	[3]

The goal entry in column 3 is transferred to guide column 4 and also entails the *T* in column 5. Because a true disjunction must have at least one true disjunct, the entries in columns 1 and 4 show that 'R' will receive the value *T* (recorded in 6), and this in turn places an *F* in column 7. But now the second premise has a true antecedent and a false consequent; so it is given an *F*—which contradicts its initial assignment.

For a final example I assess argument 83 (chapter seven):

I A T O	I → A	(~I → T) & (T → O)	I ∨ ~I	⊢ A ∨ O
F F T F	T T	T T T T T T T F	T	F F F
		F		
[9] [7] [11] [8]	[1]	[10] [5] ·[2]	[6] [3]	[4]

Study this table (in the order of column numbers) until you understand how the initial goal assignment led to the contradiction in column 6. If you do not follow it, read the footnote.[3]

[2]Roger A. MacGowan and F. I. Ordway, *Intelligence in the Universe* (Englewood Cliffs, N.J.: Prentice-Hall, 1966), p. 289.

[3]P2 (Principle 2 in section 10.1) and entry 2 entail 5 and the top entry in 6.
P3 and entry 4 entail 7 and 8.
P4 and entries 1 and 7 entail 9.
P1 and entry 9 entail 10.
P4 and entries 5 and 10 entail 11.
P4 and entries 11 and 8 entail the bottom entry in 6.

Occasionally you will encounter a valid argument where the initial goal assignment does not force other truth-value assignments. Here is an example from chapter six:

$$M \leftrightarrow G \vdash G \leftrightarrow M$$

Since there are two cases in which a biconditional is true, the assignment of T to the premise forces no other values. And because there are two cases in which a biconditional is false, the assignment of F to the conclusion forces no further assignments. In other cases the initial goal assignment entails some additional assignments but leaves others unforced. The brief-truth-table technique for establishing validity (as explained in this book) applies only to those arguments where the initial goal assignments dictate all of the remaining assignments. The method does apply to the vast majority of valid propositional arguments you will meet, and substituting it for the full-truth-table technique will usually effect a significant savings in time and workspace.

What has been explained for pedagogical reasons as two brief-truth-table techniques may also be viewed as one method summarized in this way:

Make a goal assignment of T to each premise of the argument and F to the conclusion. If the remaining assignments are completed without contradiction, the argument is invalid. If the goal assignment forces a contradictory assignment, the argument is valid.

Note that while being "forced" at each step is a requirement for proving validity, it is not a requirement for demonstrating invalidity.

EXERCISES

127. Use the brief-truth-table procedure to establish the invalidity of these arguments in the exercise set for chapter ten:

    (a)   Exercise 115
    (b)   Exercise 116
  *(c)   Exercise 118
    (d)   Exercise 120
    (e)   Exercise 123

128. Use the brief-truth-table procedure to establish the validity of these arguments in the exercise set for chapter nine:

    (a)   Exercise 103

(b)   Exercise 109

*(c)   Exercise 104

(d)   Exercise 102

(e)   Exercise 108

Instructions for exercises 129 through 138: Symbolize each argument and test it by the brief-truth-table method. Indicate whether it is valid or invalid.

129.   Some lyrics from "King Herod's Song" in the rock opera *Jesus Christ Superstar*:

So you are the Christ, you're the great Jesus Christ
Prove to me that you're divine — change my water into wine
That's all you need do and I'll know it's all true
. . .
Or has something gone wrong? Why do you take so long?
C'mon King of the Jews
. . .
You're a joke, you're not the Lord —
    you are nothing but a fraud
Take him away — he's got nothing to say![4]

Herod reasons:

If Jesus changes my water into WINE, then he's DIVINE.
Therefore, he is not divine because he did not change my
water to wine.

*130.   The doctor in the "Wizard of Id" strip presents an argument with this unstated conclusion: 'He pollutes the WATER or the AIR'. Let *B* abbreviate 'He washes'.

September 15, 1971. By permission of John Hart and Field Enterprises, Inc.

[4]"King Herod's Song" from *Jesus Christ Superstar: A Rock Opera* by Andrew Lloyd Webber and Tim Rice. © 1970 by Leeds Music Ltd., London, England. Sole selling agent, Leeds Music Corporation, 445 Park Ave., New York, N.Y., for North, Central, and South America. Used by permission. All rights reserved.

131.   A letter to "Dear Abby" includes this paragraph:

> *. . . One woman who tried to call her husband at his place of business and found his line busy, then attempted to call a lady she knew, and when HER line was also busy, this wife assumed that her husband and this lady were talking to each other! She then began to call this lady on the phone and harass her with all sorts of vile accusations.* [5]

Perhaps the jealous wife used this argument:

> My HUSBAND'S phone is busy. SO-AND-SO's telephone is also busy. If they are TALKING with each other on the phone, then, of course, both phones are busy. Therefore, my husband and so-and-so are conversing over the phone.

132.   When the Metropolitan Community Church, a homosexual congregation in Miami, petitioned the local council of churches for membership, a minister on the council remarked:

> *I feel we're damned if we do [admit this church, because it sanctions illegal homosexual marriages] and damned if we don't [for rejecting them would be un-Christian].* [6]

Does the minister's remark entail that the council will be damned (which in this context means that the council will be severely criticized)? Use these symbols:

> D = The council is damned
> A = The council admits the homosexual congregation

133.   A foreign student I know advanced the following argument as evidence for the spuriousness of Christianity:

> If [the Christian] God loves ALL people, then he doesn't love only ONE. And if he loves only one person, then he doesn't love all people. Thus, he does not love all people.

* 134.   This passage occurred in a term paper on the philosophy of science:

> *The instrumentalist interpretation of quantum theory is implied by positivism; positivism is false; hence, we must interpret quantum theory in a realistic fashion.*

---

[5] Abigail Van Buren, "Dear Abby" (Chicago Tribune-New York News Syndicate, Inc.), *Miami News* (January 7, 1972), p. 8-C.

[6] Bob Wilcox, "Council Won't Admit Homosexual Church," *Miami News* (March 26, 1971), p. 6-A.

I believe the student was reasoning as follows:

Either INSTRUMENTALISM or REALISM is correct. If POSI-
TIVISM is true, instrumentalism is correct. But positivism is
false. Hence, realism is correct.

135.   A sports story on a high-school baseball tournament includes the following:

*Columbus (9-9 in conference) — lost yesterday: definitely will participate in the
playoffs. . . .*
    *If Beach loses tonight, Columbus and Gables will be third- and fourth-place
representatives from the GMAC Southern Division. . . .*
    If Beach wins, Beach and Columbus will qualify.[7]

The conclusion of the argument contained in this passage is asserted
in the first paragraph. Use these abbreviations:

    C = Columbus will qualify
    W = Beach wins tonight
    G = Gables will qualify
    B = Beach will qualify

Ties in baseball are rare; for simplicity, let's equate *not winning* with
losing.

136.   A William Safire column begins with this paragraph:

*If President Carter's brother told the truth to the committee investigating his
Libyan influence-peddling, then two Justice Department officials and an FBI
agent should face charges of malfeasance. If the law enforcement officials have
been writing the truth in their memoranda about two interviews with Billy
Carter, then the President's brother should be indicted for perjury.*[8]

Safire does not draw a conclusion from these conditionals, but one
might (with the help of an obvious additional premise):

If BILLY told the truth, certain officials should be charged
with MALFEASANCE. If the OFFICIALS are telling the truth,
then Billy should be indicted for PERJURY. Thus, either the
officials should be charged with malfeasance or Billy should
be indicted for perjury since Billy and the officials are not
both telling the truth.

---

[7]"District Baseball: It's Loaded with 'Ifs'," *Miami News* (April 17, 1971), p. 2-B.

[8]"Somebody's Lying in This Billy Business," *Miami News* (September 6, 1980),
p. 10-A. ©1980 by the New York Times Company. Reprinted by permission.

137.   Ray is in a jam that is expressed by this argument:

> I take Maxine to the CONCERT iff I WIN this pool game. If I win this game I will be beaten UP. If I don't take Maxine to the concert, BERNARD will take her. Therefore, either I get beaten up or Maxine goes to the concert with Bernard.

© 1981 United Feature Syndicate, Inc.

138.   I reviewed a manuscript for a logic textbook in which the following argument was used:

> Abstract argument X is formally UNSOUND iff it is VALID and has at least one FALSE premise. X has one or more false premises only if the CONJUNCTION of its premises is logically absurd. So, X is formally unsound if the conjunction of its premises is logically absurd.

Let U abbreviate 'X is formally unsound'.

239.   (SEMICHALLENGE) Use the brief-truth-table procedure to establish the validity of these arguments:

(a)   Exercise 225 (chapter seven)
(b)   Exercise 98 (chapter eight)

240.   (CHALLENGE) The brief-truth-table method for establishing validity explained in section 11.2 does not apply to exercise 234 (chapter nine). Develop a modification that will demonstrate the validity of 234. Explain and illustrate your technique.

12

Statements

12.1
Logical Truths

Once upon a time there was a meteorologist named Wallace Drizzle who could not stand to have his weather predictions turn out false. In the 1950s he would make predictions such as "It will rain today in Middletown." During those evenings when his prediction had proved wrong he would sulk at home, drinking martinis. The situation improved in the 1960s and 1970s after the weather bureau altered the form of its forecasts. During this period Wally made predictions such as "There is a 40 percent chance of rain in Middletown today." He reduced his martini consumption during this period, but it was occasionally obvious (when the percentage employed in his forecast was quite high or quite low) that he had made a mistaken prediction. Then, one day in the 1980s, he hit upon the idea of issuing this "prediction":

> (S1) Either it will RAIN in Middletown today or it
> will not rain in Middletown today.

The beauty of S1, of course, is that it is true regardless of the condition of the weather. It cannot be falsified. For two weeks Wally was euphoric — then the weather bureau sacked him. Residents of Middletown had complained that his current "predictions" did not help them decide whether to carry umbrellas to work.

A statement whose falsity is logically impossible is called a *logical truth*.[1] The virtue of a logical truth is that it *must* be true; its weakness is that it conveys no factual information. Wally Drizzle favored the logical truth S1 because it was guaranteed true; the townspeople disliked S1 because it gave them no information about the weather.

A few sample (abstract) logical truths:

$$A \vee \sim A$$
$$B \rightarrow B$$
$$C \leftrightarrow C$$
$$\sim(D \,\&\, \sim D)$$
$$E \leftrightarrow \,\sim \sim E$$
$$(F \,\&\, G) \rightarrow F$$
$$H \rightarrow (H \vee I)$$

There is a truth-table method as well as a formal-proof method for demonstrating that a statement is a logical truth. I will explain these methods in turn. A statement is ~~logically true~~ a tautology iff the column (in a full truth table) under its principal symbol is composed exclusively of *T*'s.[2] I will illustrate with this truth table for S1:

R	R v ~R
T	T F
F	T T
	*

For a second example, consider this statement from a toy carton:

If these animals could TALK, they could WALK and TALK, if only they could WALK!

This may be symbolized:

$$T \rightarrow [W \rightarrow (W \,\&\, T)]$$

(Note that 'if only' and 'only if' are not synonymous.) The truth table for this logical truth:

T	W	T →	[W →	(W & T)]
T	T	T	T	T
F	T	T	F	F
T	F	T	T	F
F	F	T	T	F
		*		

[1] Logical truths belonging to propositional logic are often called *tautologies*.

[2] In the present chapter we concentrate on statements that can be satisfactorily analyzed with the techniques of propositional logic. This restriction should be understood even though it is frequently unstated.

The formal-proof method for establishing that a statement is a logical truth is to construct a proof (complete with assumption-dependence column) in which that statement occurs with *no* assumption dependence.

Such a proof will incorporate at least one of the rules of inference that reduce assumption dependence — namely, Arrow In, Tilde In, and Tilde Out. Obviously, the Arrow In strategy is appropriate for demonstrating the logical truth of conditionals, the Tilde In strategy for logically true negations, and the Tilde Out strategy for other logical truths. The following Tilde Out proof establishes that S1 is a logical truth:

1	(1)	$\sim$(R v $\sim$R)	PA
1	(2)	$\sim$R & $\sim$ $\sim$R	1 DM
	(3)	R v $\sim$R	1-2 $\sim$O

Line 3 in this proof depends on whatever assumptions line 2 depends on, less line 1 — so line 3 depends on no assumptions at all. The assumption-free status of line 3 is indicated by the absence of an entry in the assumption-dependence column. The proof shows that S1 is a logical truth, because only logical truths can be derived assumption-free. A statement that can be proved without assumptions is one that is true on logical grounds alone.

A second example of a proof of logical truth involves the "walk-talk" statement considered above.

1	(1)	T	PA
2	(2)	W	PA
1,2	(3)	W & T	2,1 &I
1	(4)	W $\rightarrow$ (W & T)	2-3 $\rightarrow$I
	(5)	T $\rightarrow$ [W $\rightarrow$ (W & T)]	1-4 $\rightarrow$I

My last example of a proof of a logical truth is provided by a politician in Lincoln County, Maine, who said:

If you take government away from the people, you're taking government away from the people.

Symbolized:

T $\rightarrow$ T

One way to construct a proof for this statement:

1	(1)	T	PA
1	(2)	$\sim$ $\sim$T	1 DN
1	(3)	T	2 DN
	(4)	T $\rightarrow$ T	1-3 $\rightarrow$I

For a given argument, a *corresponding conditional* can be formulated by employing this recipe:

> If the argument has one premise, make that premise the antecedent of a conditional whose consequent is the conclusion of the argument. If the argument has two or more premises, conjoin all premises and make the resulting conjunction the antecedent of a conditional whose consequent is the conclusion of the argument.

Two examples:

ARGUMENT	CORRESPONDING CONDITIONAL
$L \leftrightarrow M \vdash M \leftrightarrow L$	$(L \leftrightarrow M) \rightarrow (M \leftrightarrow L)$
$N \rightarrow O, N \vdash O$	$[(N \rightarrow O) \& N] \rightarrow O$

Every argument has a corresponding conditional, and every conditional corresponds to some argument. This logical principle emerges:

> An argument is valid iff its corresponding conditional is a logical truth.

Thus, it is possible to test arguments by examining conditionals and vice versa.

Some arguments contain premises that are logically true; exercise 83 (chapter seven) is such an argument. Because logical truths are without content, a logically true premise may be dropped from an argument without affecting the argument's validity (or invalidity). Can you construct a formal proof for exercise 83 that ignores its logically true premise?

12.2
Contradictions

A newspaper article included this sentence:

> (S1) Ralph was not white but he attended an all-white school.

If we interpret the expression 'all-white' strictly, so that it means "100 percent white," we must judge S1 false. We need not know Ralph's race or the racial composition of his school to know that S1 is false. S1 is false as a matter of logic; its truth is impossible. Statements whose truth is logically impossible are called *contradictions*.[3] Our present concern is with contra-

---

[3]Other labels: *logical contradictions*, *self-contradictions*, and *logically false statements*.

dictions falling within the scope of propositional logic; S1 is thus excluded. Some sample (abstract) propositional contradictions:

$$P \& \sim P$$
$$\sim Q \& \sim \sim Q$$
$$R \leftrightarrow \sim R$$
$$\sim (S \rightarrow S)$$
$$(T \rightarrow U) \& (T \& \sim U)$$

The denial of any logical truth is a contradiction, and the denial of any contradiction is a logical truth.

Since chapter five we have been using the concept of "standard contradiction." How does this concept relate to the just-introduced notion of "contradiction"? A standard contradiction is a special kind of contradiction—namely, a conjunctive contradiction whose right conjunct is the negation of its left conjunct. Standard contradictions are useful because they are easily identified by their form.

There is a truth-table method and a formal-proof method for showing that a statement belonging to propositional logic is a contradiction. Such a statement is a contradiction iff the column (in a full truth table) under its principal symbol is composed exclusively of F's. I'll illustrate the method with this statement:

> (S2) It is RAINING, but neither raining nor SNOWING.

The truth table:

R	S		R &	~(R ∨ S)	
T	T		F	F	T
F	T		F	F	T
T	F		F	F	T
F	F		F	T	F
				*	

The formal-proof method for demonstrating that a statement is a contradiction is to construct a proof in which the statement being evaluated occurs as an assumption and in which a *standard* contradiction is shown to depend on that assumption alone.

The justification for this method will be set forth in section 13.1. This formal proof shows that S2 is a contradiction:

(1)	R & ~(R ∨ S)	A
(2)	R	1 &O
(3)	~(R ∨ S)	1 &O
(4)	~R & ~S	3 DM
(5)	~R	4 &O
(6)	R & ~R	2,5 &I

As line 1 is the sole assumption in the proof, it is clear that the standard contradiction on line 6 depends only upon it.

A more complicated proof is required to demonstrate that S3 is a contradiction.

(S3) It is RAINING iff it is not raining.

The proof:

1	(1)	R ↔ ~R	A
1	(2)	R → ~R	1 ↔O
1	(3)	~R → R	1 ↔O
4	(4)	R	PA
1,4	(5)	~R	2,4 →O
1,4	(6)	R & ~R	4,5 &I
1	(7)	~R	4-6 ~I
1	(8)	R	3,7 →O
1	(9)	R & ~R	8,7 &I

An assumption-dependence column is required because the proof involves a provisional assumption. The proof could not be concluded on line 6 even though a standard contradiction was reached, for line 6 depends (partly) on an assumption other than line 1.

12.3
Contingent Statements

Statements that are neither logical truths nor contradictions are called *contingent*.[4] These are statements whose truth (or falsity) is not a matter of logic but is dependent or contingent on the way the world is actually structured. Consider S1 as an example.

(S1) Ted Kennedy is a Democrat.

S1 is true, but it is not logically true. It is true because it asserts to be the case something that happens to be the case. Most of the statements we encounter are contingent.

There is a truth-table method for establishing contingency, but there is no convenient formal-proof procedure for doing so. According to the truth-table test, a statement is contingent iff the column under its principal symbol contains at least one *T* and at least one *F*. To illustrate the method, let us examine S2.

[4]Other labels: *synthetic, factual.*

(S2) Ted Kennedy is a DEMOCRAT and a
          CATHOLIC.

The truth table:

D	C	D & C
T	T	T
F	T	F
T	F	F
F	F	F

The presence of both T's and F's in the third column indicates that S2 is contingent.

It should be clear from the definitions provided in this chapter that every statement is either a logical truth, a contradiction, or a contingent statement, and that no statement falls in two (or all three) of these categories. In logical terminology, the categories are *exhaustive* and *exclusive*.

The three truth-table tests explained in the chapter can be redescribed as one test:

Construct a full truth table for the statement to be tested. If the column under its principal symbol consists of T's only, the statement is logically true; if it consists of F's only, it is contradictory; and if it consists of both T's and F's, it is contingent.

The following table summarizes the material presented in the chapter:

	Statements			
	Truths		Falsities	
	LOGICAL TRUTHS	CONTINGENT TRUTHS	CONTINGENT FALSITIES	CONTRA-DICTIONS
Examples:	Either Kennedy is a Democrat or he is not a Democrat.	Kennedy is a Democrat.	Kennedy is a Republican.	Kennedy is a Democrat and he is not a Democrat.
Tests:	truth table, formal proof	~~truth table~~		truth table, formal proof

EXERCISES

Instructions for exercises 139 through 148: Symbolize the concrete statements. Test each statement by constructing a full truth table, and indicate whether it is ~~logically true~~ tautological, *contradictory, or contingent. Construct formal proofs for the* ~~logically true~~ tautological *and contradictory statements.*

> 139. When the head of the Longshoreman's Union was asked whether his union would boycott shipments to England if that country did not give autonomy to Northern Ireland, he answered:
>
> *I don't think we'll have to go that far unless we have to.*
>
> Let *H* abbreviate 'We have to go that far'.

> *140. Book advertisement blurb:
>
> *Scepticism and realism are each true, and mutually contradictory.*
>
> This may be paraphrased:
>
> SCEPTICISM and REALISM are each true, but it is not the case that they are both true.

> 141. If at least one of the children (Michael and Amy) is telling the truth, then both of them are.
>
> Use these symbols for exercises 141 through 143:
>
> *M* = Michael is telling the truth
> *A* = Amy is telling the truth

> 142. If both of the children (Michael and Amy) are telling the truth, then at least one of them is.

> 143. Both of the children (Michael and Amy) are telling the truth although at least one of them isn't.

> 144. $\sim[A \rightarrow (B \lor A)]$

> *145. $[(C \rightarrow D) \rightarrow C] \rightarrow C$

> 146. A television reporter describing a dilemma facing government officials said:
>
> *They're damned if they do or damned if they don't.*

Use these abbreviations:

A = They are damned
B = They do [take the action in question]

147.   The philosopher G. E. Moore[5] regards this statement as a contradiction:

If A had not had P, it would not have been true that A did not have P.

Is Moore correct? Let H abbreviate 'A has P' in this exercise and the next.

148.   A does not have P iff it is not true that A does not have P.

241.   (CHALLENGE) Each of the valid arguments listed below has a logically true premise. Construct a formal proof for each that ignores the logical truth.

(a)   Exercise 83 (chapter seven)
(b)   Exercise 125 (chapter ten)
(c)   Exercise 225 (chapter seven)

242.   (CHALLENGE)

(a)   Think of a monadic English statement connective that will produce a logical truth when prefixed to any statement.
(b)   Think of a monadic English statement connective that will produce a contradiction when prefixed to any statement.
(c)   Think of a dyadic English statement connective that will produce a logical truth when placed between any two statements.
(d)   Think of a dyadic English statement connective that will produce a contradiction when placed between any two statements.

[5]See *Philosophical Studies* (Totowa, N.J.: Littlefield, Adams, 1965), p. 283.

13

Logical Relations

13.1
Entailment

In this chapter we shall examine closely two logical relations that can obtain between statements: entailment and logical equivalence.[1] These relations were introduced in section 3.3 and have been mentioned frequently in succeeding chapters. *Entailment* is the more fundamental relation; its definition:

> One statement entails a second iff it is logically impossible for
> the first to be true and the second false.

The concepts of "entailment" and "validity" are tightly related. The premise of a one-premised argument entails its conclusion when and only when the argument is valid. We can show that one statement entails another by devising a full or brief truth table or a formal proof; we can establish that some statement does *not* entail another by constructing a full or brief truth table.

---

[1] We shall concentrate on pairs of statements whose logical relationships can be satisfactorily determined within propositional logic. This restriction should be understood even though it is frequently unstated.

Two properties of entailment should be noted:

1. Every statement entails itself.
2. Whenever one statement entails a second and the second entails a third, the first entails the third.

In logicians' terminology the relation of entailment is (1) *reflexive* and (2) *transitive*.

When we combine the concept of "entailment" with the concepts of "logical truth" and "contradiction," four more logical principles result:

3. Any statement entails a logical truth.
4. A logical truth entails only logical truths.
5. A contradiction entails any statement.
6. Only contradictions entail a contradiction.

Principles 3 and 4 conform to the observation made in chapter twelve that a logical truth lacks informative content. The last two principles correspond to the observation that a contradiction has maximum content; it claims more than can possibly be true.

Principle 5 is captured in the familiar aphorism, "Anything follows from a contradiction." The other three principles, though not part of our heritage of common sense, are equally sound. I will defend principles 3 and 4; you can argue for 5 and 6.

A defense of principle 3:

Let *L* be some logical truth and *A* a statement selected at random. It is logically impossible for L to be false. So, clearly, it is logically impossible for A to be true and L false. Therefore (by the definition of *entailment*), A entails L.

The following abstract argument, which has a logically true conclusion, is an instance of principle 3:

$$A \vdash B \lor \sim B$$

It might be instructive to establish its validity by truth table or formal proof or both. My proof has six lines.

A justification of principle 4:

Let *L* be some logical truth and *A* a randomly selected statement that is not a logical truth. Then, it is logically possible for A to be false. So (as L is true no matter what), it is logically possible for L to be true and A false. Therefore (by the definition of *entailment*), L does not entail A.

Exercise 212 (in chapter five) concerned this abstract argument:

$$A \ \& \sim A \vdash B$$

Its validity is an instance of principle 5. You may want to demonstrate its validity by truth table or (if you have not already done so) by formal proof.

In section 12.2 I explained a method for proving that a statement is a contradiction. The method involves showing that the statement entails a standard contradiction. Principle 6 provides the rationale for this procedure. Since only contradictions entail a contradiction, any statement that entails a standard contradiction must itself be a contradiction.

13.2
Logical Equivalence

Logical equivalence may be defined in terms of "entailment":

> One statement is logically equivalent to a second iff each entails the other.

So logical equivalence is mutual entailment. If one statement is logically equivalent to another, the two statements have the same content — they make the same claim. Examples may be useful. Each wff in the following lists is logically equivalent to the other wff on the same row:

A	A & A
A	A ∨ A
A	~A → A
B & C	C & B
D ∨ E	E ∨ D
F ↔ G	G ↔ F
F ↔ G	~F ↔ ~G
H ↔ ~I	~(H ↔ I)
H ↔ ~I	~H ↔ I
J & (K & L)	(J & K) & L
M ∨ (N ∨ O)	(M ∨ N) ∨ O
P ↔ (Q ↔ R)	(P ↔ Q) ↔ R
S → (T → U)	(S & T) → U
S → (T → U)	T → (S → U)

Many of these examples are old friends from earlier chapters (where the issue was entailment rather than logical equivalence). The derived inference rules of Double Negation, DeMorgan's Law, Arrow, and Contraposition suggest twelve additional examples of pairs of logically equivalent statements.

There is a formal-proof method as well as a truth-table method for establishing that one statement is logically equivalent to another. The former method consists in constructing two proofs which show that each statement entails the other. There are two main cases of the principle of distribution:

$$A \& (B \lor C) \quad (A \& B) \lor (A \& C)$$
$$D \lor (E \& F) \quad (D \lor E) \& (D \lor F)$$

The logical equivalence of the first pair of wffs was demonstrated in chapter seven. I now prove the equivalence of the second pair of wffs by constructing two proofs. I use the Arrow strategy (twice in the first proof and once in the second).

1	(1)	D ∨ (E & F)	A
2	(2)	~D	PA
1,2	(3)	E & F	1,2 DA
1,2	(4)	E	3 &O
1	(5)	~D → E	2-4 →I
1	(6)	D ∨ E	5 AR
1,2	(7)	F	3 &O
1	(8)	~D → F	2-7 →I
1	(9)	D ∨ F	8 AR
1	(10)	(D ∨ E) & (D ∨ F)	6,9 &I

1	(1)	(D ∨ E) & (D ∨ F)	A
2	(2)	~D	PA
1	(3)	D ∨ E	1 &O
1,2	(4)	E	3,2 DA
1	(5)	D ∨ F	1 &O
1,2	(6)	F	5,2 DA
1,2	(7)	E & F	4,6 &I
1	(8)	~D → (E & F)	2-7 →I
1	(9)	D ∨ (E & F)	8 AR

The truth-table test for logical equivalence employs this principle:

One statement is ~~logically~~ TF- equivalent to another iff there is no row where one statement is true and the other false.

I promised in section 7.1 to demonstrate that F1 is logically equivalent to F2.

(F1) (C ∨ M) & ~(C & M)
(F2) C ↔ ~M

I satisfy that promise now with this truth table:

C M	(C ∨ M)	& ~ (C & M)	C ↔ ~M	
T T	T	F F	T	F F
F T	T	T T	F	T F
T F	T	T T	F	T T
F F	F	F T	F	F T
		*		*

On no row does one starred column contain a *T* and the other column an *F*; so, each wff is logically equivalent to the other.

In section 2.2 I claimed that F3 is not logically equivalent to F4.

    (F3) A → (B → C)
    (F4) (A → B) → C

We can support that claim with this truth table:

A B C	A → (B → C)		(A → B) → C	
T T T	T	T	T	T
F T T	T	T	T	T
T F T	T	T	F	T
F F T	T	T	T	T
T T F	F	F	T	F
F T F	T	F	T	F
T F F	T	T	F	T
F F F	T	T	T	F
	*			*

Either circled row is sufficient to establish that F3 is not logically equivalent to F4.

We can also demonstrate nonequivalence by constructing a brief truth table. The procedure:

Make a goal assignment of *T* to (either) one of the statements and *F* to the other statement. If the remaining assignments are completed consistently, the statements are not logically equivalent.

Some of the properties of logical equivalence:

1. Every statement is logically equivalent to itself.
2. Whenever one statement is logically equivalent to a second and the second is logically equivalent to a third, the first is logically equivalent to the third.
3. Whenever one statement is logically equivalent to a second, the second is logically equivalent to the first.

That is, the relation of logical equivalence is (1) reflexive, (2) transitive, and (3) *symmetrical*. (Note that entailment is *not* symmetrical.) Because logical equivalence is symmetrical, an alternative way of claiming that one statement *is logically equivalent to* another is to say that the two statements *are logically equivalent*. This latter phrase was used regularly in preceding chapters.

When we combine the concept of "logical equivalence" with the concepts of "logical truth" and "contradiction," two more principles result:

4.   Any two logical truths are logically equivalent.
5.   Any two contradictions are logically equivalent.

Principle 4 is a consequence of the fact that any statement entails a logical truth, taken together with the definition of *logical equivalence*. Principle 5 follows from the fact that a contradiction entails any statement, in conjunction with the definition. You should study these two claims until you understand them.

For any pair of statements a *corresponding biconditional* can be formed by placing a double arrow between them. This logical principle holds:

Two statements are logically equivalent iff the biconditional formed from them is logically true.

So, it is possible to test for logical equivalence by examining a biconditional.

Entailment and logical equivalence are not the only logical relations that can hold between a pair of statements. Of the remaining relations, I will comment on *consistency*. A definition:

One statement is consistent with a second iff it is logically possible for both statements to be true.

The relation of consistency is symmetrical but neither reflexive nor transitive.

Consistency can be checked by a full truth table:

One statement is consistent with a second iff there is a row where both statements are true.

Lack of consistency — that is, *inconsistency* — can be established by the procedure just described. It can also be demonstrated by the formal-proof method:

One statement is inconsistent with a second if a standard contradiction is derived from them.

The standard contradiction, of course, must depend on no other assumptions.

Since consistency and inconsistency are symmetrical relations, expressions like 'mutually consistent' and 'mutually inconsistent' (or 'mutually contradictory') are redundant.

EXERCISES

Instructions for exercises 149 through 155 (and 243-44): Symbolize where required. Test each pair of statements for logical equivalence by constructing a full truth table. If they are equivalent, redemonstrate this with two formal proofs.

149. In section 3.3 I asked whether the arrow is a *commutative* connective. That amounts to asking whether F1 and F2 are logically equivalent. Are they?

(F1) A → B
(F2) B → A

150. A news story carries this headline:

Teachers could EXPEL, SPANK only if law were CHANGED[2]

F1 is one correct symbolization of this headline.

(F1) (E → C) & (S → C)

The first paragraph of the story begins:

Changes in the law would be required to allow teachers to expel students or paddle them.

This sentence may be symbolized by F2.

(F2) (E v S) → C

Do the headline and the lead sentence make the same claim? Find out by determining whether F1 and F2 are logically equivalent.

*151. Matthew 6:14-15:

. . . If YOU forgive men their trespasses, your heavenly FATHER also will forgive you; but if you do not forgive men their trespasses, neither will your Father forgive your trespasses.[3]

[2]*Miami News* (April 8, 1971), p. 6-A.
[3]Revised Standard Version (New York: Thomas Nelson & Sons, 1952).

Are the two conjuncts logically equivalent (thereby making the passage redundant)?

152. Exercise 219(d) involves symbolizing this sentence:

A 'no' from one of us (MOTHER and FATHER) means a 'no' from both of us.

Here are two symbolizations:

(M v F) → (M & F)
M ↔ F

Are they equivalent?

153. The University of Miami *Faculty Manual* proclaims:

The decision [to use faculty-produced teaching material] shall be made by the instructor or by the department and approved by the department chairman.[4]

This ambiguous sentence could be understood in either of the following ways (the author doubtless intended S1).

(S1) The decision shall be made by the INSTRUCTOR or the DEPARTMENT, and it shall be APPROVED by the department chairman.

(S2) Either the decision shall be made by the instructor, or it shall be made by the department and approved by the department chairman.

Are S1 and S2 logically equivalent?

* 154. In his article, "Ifs, Cans and Causes,"[5] philosopher Keith Lehrer is anxious to show that the statement 'I can' is not properly analyzed as 'I shall, if I choose'. In the middle of an extended argument he makes the claim that the following two statements are logically equivalent:

(S1) I SHALL, if I CHOOSE.
(S2) I shall if I choose, if I choose.

His argument depends on the logical equivalence of S1 and S2. Are they equivalent?

---

[4]*Faculty Manual 1980-81*, p. 53.
[5]*Analysis*, XX (1960), 122-24.

155. Bertrand Russell writes:

> . . . *State ownership of land . . . was no advance unless the State was democratic, and even then only if methods were devised for curbing the power of officials.*[6]

This wff is one correct symbolization of Russell's claim:

$(\sim D \rightarrow \sim A)\ \&\ [D \rightarrow (A \rightarrow C)]$

Is Russell's statement logically equivalent to the following simpler statement?

State ownership of land is an ADVANCE only if the state is DEMOCRATIC and methods are devised for CURBING the power of officials.

156. Philosopher Ramon Lemos concludes an argument with this assertion:

> . . . *Both [the teleological and the deontological] forms of egoism are false if either [the teleological or the deontological] form of non-egoism is true, and both forms of non-egoism are false if either form of egoism is true.*[7]

Is there a difference in content between the two conjuncts in this statement, or are the conjuncts logically equivalent? Use these symbols:

A = Teleological egoism is true
B = Deontological egoism is true
C = Teleological non-egoism is true
F = Deontological non-egoism is true

Make an intuitive assessment; then, either establish logical equivalence by means of formal proofs or demonstrate nonequivalence by devising a brief truth table. In this way you avoid constructing a 16-row full truth table.

243. (CHALLENGE) On a logic test I asked my students to symbolize this statement:

[6] *The Autobiography of Bertrand Russell* (Boston: Little, Brown, 1968), II: 277.
[7] "Egoism and Non-egoism in Ethics," *Southern Journal of Philosophy*, IX (Winter, 1971), 382.

At least two of these three will come: AL, BILL, and CHARLIE.

I expected them to employ F1, but one student offered F2.

(F1)   [(A & B) v (A & C)] v (B & C)
(F2)   [~ A → (B & C)] & [A → (B v C)]

Given my grading policy that a symbolization is worth full credit iff it is equivalent to a correct answer, and given that F1 is correct, how should I have graded F2?

244.   (CHALLENGE) This sentence appeared on another logic exam:

Exactly two of these people will participate: TED, JOHN, and NORBERT.

I expected F1, but one student used F2.

(F1)   {[(T & J) v (T & N)] v (J & N)} & ~ [(T & J) & N]
(F2)   {[(T & J) & ~ N] v [(T & N) & ~ J]} v [(J & N) & ~ T]

Are these wffs equivalent?

245.   (CHALLENGE) In exercise 28 (at the end of chapter four) I note that

. . . every *statement is logically equivalent to some — perhaps quite involved — conditional formula.*

Formulate a conditional wff that is logically equivalent to S1.

(S1)   It is RAINING.

Devise a second such wff.

246.   (CHALLENGE) A bumper sticker proclaims:

(S1)   If you ain't country, you ain't shit.

This seems to be logically equivalent to S2:

(S2)   If you're shit, you're country.

Yet while S1 is *pro*country, S2 is obviously *anti*country. Resolve this puzzle.

247.   (CHALLENGE) Solve the puzzle.

1 Y	2 E	3 S	■	4 E	5 R	6 R
7 E	E	E	■	8 A	D	U
9 T	D	E	■	10		
■	■	11			■	■
12	13		■	14	15	16
17			■	18		
19			■	20		

ACROSS

1. Is 'P → Q' true if 'Q' is true?
4. What you do if you try to apply a primitive rule to part of a line.
7. Logically equivalent to '~(~E ∨ ~R)'.
8. Inconsistent with '~A & U'.
9. Digit.
10. Sea terror.
11. She cannot help you with logic.
12. Paris pal.
14. A wff full of arrows.
17. Entailed by 'S & Y'.
18. From 'E' by VI.
19. French summer.
20. Conjunction words (Fr.).

DOWN

1. Conjunction word.
2. Logically equivalent to 'E & O'.
3. Assumption.
4. Assumption.
5. A is a *sine qua non* for I.
6. Does '~(L & M)' entail '~(L ∨ M)'?
12. Is '~(K & S)' false if 'K' is true and '~S' is false?
13. We'll see a MOVIE this week iff we receive our TAX refund.
15. Entailed by 'T ↔ ~F'.
16. Is "consistency" symmetrical?

14

Natural Arguments

14.1
Identification

Deductive arguments occur in every medium involving language. They crop up in conversations, editorials, lectures, comic strips, novels, television programs, poems, scriptures, films, posters, and so on. Such sources constitute the natural habitat of arguments. Let's call arguments occurring in these sources *natural arguments*. Natural arguments differ in significant ways from *artificial arguments*, which have been invented by logicians to illustrate various logical forms or to provide practice in employing logical methods. The major difference between a natural argument and an artificial one is that the former was actually advanced by someone as an argument while the latter was not. This fact adds to the interest of natural arguments. Natural arguments often differ in other ways from their artificial cousins. Artificial arguments are usually stated in "standard form." Every essential element is explicitly expressed; no extraneous material is present; the conclusion is written after the premises. Natural arguments are almost never in standard form. Important parts may be missing, and material that is irrelevant from the standpoint of logic is probably included; the conclusion may appear before, after, or in the midst of the premises.

The main aim of a course in applied logic is to enhance the student's skill in assessing natural arguments. But natural arguments cannot be assessed unless they are identified as arguments. Familiarity with artificial arguments does not guarantee the ability to spot arguments in the "wild." Many conventional texts contain only artificial examples and exercises; they may provide excellent instruction in pure logic, but they do not help the reader *apply* the logic that has been learned.

In writing this text, I have done two things designed to help you apply propositional logic to natural arguments. First, I have in the exercises and examples of preceding chapters frequently presented natural arguments by using direct quotations. Often, these natural arguments were followed by my reformulations. I hoped by doing this to familiarize you with the style of natural arguments and to emphasize the differences between natural arguments and their purified reformulations. The second effort I have made to help you apply propositional logic is to include (in the present chapter) suggestions for identifying, formalizing, and assessing natural arguments.

The proof of the pudding is in the eating; the test of your skills in handling natural arguments is in your working through the exercise set at the end of this chapter. That exercise set contains a number of natural arguments belonging to propositional logic. I hope that you can assess most of them with little difficulty.

The task of assessing a natural argument may be broken down for pedagogical purposes into four subtasks:

1. identification
2. formalization
3. evaluation of form
4. evaluation of content

The first three jobs fall within the scope of logic; to each of these I devote one section of this chapter. The fourth task involves judging the truth-value of the premises of the argument. As natural arguments cover all conceivable topics, skill in this area cannot be taught in one course or one book. Your total education (not just formal schooling) contributes to your ability to accurately assess the content of natural arguments.

How does one determine that a section of discourse contains an argument? In the main, one recognizes that a passage is argumentative by (a) having a grasp of the nature of argument and (b) understanding the passage in question. There are no foolproof clues—no certain indicators—of the presence of an argument. Nevertheless, the premise-introducing terms (such as 'since') and conclusion-introducing words (like 'therefore') are fairly reliable indicators. They are not foolproof clues for two reasons: (1) many argumentative passages contain none of these terms; and (2) some passages that contain one or more of these words do not express arguments.

Some dialogue from the film *Star Wars*[1] provides an example of argumentative discourse that lacks these indicator terms. Darth Vader and his storm troopers board Princess Leia's rebel starship and confront members of the crew.

> DARTH VADER: Where are those transmissions you intercepted?
>
> [*Vader grips the rebel by the throat.*]
>
> REBEL: We intercepted no transmissions. This is a consular ship. We're on a diplomatic mission.
>
> VADER: If this is a consular ship, where is the ambassador?
>
> [*Vader chokes the rebel to death.*]

How do we recognize that an argument is being employed here? In following the dialogue we realize that Vader is rejecting a claim made by the rebel and that he is giving a reason supporting the rejection. Of course, giving a reason involves advancing an argument. I shall discuss the structure of this argument in the next section.

An example of a passage which employs a conclusion-introducing word ('so') but which does not present an argument comes from a children's book:

> The sun was very hot and Harry had walked a long way from the main beach. He was tired, so he sat down at the water's edge.[2]

Even though these clues are fallible, they are definitely worth bearing in mind.

A second group of indicator words is composed of statement connectives such as 'if . . . then', 'and', and so on. This set of clues is less reliable than the indicators just discussed. Quite often, compound statements occur in nonargumentative discourse. Nevertheless, because virtually every propositional argument contains one or more of these statement connectives, they provide useful clues. Note that Darth Vader's remark contained an 'if'.

In chapter one we defined an *argument* as a set of statements, one of which (the conclusion) supposedly follows from the others (the premises). The most common use of an argument is to support the statement that occurs as the argument's conclusion — to provide a reason for thinking the conclusion true. The person advancing the argument hopes that the premises will be recognized as true and that this recognition will lead to an acceptance of the conclusion. If you determine that in a given block of discourse the author (speaker) aims to convince the reader (listener) of the truth of something, then this piece of discourse probably contains one or more arguments.

[1]Written and directed by George Lucas. A Lucasfilm Ltd. Production. A Twentieth-Century-Fox Release.

[2]Gene Zion, *Harry by the Sea* (New York: Harper & Row, Pub., 1965), no pagination.

Providing support for statements is the primary use to which arguments are put, but it is not their sole use. Sometimes we employ arguments to provide *explanations* of already granted facts. The purpose in such an instance is not to establish some statement as true but (assuming that it is true) to explain *why* it is true. The statement being explained appears as the conclusion of the argument; the premises constitute the explanation. Consider an example from a sports story on Superbowl XIV:

> *To win, the Cowboys knew they had to rush Bradshaw, not give him any time to look for his receivers and get his passes off. Thanks to the joint effort by Kolb and Davis in holding off White and Martin, Bradshaw had all the time he needed, and he used it to set a pair of Superbowl passing records by passing for 318 yards and four touchdowns.* [3]

We can pick out this argument:

> Rushing Bradshaw was a necessary condition for a Cowboy victory. Bradshaw was not rushed. Hence, the Cowboys did not win.

Notice that the point of the passage is not to *prove* that the Cowboys lost. The point is to *explain* the loss. Passages that convey explanations are likely to contain arguments.

14.2
Formalization

Having determined that some piece of discourse contains an argument, the next task is to *formalize* that argument—that is, to abstract from the passage a purified or regularized version of the argument. Formalizing an argument may involve any or all of the following:

1. identifying the premises and conclusion (and placing the latter last)
2. rephrasing so as to make apparent the connections between statements
3. eliminating extraneous material
4. expressing elements that, although not stated in the original, are essential parts of the argument.

When an argument has been adequately formalized, it is ordinarily easy to symbolize.

I will illustrate this process of formalization with several examples.

---

[3] *Valley News Dispatch* (January 23, 1979), p. 3-D.

While walking through Long Pine Key Campground in Everglades National Park, my son Mike (aged five) pointed to a travel trailer and said:

That one has TV because it has an antenna.

He was giving a reason for believing that a certain travel trailer (call it *A*) sports a television set. A little effort results in this incomplete formalization:

> A has an antenna.
> So A has a TV.

It is clear that this version of the argument lacks a crucial premise — one that notes a connection between being equipped with an antenna and possessing a TV. Although no premise of this sort was overtly asserted by Mike, it is reasonable to suppose that he took some such premise for granted. What is the suppressed premise? Two candidates:

> (P1) If A has an antenna, then it has a TV.
> (P2) If A has a TV, then it has an antenna.

How do we choose between these statements? If we select P1, the resulting argument will be àn instance of *modus ponens*; if we select P2, the argument will commit the fallacy of affirming the consequent. In view of the fact that people use valid deductive arguments much more often than invalid ones, and in the absence of any indication that Mike was committing a logical error, we adopt P1. We thereby settle on formulation A1:

> (A1) A has an antenna.
> If A has an antenna, then it has a TV.
> So A has a TV.

(The order of the premises is unimportant.)
  Mike's argument could also be formulated in a rather different way:

> (A2) A has an antenna.
> A is a travel trailer.
> All travel trailers that have antennas have
>   TVs.
> So A has a TV.

A2 is a valid deductive argument that falls outside the scope of propositional logic. (Notice that it does not contain a single compound statement.) Both A1 and A2 are plausible formalizations of Mike's argument. Without questioning Mike, it is probably impossible to determine which better represents his inference. Because we are studying propositional logic, we naturally prefer A1. If we had also examined the logic of A2, then the choice between the two formulations might be a tossup.

An argument with one or more missing elements is called an *enthymeme*.[4] Most natural arguments are enthymemes. The missing parts may be premises or the conclusion or both. In the original version of the "antenna" argument a premise was suppressed. Darth Vader's argument has an unstated premise and an unstated conclusion. Vader asks the question, 'If this is a consular ship, where is the ambassador?' He is refuting the rebel's claim that the cruiser is a consular ship, citing as evidence the absence of an ambassador. Vader's inference is *modus tollens*:

> If this is a consular ship, there is an ambassador on board.
> There is no ambassador on board.
> Therefore, this is not a consular ship.

One could also give a more complex interpretation of Vader's reasoning with an argument whose conclusion is reflected in Vader's act of killing the rebel.

> If you are telling the truth, this is a consular ship. If this is a consular ship, there is an ambassador on board. There is no ambassador on board. If you are not telling the truth, you are a rebel. Therefore, you are a rebel.

A final example of an enthymematic argument derives from a conversation with a colleague concerning a mutual acquaintance. My colleague said:

> *Royer's degree must not be in philosophy because Bowling Green does not give the Ph.D. in philosophy.*

A first attempt at formalization yields the following:

> Bowling Green does not give the Ph.D. in philosophy.
> Royer's Ph.D. is from Bowling Green.
> Thus, Royer's Ph.D. is not in philosophy.

Notice that no simple statement occurs more than once in this formalization. An additional premise joining the parts of the argument is required for satisfactory treatment by propositional logic. A little thought suggests this premise:

> If Royer's Ph.D. is in philosophy and from Bowling Green, then Bowling Green does give the Ph.D. in philosophy.

When we add this obviously true premise, the resulting argument is assessed as valid by the methods of propositional logic.

[4]Pronounced "EN'-THI-MEEM."

I shall conclude this discussion by comparing the process of formalization with the translation of a passage from one natural language (say, English) to another (German). It is not true that there is just one correct German translation of a given English passage; there can be several. But, on the other hand, it is not the case that *any* translation is as good as any other; some will definitely be defective. In the same way there will ordinarily be several distinct satisfactory formalizations of the argument contained in some passage; yet, some formalizations will obviously be incorrect. A further analogy between formalization and translation should be noted: in both activities skill is gained largely through practice. The passages at the end of this chapter will provide practice in the art of formalizing arguments.

14.3
Evaluation

Having formalized an argument, you should be able to judge whether it falls within the scope of propositional logic. If the argument is not propositional, then (at this stage in your study of logic) you are forced to fall back upon your native logical intuition. The chances are that this intuitive assessment will be correct. If this approach leaves you unsatisfied, you will want to explore additional branches of logic. One area of logic which is built upon propositional logic and which can adequately treat many arguments that are beyond the capacity of propositional logic is called *predicate logic* or *quantificational logic*.

If the formalized argument in question is propositional, it should be symbolized. The argument may exhibit a familiar pattern whose validity (or invalidity) you have established; in this case further testing is unnecessary.[5] Although there is an infinite variety of forms of valid propositional arguments, most of the valid propositional arguments one encounters can be sorted out among a small group of argument patterns. Likewise, although there exists an infinite variety of forms of invalid propositional arguments, most of the invalid propositional arguments one actually encounters exhibit one or another of a few basic forms. The most common valid and invalid patterns are listed in the table below. Each pattern was discussed in some earlier chapter.

If the argument under examination is propositional but exhibits an unfamiliar logical form, you can evaluate it with the formal-proof or truth-table methods that we have examined in detail in the preceding chapters.

[5]At the end of section 9.3 I noted that it is possible for a valid argument to be a substitution instance of an invalid argument-form. In practice this possibility can be safely ignored.

Common Argument Patterns

	Valid	Invalid	
NAME	PATTERN	PATTERN	NAME
modus ponens	$P{\to}Q,\ P \vdash Q$	$P{\to}Q,\ Q \vdash P$	affirming the consequent
modus tollens	$P{\to}Q,\ {\sim}Q \vdash {\sim}P$	$P{\to}Q,\ {\sim}P \vdash {\sim}Q$	denying the antecedent
disjunctive argument	$P{\vee}Q,\ {\sim}P \vdash Q$ $P{\vee}Q,\ {\sim}Q \vdash P$	$P{\vee}Q,\ P \vdash {\sim}Q$ $P{\vee}Q,\ Q \vdash {\sim}P$	affirming a disjunct
conjunctive argument	${\sim}(P\&Q),\ P \vdash {\sim}Q$ ${\sim}(P\&Q),\ Q \vdash {\sim}P$	${\sim}(P\&Q),\ {\sim}P \vdash Q$ ${\sim}(P\&Q),\ {\sim}Q \vdash P$	denying a conjunct
chain argument	$P{\to}Q,\ Q{\to}R \vdash P{\to}R$		
dilemma	$P{\to}Q,\ R{\to}Q,\ P{\vee}R \vdash Q$ $P{\to}Q,\ R{\to}S,\ P{\vee}R \vdash Q{\vee}S$		

EXERCISES

Instructions for exercises 157 through 180 (and 248-49): For each passage determine whether it contains an argument. Label nonargumentative passages 'No Argument'. For argumentative passages follow steps (1) through (3). (1) Formalize the argument taking care to supply any suppressed elements. (2) Symbolize the argument, indicating for each capital employed the statement it abbreviates. (3) Make an intuitive assessment; then, either demonstrate the argument's validity by formal proof or full (or brief) truth table, or establish invalidity by truth table.

157. "If the stock market never fluctuated, then stock would have no market risk. Of course, the market does fluctuate, so market risk is present."

— Eugene F. Brigham, *Fundamentals of Financial Management* (Hinsdale, Ill.: Dryden Press, 1978), p. 116.

*158. A radio advertisement for American Motors cars extols their warranty, then delivers this slogan:

If we weren't building them better, we couldn't back them better.

159. On an episode of the television series *Battlestar Galactica*, Commander Adama (played by Lorne Green) says:

If we don't have seeds we can't have food. If we don't have food we'll all perish.

*160. "He discovered that he had a scorching thirst. His face was so dry and grimy that he thought he could feel his skin crackle. Each bone of his body had an ache in it, and seemingly threatened to break with each movement. His feet were like two sores. Also, his body was calling for food. It was more powerful than a direct hunger. There was a dull, weightlike feeling in his stomach, and, when he tried to walk, his head swayed and he tottered."

> — Stephen Crane, *The Red Badge of Courage and Selected Stories*
> (New York: New American Library, 1980), p. 70.

161. "I'm getting married on December 31 in Dallas but I won't get to Texas in time to have a blood test taken there. If I can't get a blood test, I can't get a license. No license — no wedding. I'm in a jam. What do I do? — J. B."

> — "Action Line," *Miami Herald* (December 5, 1977), pp. 23-A.

162. "But of course mice are famous for something," [Maximilian said].
        "Don't be so sure," said the monkey as Maximilian turned to go. "If you're famous, why aren't you in the zoo?" called the monkey as Maximilian scampered away.
        ". . . They're right," he decided. "If mice were famous for anything, they'd have one in the zoo. And they don't."

> — Florence Heide, *Maximilian Becomes Famous*
> (New York: Funk & Wagnalls, 1969), no pagination.

163. "IF YOU LIKE THE POSTAL SERVICE YOU'LL LOVE NATIONALIZED GAS."

> — Automobile bumper sticker.

164. ". . . (i) If the thing b has the disposition D_{SR} and the condition S is fulfilled for b, then . . . the result R holds for b.
        "Therefore:
        "(ii) If S holds for b, but R does not, then b cannot have the disposition D_{SR}."

> — Rudolf Carnap, "The Methodological Character of Theoretical
> Concepts," in *Minnesota Studies in the Philosophy of Science*,
> ed. Herbert Feigl and Michael Scriven (Minneapolis:
> University of Minnesota Press, 1956), I: 67.

165. "In his last public statement before the Hanoi offensive, President Nixon said that if the South Vietnamese lines do not 'break' under attacks from the North, 'it will be the final proof that Vietnamization has succeeded.' Therefore, if the lines do break, the converse

would presumably be true, and Mr. Nixon would have to concede that Vietnamization has indeed failed."

—Victor Zorza, "Hanoi Points to General Uprising,"
Christian Science Monitor (Boston) (April 5, 1972), p. 16.

166.   "And when they drew near to Jerusalem and came to Bethphage, to the Mount of Olives, then Jesus sent two disciples, saying to them, 'Go into the village opposite you, and immediately you will find an ass tied, and a colt with her; untie them and bring them to me. If anyone says anything to you, you shall say, "The Lord has need of them," and he will send them immediately.'"

—Matthew 21:1-3, Revised Standard Version
(New York: Thomas Nelson & Sons, 1952).

167.   "CHICAGO—A tip on the eventual victor tonight should come in the early moments of the annual game between the pro football champions, this time the Pittsburgh Steelers, and the College All-Stars. . . .

"'If we can't protect the passer, we'll have very little chance,' [All-Stars coach John] McKay said. 'If we can't run it'll be almost impossible to protect the passer because they'll know he's going to pass and just tee off on him.'"

—"Stars Bid to Upset Steelers,"
Miami Herald (August 1, 1975), p. 1-F.

168.   "So, if utilitarianism is true, . . . then it is better that people should not believe in utilitarianism. If, on the other hand, it is false, then it is certainly better that people should not believe in it. So, either way, it is better that people should not believe in it."

—Bernard Williams, *Morality: An Introduction to Ethics*
(New York: Harper & Row, Pub., 1972), p. 107.

169.

© King Features Syndicate, Inc., 1977.

170. "Hayden oil coolers — If you've got money to burn, you don't need one."

— Radio advertisement.

171. "Finally, if stress and cancer are linked, wouldn't people subjected to unusual degrees of stress — prisoners of war, for instance — show higher rates of cancer later on in their lives? Robert J. Keehn of the Medical Follow-up Agency of the National Academy of Sciences National Research Council recently looked at this particular phenomenon. After studying former World War II and Korean War prisoners, Keehn found their cancer death rates were no different from cancer death rates in the population at large."

— M. Scarf, "Images That Heal,"
Psychology Today, XIV (September, 1980), 43.

172.

MILES TO GO by Phil Frank. ©1982. Field Enterprises, Inc.
Courtesy of Field Newspaper Syndicate.

173. "We find puzzling the extent to which liberals often seem impelled to weaken the economic structure on which not just social progress, but indeed our national livelihood depends. To them we suggest the following, oversimplified but nevertheless pointing up the heart of the matter:

"Without adequate profits, no businesses.

"Without businesses, no jobs.

"Without jobs, no social programs."

— Part of a Mobil Oil Corporation advertisement in the
New York Review of Books (June 15, 1978),
p. 11. © 1978 Mobil Corporation.

174. "And he went on from there, and entered their synagogue. And behold, there was a man with a withered hand. And they asked him, 'Is it lawful to heal on the sabbath?' so that they might accuse him.

He said to them, 'What man of you, if he has one sheep, and it falls into a pit on the sabbath, will not lay hold of it and lift it out? Of how much more value is a man than a sheep! So it is lawful to do good on the sabbath.' "

> —Matthew 12:9-12, Revised Standard Version
> (New York: Thomas Nelson & Sons, 1952).

175.

By permission of Johnny Hart and Field Enterprises, Inc.

176.   "President Reagan is back in Washington after what arguably was the most extraordinary 10 days of his Presidency to date. For the first time since he assumed the mantle of leader of the Western world, Ronald Reagan embarked upon what once was known as 'the Grand Tour.' His performance earned mixed reviews, yet on balance the experience seems decidedly worthy."

> —"Presidential Tour," *Miami Herald* (June 13, 1982), p. 2-E.

177.   "I was particularly anxious to learn . . . why the Nile, at the commencement of the summer solstice, begins to rise, and continues to increase for a hundred days—and why, as soon as that number is past, it forthwith retires and contracts its stream, continuing low during the whole of the winter until the summer solstice comes round again. On none of these points could I obtain any explanation from the inhabitants. . . .

"Some of the Greeks, however, wishing to get a reputation for cleverness, have offered explanations of the phenomena of the river. . . . One pretends that the Etesian winds cause the rise of the river by preventing the Nile-water from running off into the sea. But . . . if the Etesian winds produced the effect, the other rivers which flow in a direction opposite to those winds ought to present the same phenomena as the Nile, and the more so as they are all smaller streams, and have a weaker current. But these rivers, of which there are many both in Syria and Libya, are entirely unlike the Nile in this respect."

> —Herodotus, *History*, trans. George Rawlinson
> (New York: Dutton, 1910), Vol. I, Book II, Chapters 19-20.

178.

April 16, 1972. © 1972 United Feature Syndicate, Inc.

179.   A film about the French Foreign Legion, *Desert Sands* (United Artists), includes this dialogue:

CAPTAIN: Well, Lieutenant, I guess we'd better turn in.

LIEUTENANT: Sir, I thought we'd wait up for the [relief] column.

CAPTAIN: Oh, sitting up all night may sound more romantic, Lieutenant, but it's not going to help them much. If everything is all right, then we've lost a lot of sleep for nothing. If it isn't — I'd rather we got some sleep now. Good night, Lieutenant.

180.   "NEW YORK — (UPI) — If it was the greatest bar mitzvah you ever attended and the filet mignon was delicious, well then, Mrs. Bess Myerson Grant says something isn't kosher.

"The New York City consumer affairs commissioner said that many supposedly kosher catering firms are violating Jewish dietary laws by serving filet mignon at bar mitzvahs and weddings.

"Mrs. Grant pointed out that filet mignon is not a kosher cut of meat, which represents a fraud. If the caterers are substituting another kosher cut and calling it 'filet mignon' it's still fraud. . . .

" 'Either they are substituting a different, probably cheaper, cut of meat, or they are violating their contractual obligation to prepare meals in accordance with Hebrew dietary requirements,' she said.

. . .

"'One way or another, they're acting against the law,' she said."

— "Something Isn't Kosher: Caterers Rapped for Unkind Cuts"
(United Press International), *Miami Herald*
(October 24, 1970), p. 9-A.

248. (CHALLENGE) "Many theories . . . have been advanced to explain the origin of the cuckoo laying its eggs in other birds' nests. M. Prévost alone, I think, has thrown light by his observations on this puzzle: he finds that the female cuckoo, which, according to most observers, lays at least from four to six eggs, must pair with the male each time after laying only one or two eggs. Now, if the cuckoo was obliged to sit on her own eggs, she would either have to sit on all together, and therefore leave those first laid so long, that they probably would become addled; or she would have to hatch separately each egg or two eggs, as soon as laid: but as the cuckoo stays a shorter time in this country than any other migratory bird, she certainly would not have time enough for the successive hatchings. Hence we can perceive in the fact of the cuckoo pairing several times, and laying her eggs at intervals, the cause of her depositing her eggs in other birds' nests, and leaving them to the care of foster-parents."

— Charles Darwin, *The Voyage of the Beagle*
(London: Dent, 1959), pp. 50-51.

249. (CHALLENGE) "Let me summarize . . . [my formulation of St. Anselm's second ontological] proof. If God, a being a greater than which cannot be conceived, does not exist then He cannot *come* into existence. For if He did He would either have been *caused* to come into existence or have *happened* to come into existence, and in either case He would be a limited being, which by our conception of Him He is not. Since He cannot come into existence, if He does not exist His existence is impossible. If He does exist He cannot have come into existence (for the reasons given), nor can He cease to exist, for nothing could cause Him to cease to exist nor could it just happen that He ceased to exist. So if God exists His existence is necessary. Thus God's existence is either impossible or necessary. It can be the former only if the concept of such a being is self-contradictory or in some way logically absurd. Assuming that this is not so, it follows that He necessarily exists."

— Norman Malcolm, "Anselm's Ontological Arguments,"
Philosophical Review, LXIX (1960), 49-50.

250. (CHALLENGE) Locate in newspapers, magazines, books (other than logic texts), films, television broadcasts, or radio broadcasts five natural arguments that fall within the scope of propositional

logic. For each argument provide (1) an accurate quotation of the argument in its original form;[6] (2) a reference to the source (including title, date, and page number); (3) your formalization of the argument (with needed suppressed elements supplied); (4) a symbolization of your formalization (including a "dictionary" that indicates for each capital the statement it abbreviates); and (5) an assessment of the argument which employs some technique explained in this book.

---

[6]Consider clipping or photocopying long passages.

Is Propositional Logic Reliable?

Consider this argument:[1]

> If I will have ETERNAL life if I BELIEVE in God, then GOD must exist. I do not believe in God. Therefore, God exists.

It is possible for this argument to have true premises and a false conclusion; hence, it is invalid. The inference's propositional symbolization:

$$(B \rightarrow E) \rightarrow G, \; {\sim}B \vdash G$$

You can establish by formal proof or truth table that this symbolized argument is valid! We have here an invalid English argument whose symbolization is valid.

The so-called "paradoxes of material implication" provide additional examples. Consider exercises 206 and 213 (from chapters four and five):

206. $M \vdash T \rightarrow M$
213. ${\sim}T \vdash T \rightarrow M$

(I use new letters here.) These symbolized arguments are demonstrably valid, but consider two English counterparts:

[1]This is an adaptation of an example given me by Charles L. Stevenson.

214

206E. Jane Fonda is monogamous. Hence, if she
has two husbands she is monogamous.

213E. Jane Fonda does not have two husbands.
Hence, if she has two husbands she is
monogamous.

The premises of both English arguments are clearly true, but the conclusions seem to be false. And if they are false, they do not follow from true premises. How are these anomalies to be explained?

The basic explanation in each case is that the symbolized argument is not a wholly satisfactory translation of the natural-language argument. The major symbols in propositional logic are the five statement connectives. How do these symbols acquire their meanings? Are they simply assigned the meanings of the English connective expressions they translate? English connective expressions exhibit the vagueness characteristic of most natural-language words. Because logicians require precision in the symbols they employ, they are not content to let their logical symbols absorb the somewhat vague meanings of natural-language expressions; hence, they stipulate the meanings of their connectives. In propositional logic this stipulation commonly occurs in two ways: through stating inference rules governing the connectives and by providing a basic truth table. Both methods have been employed in this book. Fortunately, the set of inference rules we adopted in chapters two through seven completely conforms to the basic truth table presented in chapter ten. Had these two methods not conformed, we would have been assigning two distinct meanings to some or all of our connective symbols.

Now the question arises as to how closely the meanings of the connective symbols correspond to the meanings of the English expressions they translate. For example, how nearly synonymous are the logic symbol '&' and the English word 'and'? The answer is that '&' and 'and' are as nearly synonymous as could be expected. The meaning of '~' is nearly the same as the meaning of 'not', and the meaning of 'v' is similar to the meaning of 'or'. There is a somewhat greater disparity between the meanings of '→' and 'if . . . then', and there is a similar disparity between the meanings of '↔' and 'if and only if'.

Let's concentrate on the case of the arrow. Consider statement S1 and its translation into propositional notation F1:

(S1)   If Jon belongs to the COUNTRY club, then
he is WHITE.

(F1) $C \rightarrow W$

We will regard S1 as a true statement only if we believe that there is some connection between the situation described by its antecedent and the one described by its consequent. One obvious connection would be this: the country club in question has a racist membership policy. The case is different with F1. We may ascribe truth to F1 in the absence of knowledge of a connection between the antecedent and the consequent. As a result of adopting the basic truth table of chapter ten, we are prepared to attribute truth to F1 if its antecedent is false or if its consequent is true. In fact, the presence or absence of some connection between antecedent and consequent (other than a connection of truth-values) is irrelevant to the truth-value of F1. If the consequent of F1 is true but there is no nontruth-functional connection between the parts of S1, F1 will be true and S1 false. Therefore F1 does not entail S1. On the other hand, if F1 is false (having a true antecedent and false consequent) necessarily S1 will also be false. So the falsity of F1 entails the falsity of S1; but that means that S1 entails F1. In summary, S1 entails F1, but not vice versa; the meaning of 'if . . . then' in S1 is logically stronger than the meaning of the arrow in F1.

Let's return to the "God" argument discussed at the beginning of this appendix. The analysis of this argument that is provided by propositional logic fails because of a difference in meaning between the first premise of the English argument and its symbolization. Specifically, the problem is this: The second premise of the argument, S2, does not entail S3, the antecedent of the first premise. But S2 does entail F3, the symbolization of S3.

> (S2) I do not believe in God.
> (S3) I will have eternal life if I believe in God.
> (F3) B → E

Consider again the first Fonda example:

> (S4) Jane Fonda is monogamous.
> (S5) If Jane Fonda has two husbands she is monogamous.
> (F4) M
> (F5) T → M

Wff F5 is logically weaker than S5, and that explains why F5 can follow from F4 even though S5 does not follow from S4.

As the above discussion reveals, propositional logic sometimes gives incorrect results even with arguments that appear to fall within the scope of propositional logic. In view of this fact, should we scrap the propositional logic developed in this book, attempt to modify it, or retain it in its present form? I believe it should be retained. Here are five reasons in support of my view: (1) Anomalous arguments such as the "God" inference are extremely rare. (2) Every such argument I have ever encountered was invented by some logician to illustrate a defect in propositional logic. In my experience propositional logic never "misfires" on natural arguments.[2] (3) Logic can be a workable science only if it abstracts from

---

[2]I exclude from consideration natural arguments falling within the scope of some advanced branch of logic.

the complexities of natural language. The English expression 'if . . . then' has different meanings in different contexts. A logic that had a different symbol for each meaning would be too complicated to learn or use. (4) Although the meaning of the arrow is an abstraction from the meaning of 'if . . . then', it captures that part of the meaning that is crucial for logical purposes. (5) There are English conditional sentences that are perfectly translated by propositional logic. Statement S6 (uttered by sportscaster Sonny Hirsch) is an example.

> (S6) If the BALL is on the one-foot line, I'm an
>   ADMIRAL in the Swiss Navy.[3]

The only connection between the antecedent and consequent of S6 has to do with truth-values; so, it is exactly translated by F6:

> (F6) B → A

The meaning that 'if . . . then' has in S6 (which is the meaning of the arrow) is the common denominator of the various senses of this English connective.

---

[3]S6 is an enthymematic *modus tollens*. It amounts to a denial of the claim that the ball rests on the one-foot line.

appendix **2**

Alternative Symbols

Unfortunately, symbolic logic has not reached a stage of maturity where scholars can agree about the notation to be used. Hence, if you read material that treats or employs symbolic logic, you are quite likely to en-counter statement connective symbols other than the ones used in this book. The following dictionary may prove useful.

ENGLISH CONNECTIVES	SYMBOLS USED IN THIS BOOK	OTHER SYMBOLS	POLISH NOTATION
not	~	− ⌐	N
and	&	· ∧	K
or	∨		A
if	→	⊃	C
iff	↔	≡	E

In Polish notation (developed by the Warsaw school of logicians) state-ment letters are written in lower case to distinguish them from connec-tives. Also, dyadic connective symbols precede the statement letters they "connect," rather than appearing between them. Thus, for example, F1 symbolizes S1.

      (S1) If PAUL attends, then RALPH will attend.

      (F1) **Cpr**

One virtue of Polish notation is that it employs no groupers.

Solutions to Starred Exercises

Chapter Two

3. (e)   C → F

     (j)   Q → (C → R)   [also correct: C → (Q → R)]

4. (c)   If it's true that if salt is added to the solution its boiling point drops, then it is true that if salt is added to the solution it will boil sooner.

5. (d)   (5)   4,2 →O

             (6)   1,5 →O

             (7)   3,6 →O

7.   (1)   D   A

          (2)   D → P   A

          (3)   P → R   A

          (4)   P   2,1 →O

          (5)   R   3,4 →O

13.   (1)   (F → G) → (G → H)   A

          (2)   F → G   A

(3)	F	A
(4)	G → H	1,2 →O
(5)	G	2,3 →O
(6)	H	4,5 →O

The proof for exercise 13 can also be completed as follows:

(4)	G	2,3 →O
(5)	G → H	1,2 →O
(6)	H	5,4 →O

In the following only one proof for each argument will be given, even though often there will be two or more correct proofs.

Chapter Three

14. (e) (M & A) & D
    (i) (O → L) & (H → W)

15. (d) If Miami wins its last regular-season game, then New York will lose its last regular-season game and Miami will win the division championship.

16. (c)

(3)		2 &O
(4)		1 &O
(5)	F	
(6)		2 &O
(7)	E	1 &O
(8)	G	6,7 →O
(9)		5,8 &I

20.

(1)	I & F	A
(2)	I → (F → C)	A
(3)		1 &O
(4)		2,3 →O
(5)		1 &O
(6)	C	4,5 →O

Several statements have been omitted from the above proof; you should supply the missing lines. Such omissions will occur regularly in this appendix. The purpose is to encourage you to engage in proof construction, rather than passively observing the results of my work.

25.

(1)	E	A
(2)	M & V	A
(3)	E → [(V & M) → H]	A

(4)	H → I	A
(5)		3,1 →O
(6)		2 &O
(7)		2 &O
(8)		7,6 &I
(9)		5,8 →O
(10)	I	4,9 →O

Chapter Four

27. (g) R → D

(j) Without you it won't get done =
The JOB gets done only if you HELP =
J → H [incorrect: H → J]

(l) [(F & B) & (D & K)] → [(C & P) → E]

29. (b)

1	(1)		
2	(2)		
3	(3)		
1,3	(4)	D	1,3 →O
2,3	(5)		2,3 →O
1,2,3	(6)	D & E	4,5 &I

31.

1	(1)	L → P	A
2	(2)	L & E	PA
2	(3)		2 &O
1,2	(4)		1,3 →O
1	(5)	(L & E) → P	2-4 →I

35.

1	(1)	Q → (C → R)	A
2	(2)	C	PA
3	(3)	Q	PA
1,3	(4)		1,3 →O
1,2,3	(5)		4,2 →O
1,2	(6)		3-5 →I
1	(7)	C → (Q → R)	2-6 →I

38.

1	(1)	T → (L & M)	A
2	(2)	T	PA
1,2	(3)		1,2 →O
1,2	(4)	L	3 &O
1	(5)		2-4 →I
1,2	(6)		3 &O
1	(7)		2-6 →I
1	(8)	(T → L) & (T → M)	5,7 &I

Chapter Five

42. (i)   ~ (P & ~ M)   [also correct: ~ M → ~ P]
    (k)   Two nonequivalent symbolizations:

    [C & ~ (D & B)] → A
    [C & (~ D & ~ B)] → A

    The first formula is a literal symbolization of the sentence; however, the second (presumably) captures the thought the reporter intended to express.

    (m)   ~ (M & G) → E

43. (c)   Justice O'Connor is not both a Democrat and a Republican.

44. (c)

1	(1)		
2	(2)		
3	(3)		
1,3	(4)	F	1,3 →O
1,3	(5)	E & F	3,4 &I
1,2,3	(6)		5,2 &I
	(7)	~ E	

49.

1	(1)	R	A
2	(2)	R → B	A
3	(3)	~ ~ M → ~ B	A
4	(4)	~ ~ M	PA
3,4	(5)		3,4 →O
1,2	(6)		2,1 →O
1,2,3,4	(7)		6,5 &I
1,2,3	(8)	~ M	4-7 ~O

55.

1	(1)	G	A
2	(2)	T	A
3	(3)	T → U	A
4	(4)	(U & ~ R) → ~ G	A
2,3	(5)		3,2 →O
6	(6)		PA
2,3,6	(7)		5,6 &I
2,3,4,6	(8)		4,7 →O
1,2,3,4,6	(9)		1,8 &I
1,2,3,4	(10)	R	6-9 ~O

Chapter Six

58. (f)   P ↔ (~A & B)
    (g)   Two defensible (nonequivalent) symbolizations:

    L & [R → (W & E)]
    L & [R ↔ (W & E)]

59. (c)   Smith wins the batting crown if and only if he gets a hit; furthermore, Jones makes an out.

60. (c)
1	(1)		
2	(2)		
3	(3)		
1	(4)	H → (I & J)	
1,3	(5)	I & J	4,3 →O
1,3	(6)	I	5 &O
1	(7)	H →I	

65.
1	(1)	A → (B ↔ C)	A
2	(2)	~B	A
3	(3)	C	A
4	(4)		PA
1,4	(5)		1,4 →O
1,4	(6)		5 ↔O
1,3,4	(7)		6,3 →O
1,2,3,4	(8)		7,2 &I
1,2,3	(9)	~A	4-8 ~I

71.
1	(1)	S	A
2	(2)	(S & L) → ~L	A
3	(3)	(S & ~L) → L	A
4	(4)		PA
1,4	(5)		1,4 &I
1,2,4	(6)		2,5 →O
1,2	(7)	L → ~L	4-6 →I
8	(8)	~L	PA
1,8	(9)		1,8 &I
1,3,8	(10)		3,9 →O
1,3	(11)		8-10 →I
1,2,3	(12)	L ↔ ~L	7,11 ↔I

Chapter Seven

73. (c)   B v N [also correct: (B & N) v (B v N)]
    (i)   (~A v ~B) → ~C
    (m)   (P v A) → (R v B)

74. (d) Zero is either even or neither even nor odd.

75. (c)

1	(1)		
2	(2)		
2	(3)		2 vI
1,2	(4)		1,3 →O
1	(5)		2-4 →I
6	(6)	E	
6	(7)		6 vI
1,6	(8)		1,7 →O
1	(9)		6-8 →I
	(10)		5,9 &I

80.

1	(1)	~(D v E)	A
2	(2)	D	PA
2	(3)		2 vI
1,2	(4)		3,1 &I
1	(5)	~D	2-4 ~I

83.

1	(1)	I → A	A
2	(2)	(~I → T) & (T →O)	A
3	(3)	I v ~I	A
4	(4)	I	PA
1,4	(5)		1,4 →O
1,4	(6)		5 vI
1	(7)		4-6 →I
8	(8)	~I	PA
2	(9)		2 &O
2,8	(10)		9,8 →O
2	(11)		2 &O
2,8	(12)		11,10 →O
2,8	(13)		12 vI
2	(14)		8-13 →I
1,2,3	(15)	A v O	3,7,14 vO

Chapter Eight

87. (d) Not a wff. (As the formula begins with a left-hand grouper, it does not satisfy clauses one or two. Thus it is a wff only if it satisfies clause three. The formula satisfies clause three only if its fragment 'H & I' is a wff. The fragment is not a wff by any clause; therefore, the fragment is not a wff. Thus, formula (d) is not a wff.)

88. (b)

1	(1)		
2	(2)		
3	(3)		
2,3	(4)		3,2 &I

2,3	(5)		4 &O
2	(6)		3-5 →I
7	(7)		
8	(8)		
2,7	(9)		7,2 &I
2,7,8	(10)		9,8 &I
2,7,8	(11)		10 &O
2,7	(12)		8-11 ~O
2	(13)		7-12 →I
	(14)		1,6,13 vO

94.

1	(1)	F ↔ ~S	Λ
2	(2)	~F & ~S	PA
1	(3)	~S → F	1 ↔O
2	(4)		2 &O
1,2	(5)		3,4 →O
2	(6)		2 &O
1,2	(7)		5,6 &I
1	(8)	~(~F & ~S)	2-7 ~I

97.

1	(1)	S → ~M	A
2	(2)	~S → ~M	A
3	(3)	M	PA
4	(4)	S	PA
1,4	(5)		1,4 →O
1,3,4	(6)		3,5 &I
1,3	(7)		4-6 ~I
1,2,3	(8)		2,7 →O
1,2,3	(9)		3,8 &I
1,2	(10)	~M	3-9 ~I

Chapter Nine

99. (c)   1 CN; 2,3 CH; 4 AR

100. (d)   Line 3 should be 'J → I'. Line 4 should be '~I → K'. The Chain Argument Rule (employed on line 5) cannot be applied correctly to lines 3 and 4; the consequent of 3 and the antecedent of 4 are not identical.

101. (b)

(1)	~D → H	A
(2)	~H	A
(3)		1,2 MT
(4)	D	3 DN

104.

(1)	F v R	A
(2)	F → S	A

(3)	~S	A
(4)	R → B	A
(5)		2,3 MT
(6)		1,5 DA
(7)	B	4,6 →O

107. (e)

(1)	T → ~R	A
(2)	R → ~T	1 CN
(3)		2 AR
(4)	~(R & T)	3 DM

110.

(1)	(~S → D) & (S → H)	A
(2)	H → B	A
(3)	~S → D	1 &O
(4)		1 &O
(5)		3 CN
(6)		5,4 CH
(7)		6,2 CH
(8)	D v B	7 AR

Chapter Ten

114. (c)

D → E	E v F	⊢(D v F) →	(E & F)			**invalid**
T	T	T	T	T		
T	T	T	T	T		
F	T	T	F	F		
T	T	T	F	F		
T	T	T	F	F		
T	T	F	T	F		
F	F	T	F	F		
T	F	F	T	F		
			*			

117.

O ‖ O → ~O	⊢~O		**valid**
T ‖ F F	F		
F ‖ T T	T		
*			

124.

N P R ‖ [N v ~	(P v N)]	→	~ R	P	⊢R	**invalid**
T T T	T F	T	F F	T	T	
F T T	F F	T	T F	T	T	
T F T	T F	T	F F	F	T	
F F T	T T	F	F F	F	T	
T T F	T F	T	T T	T	F	
F T F	F F	T	T T	T	F	
T F F	T F	T	T T	F	F	
F F F	T T	F	T T	F	F	
	*					

Chapter Eleven

127. (c)

C	F	(C → ~F)	&	~ F	⊢C
F	F	T T	T	T T	F

128. (c)

F	R	S	B	F ∨ R	F → S	~S	R → B	⊢B
F	F	F	F	T F	T	T	T	F

130.

B	W	A	B → W	~B → A	⊢W ∨ A	valid
F	F	F	T	T T F	F	

134.

I	R	P	I ∨ R	P → I	~P	⊢R	invalid
T	F	F	T	T	T	F	

Chapter Twelve

140.

S	R	(S & R)	&	~ (S & R)	contradictory
T	T	T	F	F T	
F	T	F	F	T F	
T	F	F	F	T F	
F	F	F	F	T F	
			*		

(1)	(S & R) & ~(S & R)		A
(2)			1 DN
(3)	(S & R) & ~(S & R)		2 DN

145.

C	D	[(C → D) → C]	→ C	logically true
T	T	T T	T	
F	T	T F	T	
T	F	F T	T	
F	F	T F	T	
			*	

1	(1)	(C → D) → C	PA
2	(2)	~C	PA
1,2	(3)		1,2 MT
1,2	(4)		3 AR
1,2	(5)		4 &O
1,2	(6)		5,2 &I
1	(7)		2-6 ~O
	(8)	[(C → D) → C] → C	1-7 →I

Chapter Thirteen

151.

Y	F	Y → F	~Y → ~F			not logically equivalent
T	T	T	F	T	F	
F	T	T	T	F	F	
T	F	F	F	T	T	
F	F	T	T	T	T	
				*		

154.

C	S	C → S	C → (C → S)		logically equivalent
T	T	T	T	T	
F	T	T	T	T	
T	F	F	F	F	
F	F	T	T	T	
			*		

(1) C → S   A
(2)   1 v I
(3) C → (C → S) 2 AR

1	(1)		A
2	(2)	C	PA
1,2	(3)		1,2 →O
1,2	(4)		3,2 →O
1	(5)		2-4 →I

Chapter Fourteen

158. One acceptable solution:

(1)   If we (American Motors) do not build better cars, then we will not provide better warranties.

We do provide better warranties.

So, we build better cars.

(2)   ~C → ~W, W ⊢ C

C = We build better cars
W = We provide better warranties

(3)   (1) ~ C → ~W   A
      (2) W   A
      (3) W → C   1 CN
      (4) C   3,2 →O

160. No argument.

Index

A

Abstract argument, 21
Affirming a disjunct, 133
Affirming the consequent, 15-17
'Although', 25
Ampersand (&), 24
Ampersand In Rule, 28
   strategy, 33
Ampersand Out Rule, 30
   strategy, 33
'And', 24-27
'And/or', 96
Antecedent, 11
Argument:
   abstract vs. concrete, 21
   defined, 4
   determining gross structure, 27-28
   evaluating content, 4-6
   evaluating form, 4-6
   symbolized, 123

Argument-form, 142
Arrow (→), 11
Arrow In Rule, 46-47
    assumption-dependence principle, 48
    restrictions, 52
    strategy, 50-51
Arrow Out Rule, 18
    strategy, 32
Arrow Rule, 135
Arrow strategy, 141
Associativity:
    of ampersand, 31
    of double arrow, 152
    of wedge, 97
Assumption:
    original, 47
    provisional, 47
Assumption dependence, 48-49
    column, 48
    principles, 48, 67, 115
Assumption Rule, 47
    assumption-dependence principle, 48

B

Basic truth table, 154
'Because', 27
Biconditional:
    defined, 84
    symbolizing, 84-85
Brief truth table:
    method summarized, 174
    procedural principle, 170
    test of invalidity, 169-71
    test of nonequivalence, 192
    test of validity, 171-73
'But', 25

C

Capital, 11, 64, 120
Chain argument (pattern), 46
Chain Argument Rule, 135
Charts (*see* Tables)

Comics and cartoons, 10, 14, 21, 33, 34, 56, 60, 74, 76, 91, 109, 110,
    126, 128, 142, 146, 163, 175, 178, 208, 209, 210, 211
Common argument patterns, 206
Commutativity:
  of ampersand, 30
  of double arrow, 86
  of wedge, 101
Completeness of primitive proof rules, 116
Compound statement, 9
Conclusion-introducing terms, 27
Concrete argument, 21
Conditional:
  defined, 11
  symbolizing, 10-14, 41-45
Conjunct, 24
Conjunction:
  defined, 24
  symbolizing, 24-27
Conjunctive argement (pattern), 70
Conjunctive Argument Rule, 135
Connective (*see* Statement, connective)
Consequent, 11
'Consequently', 27
Consistency:
  defined, 193
  formal-proof test, 193
  truth-table test, 193
Consistency of primitive proof rules, 116
Contingent statement:
  defined, 184
  truth-table test, 184-85
Contradiction:
  defined, 182
  formal-proof test, 183
  standard, 66-67, 183
  truth-table test, 183
Contraposition Rule, 135
Corresponding biconditional, 193
Corresponding conditional, 182
Crossword puzzles, 80, 151, 198

D

Deductive logic, 4
DeMorgan's Law Rule, 135

Denying a conjunct, 70
Denying the antecedent, 68
Derived inference rules, 135
    strategy, 138
Dilemma, 101
Disjunct, 95
Disjunction:
    defined, 95
    symbolizing, 95-97
Disjunctive argument (pattern), 133
Disjunctive Argument Rule, 134
Distribution, 104
Double arrow (↔), 85
Double Arrow In Rule, 86
    strategy, 88
Double Arrow Out Rule, 86
    strategy, 88
Double Negation Rule, 135

E

Entailment:
    defined 31, 188
    properties, 189
Enthymeme, 204
'Even though', 25
'Exactly if', 85
Explanations, cast as arguments, 202

F

'For', 27
Formal proof:
    checking off lines, 137-40
    defined, 17, 123
    introduced, 17-20
    strategy, 32-33, 50-51, 69, 72, 88, 98, 102-3, 117-20, 137-41
    tests:
        consistency, 193
        contradiction, 183
        logical equivalence, 191
        logical truth, 181
        validity, 17
Formula, 120

G

Grouper, 11-12, 120

H

'Hence', 27
'However', 25

I

'If and only if', 84-85
'Iff', 85
'If only', 44
'If . . . then', 11-12
Inductive logic, 6-7
Inference rules:
    derived, 135
    primitive, 115
    primitive vs. derived, 134

J

'Just in case', 85

L

Logic:
    deductive, 4
    inductive, 6-7
Logical equivalence:
    defined, 31, 190
    properties, 192-93
    tests:
        brief truth table, 192
        formal proof, 191
        truth table, 191
Logical truth:
    defined, 180
    formal-proof test, 181
    truth-table test, 180

M

Modus ponens, 14-15
Modus tollens (pattern), 66
Modus Tollens Rule, 135
'Moreover', 25

N

Natural agrument, 199
'Necessary and sufficient condition', 85
'Necessary condition', 44-45
Negation:
   defined, 62
   symbolizing, 62-65
'Neither . . . nor', 99
'Not', 62-64

O

'Only if', 41-44
'Or', 95-97
   inclusive vs. exclusive, 95-97
Original assumption, 47

P

Polish notation, 218
Premise-introducing terms, 27
Primitive inference rules, 115
   strategy, 118
Proof (*see* Formal proof)
Proposition, 10
Propositional logic, 7, 10
'Provided that', 12
Provisional assumption, 47

R

Reductio ad absurdum, 73
Reflexivity:

of entailment, 189
of logical equivalence, 192-93

S

Simple statement, 9
'Since', 27
'So', 27
Standard contradiction, 66-67, 183
Statement:
  compound, 9
  connective, 10, 120
    ampersand, 24
    arrow, 11
    double arrow, 85
    dyadic, 62, 121
    monadic, 62
    scope, 12
    tilde, 62
    truth-functional, 154
    wedge, 95
  contingent, 184
  contradictory, 182
  defined, 4
  logically true, 180
  simple, 9
Strategy, formal proof, 32-33, 50-51, 69, 72, 88, 98, 102-3, 117-20, 137-41
Subjunctive mood, 14
Subproof, 51-52, 72
Substitution instance, 143
'Sufficient condition', 44-45
Symbol, 120
Symbolized argument, 123
Symmetry:
  of consistency, 193
  of logical equivalence, 192-93

T

Tables:
  alternative symbols, 218
  assumption-dependence principles for primitive inference rules, 115

Tables: (*cont.*)
   common argument patterns, 206
   derived inference rules, 135
   primitive inference rules, 115
   strategic suggestions for derived inference rules, 138
   strategic suggestions for primitive inference rules, 118
   types of statements, 185
'Therefore', 27
'Thus', 27
Tilde (~), 62
Tilde In Rule, 66
   assumption-dependence principle, 67
   restrictions, 73
   strategy, 69
Tilde Out–DeMorgan's Law strategy, 140
Tilde Out Rule, 71
   restrictions, 73
   strategy, 72
Transitivity:
   of entailment, 189
   of logical equivalence, 192-93
Truth, the, 1-228
Truth table, 156
   asterisk, 157
   basic, 154
   guide column, 156
   number of rows, 157
   principles, 155
   tests:
      consistency, 193
      contingency, 184-85
      contradiction, 183
      logical equivalence, 191
      logical truth, 180
      validity, 158
Truth-value, 154
Turnstile (⊢), 15

U

'Unless', 64-65

V

Validity:
    defined, 4
    formal-proof test, 17
    and truth, 4-6
    truth-table test, 158

W

Wedge (v), 95
Wedge In Rule, 98
    strategy, 98
Wedge Out Rule, 101
    strategy, 102
Well-formed formula, 120-22
Wff, 121-22

Y

'Yet', 25

The Ten Primitive Inference Rules

	IN	OUT
→	From the derivation of B from assumption A (and perhaps other assumptions) derive $A \rightarrow B$.	From $A \rightarrow B$ and A derive B.
&	From A and B derive $A \& B$.	From $A \& B$ derive either A or B.
v	From A derive either $A \vee B$ or $B \vee A$.	From $A \vee B$, $A \rightarrow C$, and $B \rightarrow C$ derive C.
↔	From $A \rightarrow B$ and $B \rightarrow A$ derive $A \leftrightarrow B$.	From $A \leftrightarrow B$ derive either $A \rightarrow B$ or $B \rightarrow A$.
~	From the derivation of $B \& \sim B$ from assumption A (and perhaps other assumptions) derive $\sim A$.	From the derivation of $B \& \sim B$ from assumption $\sim A$ (and perhaps other assumptions) derive A.

The Eight Derived Inference Rules

Modus Tollens (MT)	From $\mathcal{A} \rightarrow \mathcal{B}$ and $\sim\mathcal{B}$ derive $\sim\mathcal{A}$.	
Disjunctive Argument (DA)	From $\mathcal{A} \lor \mathcal{B}$ and $\sim\mathcal{A}$ derive $\mathcal{B}$. From $\mathcal{A} \lor \mathcal{B}$ and $\sim\mathcal{B}$ derive $\mathcal{A}$.	**I**
Conjunctive Argument (CA)	From $\sim(\mathcal{A} \& \mathcal{B})$ and $\mathcal{A}$ derive $\sim\mathcal{B}$. From $\sim(\mathcal{A} \& \mathcal{B})$ and $\mathcal{B}$ derive $\sim\mathcal{A}$.	
Chain Argument (CH)	From $\mathcal{A} \rightarrow \mathcal{B}$ and $\mathcal{B} \rightarrow \mathcal{C}$ derive $\mathcal{A} \rightarrow \mathcal{C}$.	
Double Negation (DN)	From $\mathcal{A}$ derive $\sim\sim\mathcal{A}$ and vice versa.	
DeMorgan's Law (DM)	From $\mathcal{A} \& \mathcal{B}$ derive $\sim(\sim\mathcal{A} \lor \sim\mathcal{B})$ and vice versa. From $\sim(\mathcal{A} \& \mathcal{B})$ derive $\sim\mathcal{A} \lor \sim\mathcal{B}$ and vice versa. From $\sim\mathcal{A} \& \sim\mathcal{B}$ derive $\sim(\mathcal{A} \lor \mathcal{B})$ and vice versa. From $\sim(\sim\mathcal{A} \& \sim\mathcal{B})$ derive $\mathcal{A} \lor \mathcal{B}$ and vice versa.	
Arrow (AR)	From $\mathcal{A} \rightarrow \mathcal{B}$ derive $\sim\mathcal{A} \lor \mathcal{B}$ and vice versa. From $\sim\mathcal{A} \rightarrow \mathcal{B}$ derive $\mathcal{A} \lor \mathcal{B}$ and vice versa. From $\mathcal{A} \rightarrow \mathcal{B}$ derive $\sim(\mathcal{A} \& \sim\mathcal{B})$ and vice versa. From $\sim(\mathcal{A} \rightarrow \mathcal{B})$ derive $\mathcal{A} \& \sim\mathcal{B}$ and vice versa.	**II**
Contra- position (CN)	From $\mathcal{A} \rightarrow \mathcal{B}$ derive $\sim\mathcal{B} \rightarrow \sim\mathcal{A}$ and vice versa. From $\mathcal{A} \rightarrow \sim\mathcal{B}$ derive $\mathcal{B} \rightarrow \sim\mathcal{A}$. From $\sim\mathcal{A} \rightarrow \mathcal{B}$ derive $\sim\mathcal{B} \rightarrow \mathcal{A}$.	